IMAGES
*of America*

# ALMA

*On the cover*: One of the first automobiles in Alma was owned by the superintendent of the Alma Springs Sanitarium, Dr. J. Henry Lancashire. He was the son-in-law of the sanitarium's owner, millionaire entrepreneur Ammi W. Wright. Not only was this vehicle the doctor's personal car, driven by his chauffeur, but, as a novelty, it provided transportation around town for guests of the spa. During the summer season, the car was parked under the sunroom porch of the sanitarium. It is pictured here, complete with uniformed driver, in Sanitarium Park, which adjoined the large sanitarium building. (Author's collection.)

IMAGES
*of America*

# ALMA

David McMacken

ARCADIA
PUBLISHING

ISBN 978-0-7385-6125-7

Published by Arcadia Publishing
Charleston, South Carolina

Printed in the United States of America

Library of Congress Catalog Card Number: 2008928992

For all general information contact Arcadia Publishing at:
Telephone 843-853-2070
Fax 843-853-0044
E-mail sales@arcadiapublishing.com
For customer service and orders:
Toll-Free 1-888-313-2665

Visit us on the Internet at www.arcadiapublishing.com

*This book is dedicated to the Alma photographers, professional and amateur, who recorded the past for the eyes of the future.*

# Contents

# ACKNOWLEDGMENTS

When this book was suggested, the author reminded the publisher that Alma already had a pictorial history, compiled years ago. Where would fresh, unpublished photographs come from? A quick inventory revealed that many of the old pictures were no longer available, their owners having passed on, and the photographs' whereabouts were now unknown.

New pictures were found, however, in both institutional and private collections. All owners of these photographs enthusiastically agreed to their publication. The generosity and cooperation of these folks have made this book possible.

Thanks go to Bryan Dinwoody, director of the Alma Public Library; Jennifer Starkey and Viki Everhart of the Alma College Library; Ann Jarrett of Alma Public Schools; Penny Daniels of Gratiot Medical Center; Joyce Rasmussen of Masonic Pathways; Esther Lobsinger of Alma Products Company; Patricia Gillis and Robert Smith of the Breckenridge-Wheeler Area Historical Society for providing Mid-West and Leonard refineries pictures; and Tom McCreery for his collection of Lobdell-Emery Company pictures.

A number of people opened their personal collections: Lucille Behler, Dale Kemler, John Kemler, Jan Caputo, Colleen Boyer, Harold and Teacel Dean, Charles and Diantha Hicks, Jim Sommerville, Tom Fortino, and Doris Amsbury.

A special thanks goes to Richard Tesman who made available his extensive collection of Alma postcards. His name appears repeatedly in photograph credit lines.

Numerous individuals also assisted by providing photographs that ultimately were not chosen, and other people provided valuable information about the ones that were. A special thanks goes to all of these helpers. Thanks also go to Pat Thelen of the Clarke Historical Library and Shada Biabani of Concept Communications who both provided valuable assistance with many scans.

My wife, Virginia, and daughter, Jordan, deserve thanks for their critical proof-reading and wise editorial suggestions.

# INTRODUCTION

In the fall of 1853, four men slogged through the ancient woods of Gratiot County following a Native American trail that snaked along the Pine River. Leaves had fallen, and an endless canopy of interlaced branches stretched overhead. The leader of the group, 33-year-old Ralph Ely, was scouting for cheap government land along the river. To be successful in starting a settlement, he needed the river for transportation and waterpower.

The party of men came upon a prime location where the river flowed between high banks. Here Ely selected his parcel of property and went off to the land office in Ionia to pay for it. He left his companions to cut trees and build a log cabin where they spent the winter, and they continued to chop trees and clear land.

In the spring of 1854, Ely brought his wife and four children to their new cabin in the wilderness. Soon he built a log store and installed a sawmill and a gristmill, both powered by small steam engines. He named his settlement Elyton.

Known also as Ely's Mills, the village grew as more settlers arrived in the wilderness. James Gargett came from Ohio in 1858. He bought and ran Ely's store. Gargett also purchased many acres of land adjoining Elyton. He platted his addition into blocks and lots and called his property Alma. Soon Gargett's section of the village absorbed Elyton, and the entire town became known as Alma, the name memorializing a battle in the recent Crimean War in Russia.

A slow-growing frontier town until the mid-1870s, Alma began to thrive after the Chicago, Saginaw and Canada Railroad arrived in 1874. Countless lumber camps above Alma on the Pine River used the railroad to ship timber. Thousands of other logs came down the river in the spring log drives, which brought prosperity and excitement to the town for 30 years. Local industries included a large sawmill as well as Gargett's towering Empire Flouring Mills and his woolen mill. Lumbering and industry aside, the overall economy rested mainly on a growing number of farmers with expanding farms who patronized the shops of Alma and sold their surplus crops to local grain dealers. Alma, in all respects, was becoming a substantial, quiet, rural village. The bucolic settlement, however, was soon to experience a major change.

When millionaire lumberman Ammi W. Wright arrived from Saginaw in the 1880s, the town took a strong and unexpected turn toward prosperity. Adopting Alma as his new home, Wright dipped into his ample resources and demonstrated what money could do. He built the Opera House Block, the Wright Hotel, the Alma Springs Sanitarium, his own substantial mansion, and the first buildings of what became Alma College. He engaged in retailing, banking, and farming, becoming Michigan's largest individual farmer. He introduced the growing of sugar beets to Gratiot farmers and established the Alma Sugar Company processing plant. His donation of the sanitarium building to the Masonic lodge brought the Masonic home for the elderly to Alma. Wright's investment of money and his philanthropic bent are chiefly responsible for what Alma has become.

The Wright era was fading when establishment of the Republic Truck Company in 1913 marked the beginning of a period of great prosperity for Alma. Frank Ruggles, superintendent of the company, designed a solid, reliable truck that gained popularity quickly. Fulfilling government contracts for hundreds of Liberty trucks during World War I, the company soon expanded into three plants and by 1920 was the largest exclusive truck manufacturer in the world. During the truck company's unfortunate decline in the 1920s, the Lobdell-Emery Manufacturing Company arrived from Onaway. This maker of wooden bicycle rims also made 80 percent of the automobile and truck steering wheels used in the United States; it offered employment to hundreds of area citizens for more than 75 years. The discovery of major oil fields in central Michigan in the late 1920s prompted the building of the Mid-West and Leonard oil refineries in Alma during the 1930s. Oil refining remained big business in Alma for more than 60 years.

During the 1930s, almost by chance, the house trailer and mobile-home industry took root in Alma, with the emergence of the Silvermoon Trailer. Unable to keep up with orders for its new trailer, the Alma Trailer Company expanded into abandoned plant No. 1 of the Republic Truck Company and began producing the New Moon Trailer. Rivalries within the company soon resulted in a second business, the Redman Trailer Company. Government orders for trailers to be used as housing at military installations during World War II resulted in several major transports of trailers from Alma to the East Coast. The mobile-home industry continued in Alma until the 1970s.

From the time of Ely to the present, the Pine River has had a powerful influence on Alma. Ely used the river to travel by transportation barge to get supplies for his store. Loggers shepherded pine logs by the thousands through the sluice in Alma's dam. Swimming, ice-skating, canoeing, and the annual tug-of-war between Alma College freshmen and sophomores all took place on the river and so did several damaging floods. A lawsuit over water rights on the Pine River dragged on for 10 years and ended up in federal court in Detroit. The river took on its own personality as an important member of the community.

A rough-and-ready town by anyone's standards in the 1870s, Alma gradually watched the settling effects of religion and education bring an element of culture that has been consistently nourished through the years. The influence of Alma College, a liberal arts Presbyterian school, coupled with an ongoing prosperity generated by industry, has given the town a rich mixture of affluence and refinement that has ground down the rough edges of the past.

The panoply of photographs in this book reflects that balance and portrays the town and the people who caused it to flourish.

# One

# EARLY YEARS

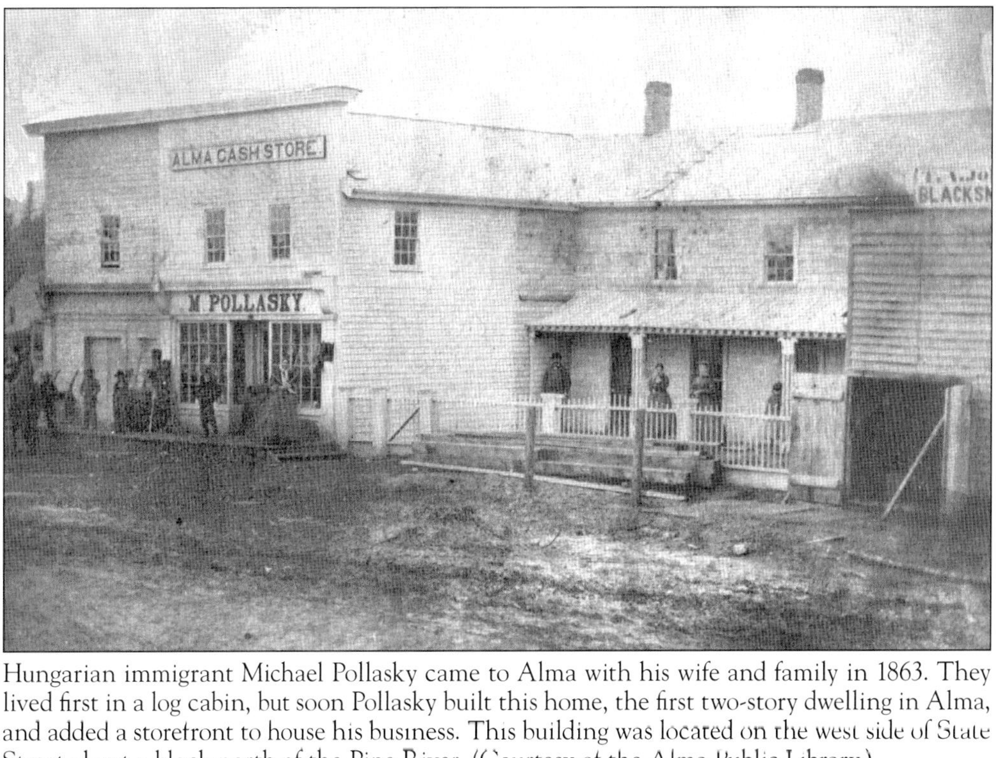


Hungarian immigrant Michael Pollasky came to Alma with his wife and family in 1863. They lived first in a log cabin, but soon Pollasky built this home, the first two-story dwelling in Alma, and added a storefront to house his business. This building was located on the west side of State Street about a block north of the Pine River. (Courtesy of the Alma Public Library.)

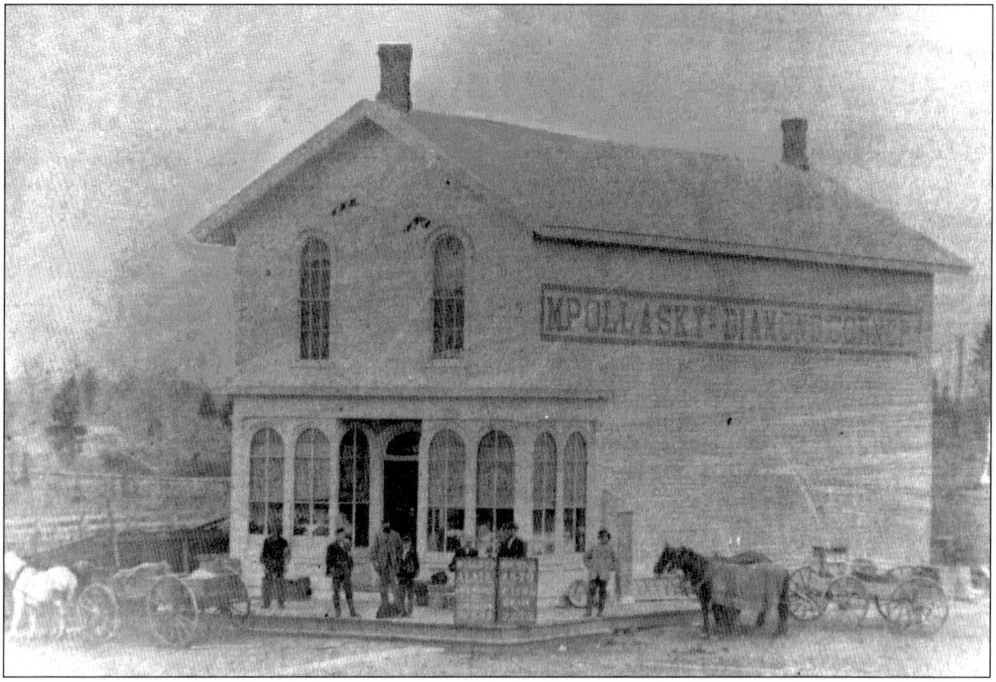


Deciding to relocate to the main intersection of Alma, Michael Pollasky built his Diamond Corner store in 1865 at the corner of Superior and State Streets. The store faced a cornfield across State Street. At this location Pollasky continued his career as a longtime Alma merchant. In this 1870 view, Pollasky's sign offers cash for grain. (Courtesy of the Alma Public Library.)

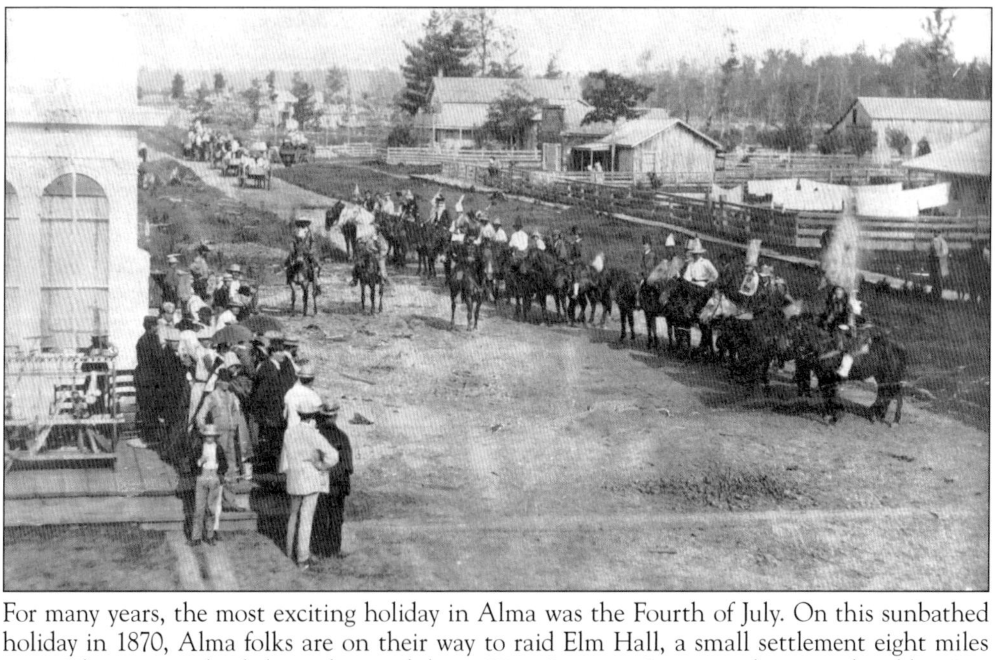

For many years, the most exciting holiday in Alma was the Fourth of July. On this sunbathed holiday in 1870, Alma folks are on their way to raid Elm Hall, a small settlement eight miles away. The carriage loads have departed down West Superior Street, and mounted "soldiers" in various costumes are ready to join the procession. Ladies have spread their parasols against the early-morning sun. (Courtesy of the Alma Public Library.)

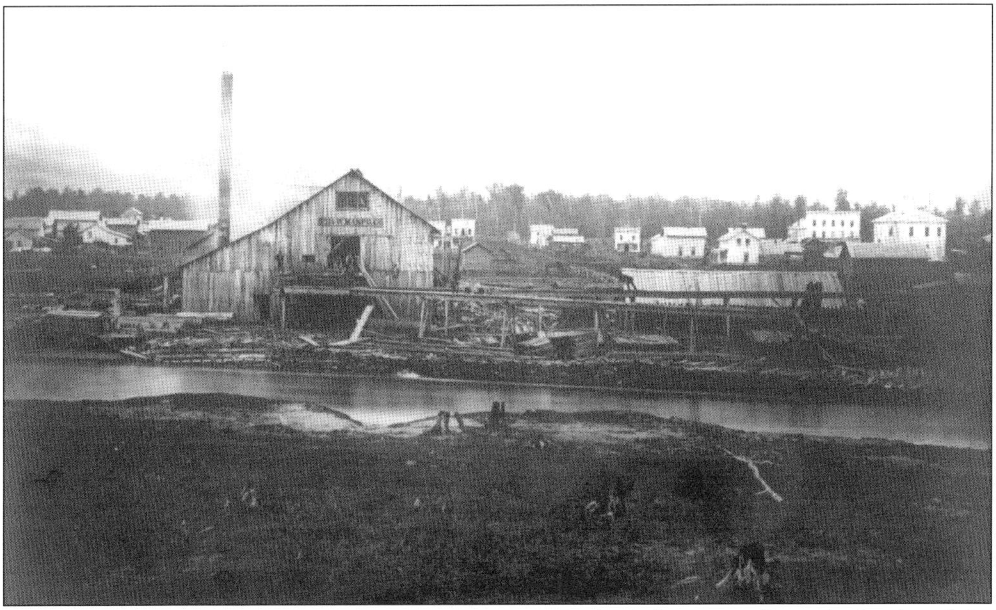

Isaac Pierce, James T. Hall, and Gerritt S. Ward established this sawmill on the banks of the Pine River around 1868. Seen here in 1875, it replaced the steam sawmill built by Ralph Ely in the early days of the settlement. At the far right stands the two-story school built in 1868. Behind the school stands the Hulbert House, a hotel and store destined to burn in a spectacular blaze in 1876. (Courtesy of the Alma Public Library.)

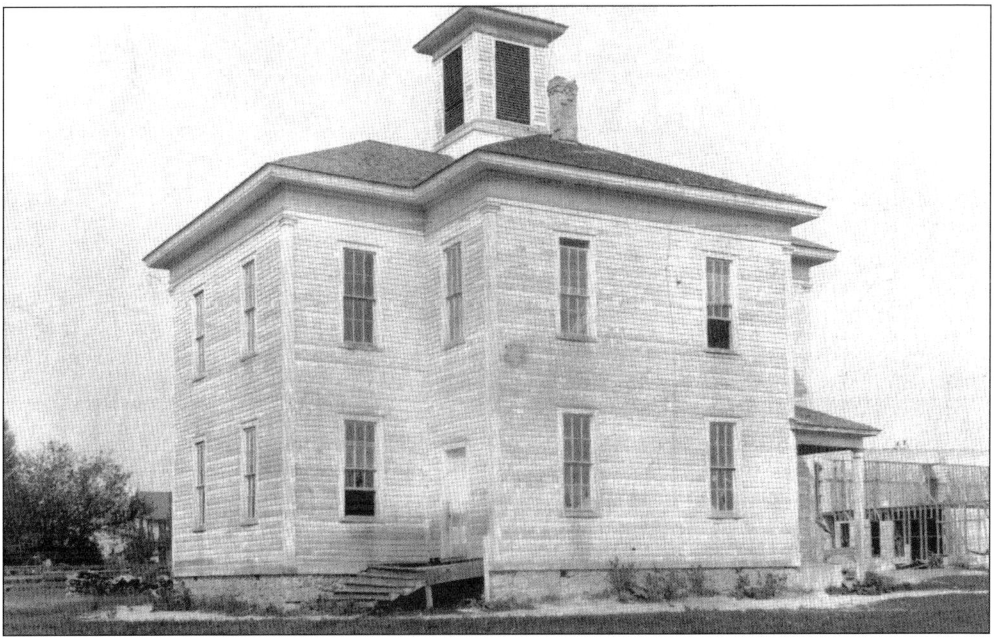

This school at Gratiot and Center Streets was built in 1868 to replace the one-story frame school at Superior and State Streets. By the early 1880s, this four-room building was crowded and was replaced by the new Union School across the river. Harrington's Table Company of St. Louis, Michigan, moved into this building that burned in 1888, destroying tools, paints, and a buggy left there to be painted. (Courtesy of the Alma Public Library.)

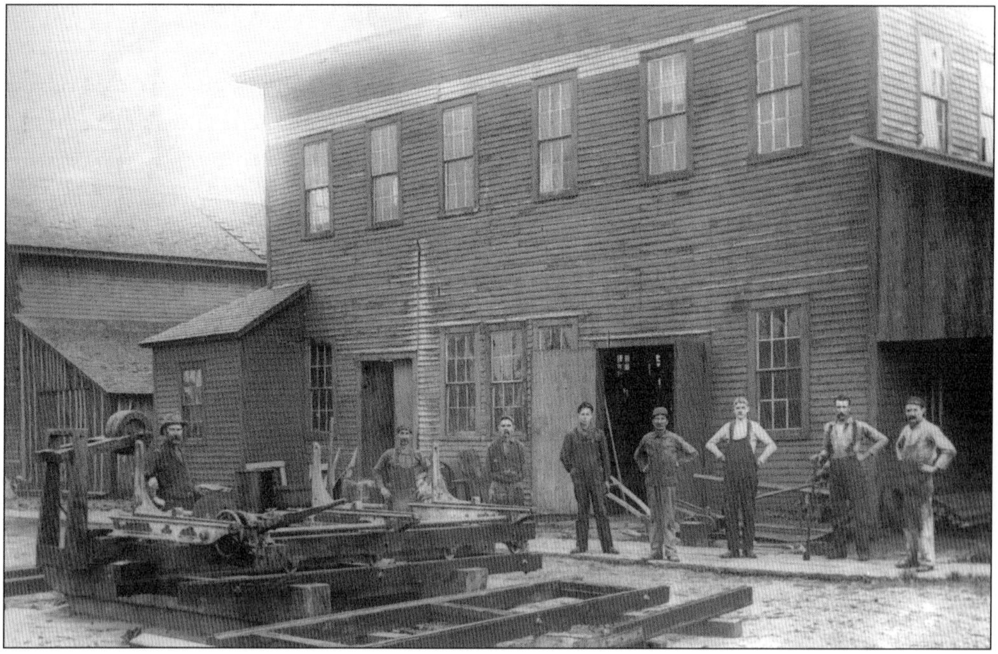

John Montigel built his machine shop and foundry on the bank of the Pine River north of Superior Street in 1871. In this picture dating from 1880, his crew is building a sawmill. The building burned in 1901, and Montigel lost his machinery, equipment, and tools as well as 50 pairs of sleighs that were being built. (Courtesy of Lucille Behler.)

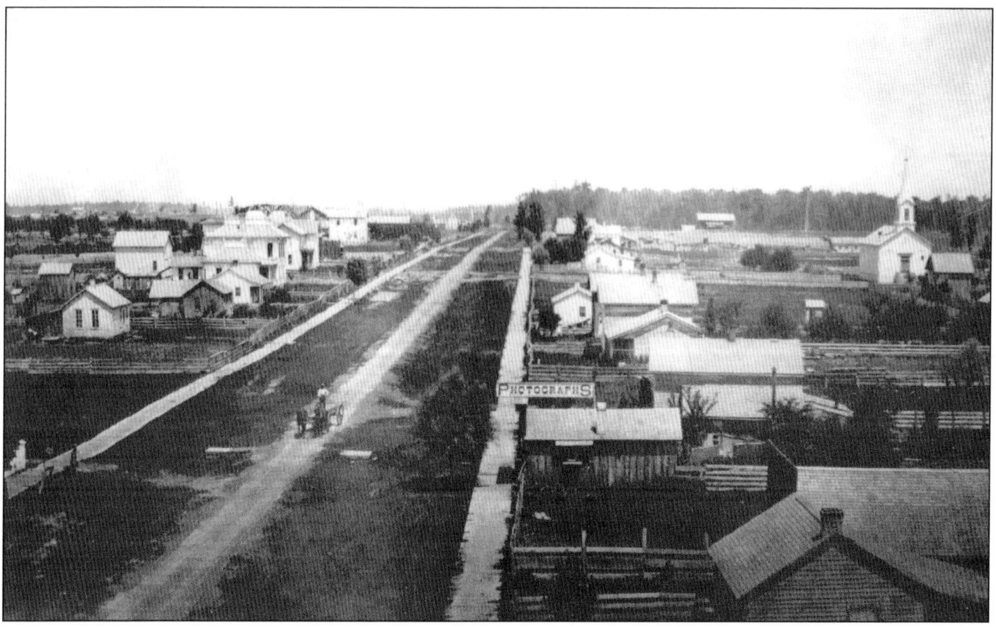


In a photograph taken in 1879 from the roof of the newly built Opera House Block, State Street stretches northward. At the far end of the dirt street on the left is the depot of Alma's first railroad, the Chicago, Saginaw and Canada. The rail line was blocks from the center of the village, an inconvenience that later was remedied when the tracks were rerouted. (Courtesy of the Alma Public Library.)

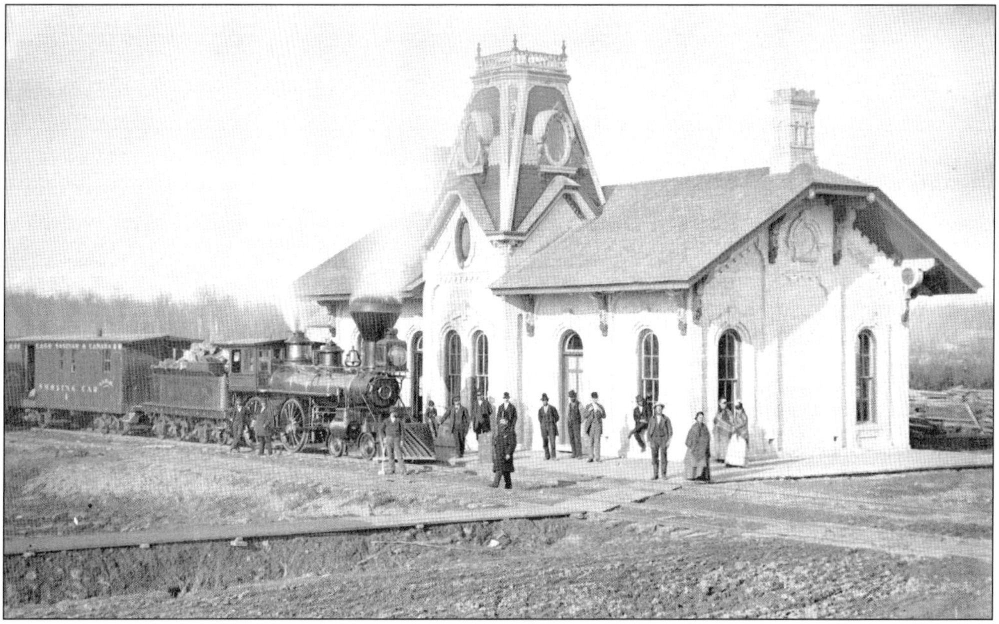

The ornate depot of the Chicago, Saginaw and Canada Railroad was located at Alma's north side, distant from the center of town. Construction of the charming building was financed by the ladies of Alma who gave several "socials," which raised $300. The building burned a few years later. The locomotive with its smoking car has arrived from Montcalm County. (Photograph by J. E. Davidson, courtesy of Tom McCreery.)

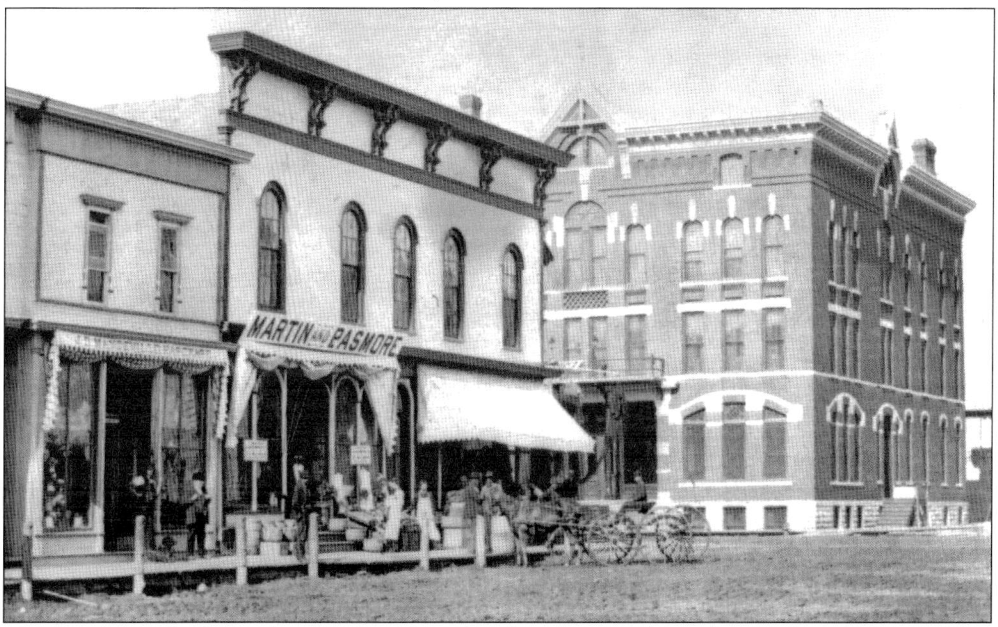


The newly finished Wright House, a first-class hotel, opened on the corner of Superior and State Streets in 1883. The site originally was occupied by Alma's first frame schoolhouse that was moved to a new location on West Superior Street to serve as a blacksmith shop. Michael Pollasky's store building, shared by Martin and Pasmore, occupies the southwest corner of the intersection. (Courtesy of the Alma Public Library.)

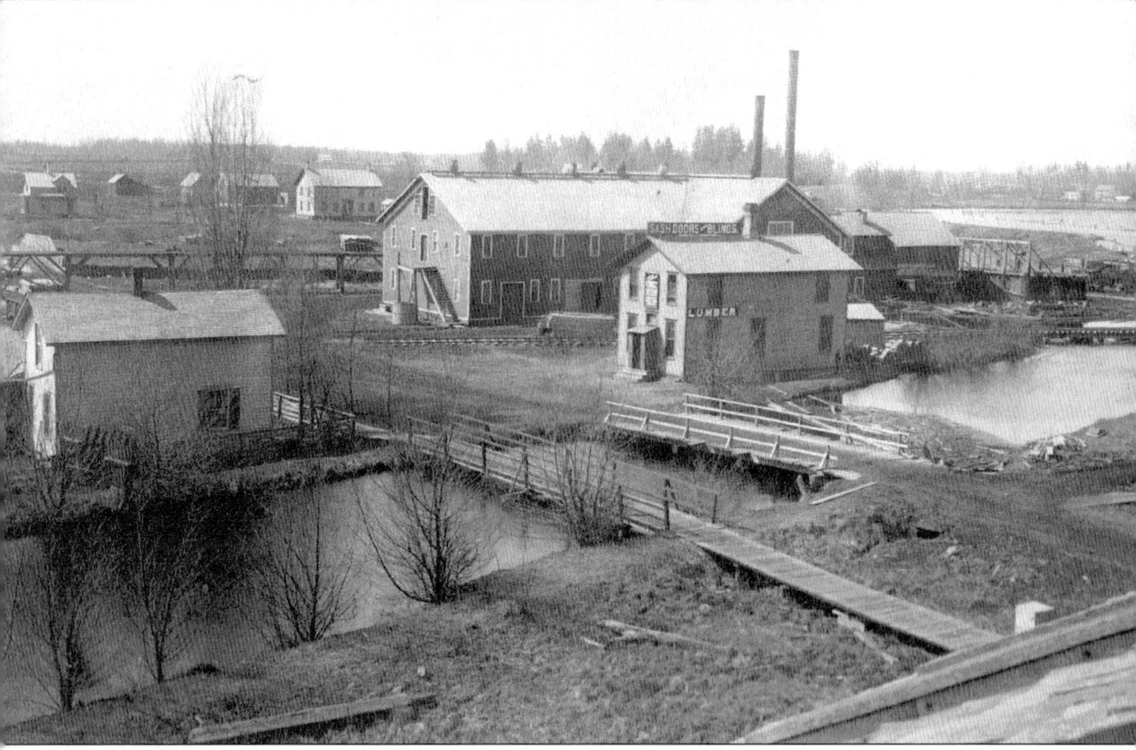


The Pierce and Ward mill was expanded to produce sashes, doors, and blinds under the firm of Tinker and Lumsden. The buildings on the left occupy the site of Ralph and Mary Ely's log cabin, the first building in Alma. Woodworth Street and its sidewalk cross the millrace, whose flowing waters power a gristmill and woolen mill downstream. (Courtesy of the Alma Public Library.)

# *Two*

# MOVERS AND SHAKERS

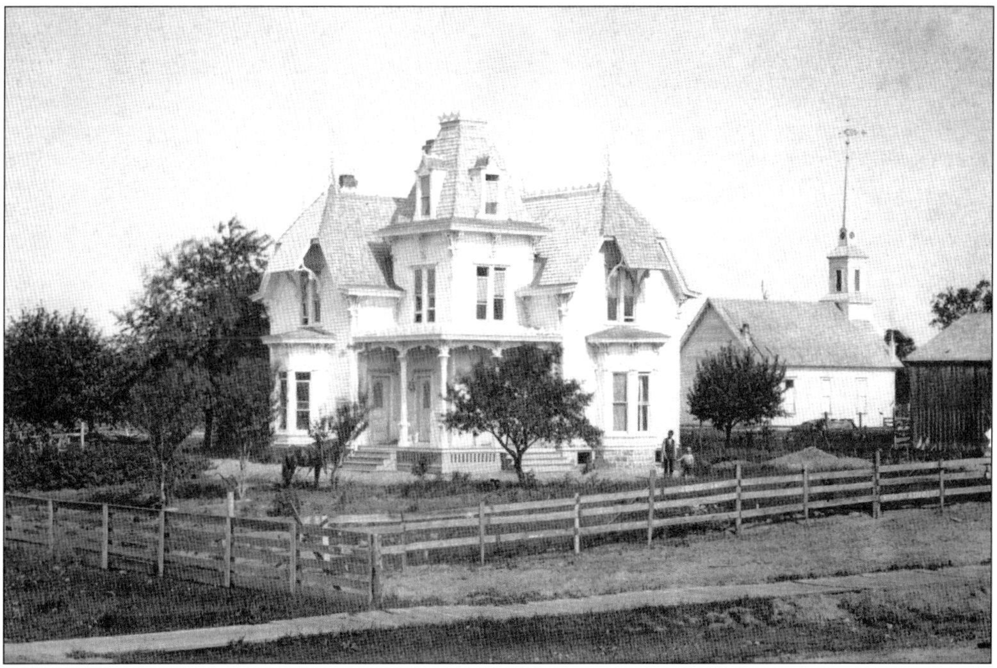

Ralph and Mary Ely, founders of Alma, lived in a log cabin during their pioneering years in the 1850s. After his service in the Civil War, where he became a brigadier general, they built this elaborate home in 1870 at the corner of Center and State Streets. Ely farmed, lumbered, and served as state senator and state auditor general. He later sold this home and moved to Petoskey to continue lumbering. He died at Cross Village in 1883 and was buried in Alma. (Courtesy of the Alma Public Library.)

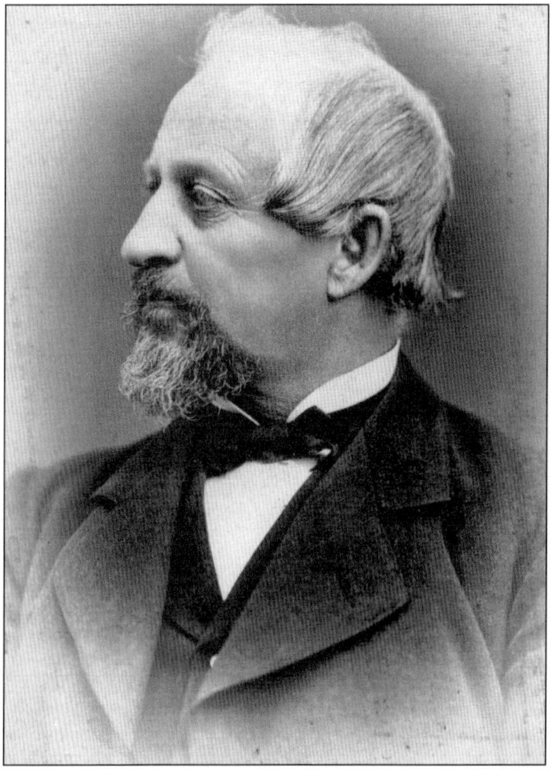

To this day, Alma owes more to Ammi W. Wright than to any other person. The wealthy Saginaw capitalist moved to Alma in the 1880s and began to pour his money into many projects. The Opera House Block, the Wright Hotel, the Alma Springs Sanitarium, the Alma Roller Mills, and Alma College were his earliest ventures. Before his death, he had brought the Masonic home to Alma and laid the foundations for the great Republic Truck Company. (Author's collection.)

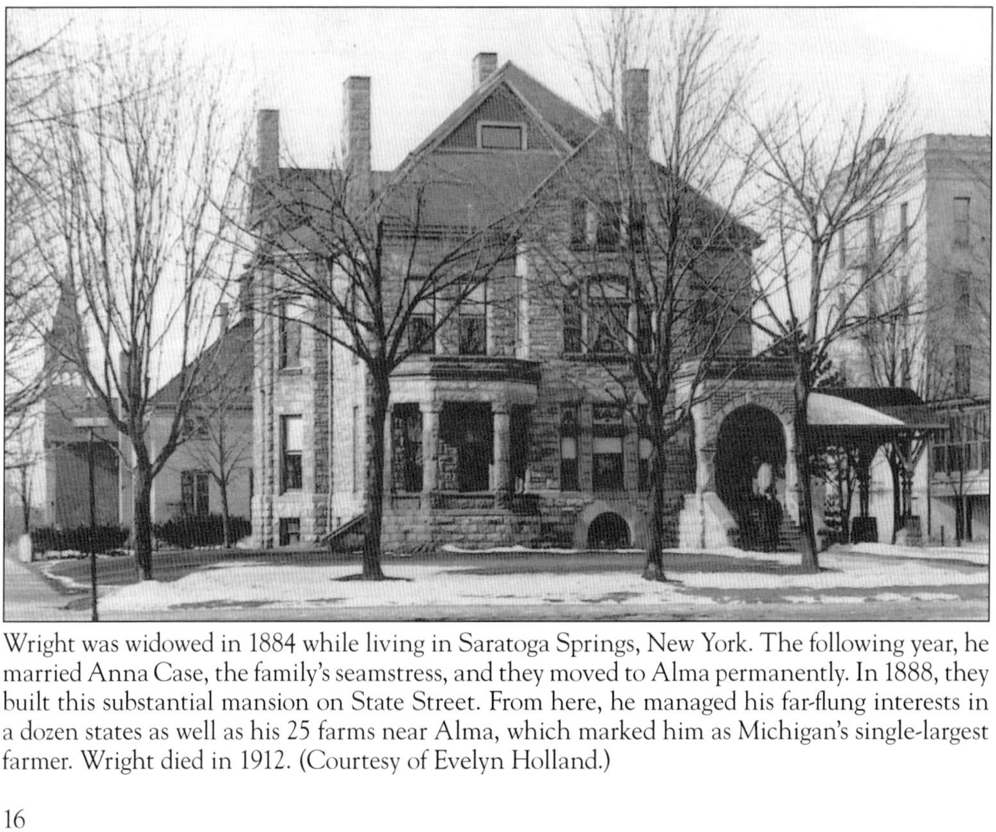

Wright was widowed in 1884 while living in Saratoga Springs, New York. The following year, he married Anna Case, the family's seamstress, and they moved to Alma permanently. In 1888, they built this substantial mansion on State Street. From here, he managed his far-flung interests in a dozen states as well as his 25 farms near Alma, which marked him as Michigan's single-largest farmer. Wright died in 1912. (Courtesy of Evelyn Holland.)

Of Wright's five children, only one survived to full adulthood. Sarah, Wright's pampered daughter, married Dr. J. Henry Lancashire of Saratoga Springs. She and her husband easily and joyfully lived the life of the wealthy, enjoying her father's largesse. She inherited the entire Wright fortune, and before her death at 84, she managed to spend virtually all of her father's millions. (Author's collection.)

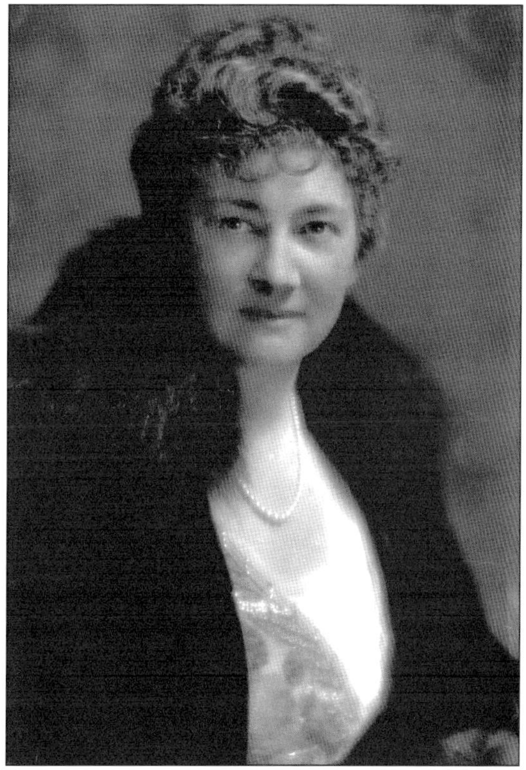

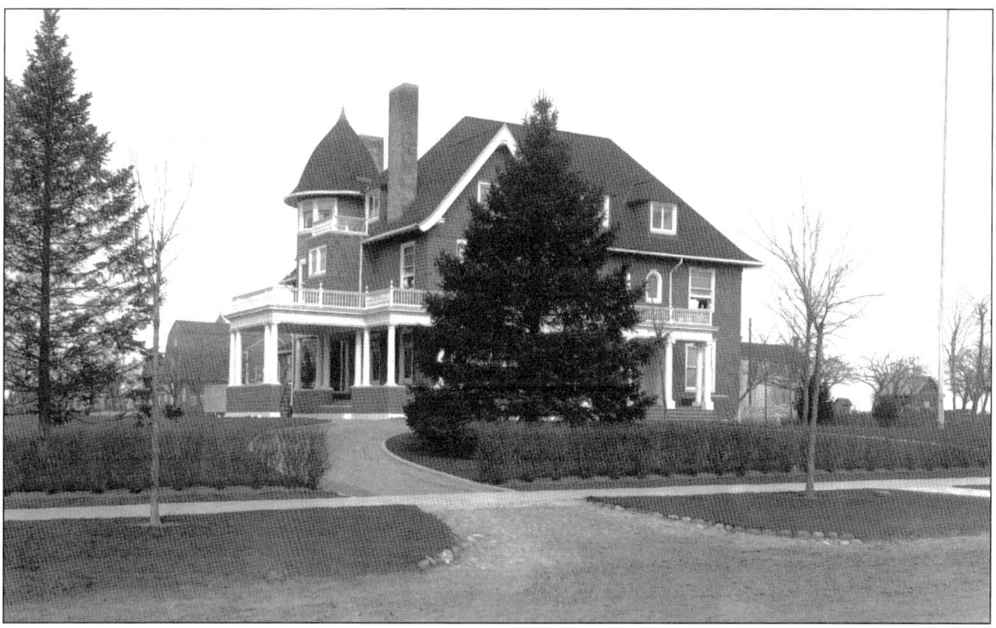

Sarah Wright Lancashire grew up in high society, and she considered the rural city of Alma to be a social wasteland. To lure his daughter to Alma, Wright built her this mansion as a belated wedding gift. The Lancashires and their four children spent several months of the year at Saravilla on State Street. They summered on the Atlantic shore north of Boston and wintered in the South. (Author's collection.)

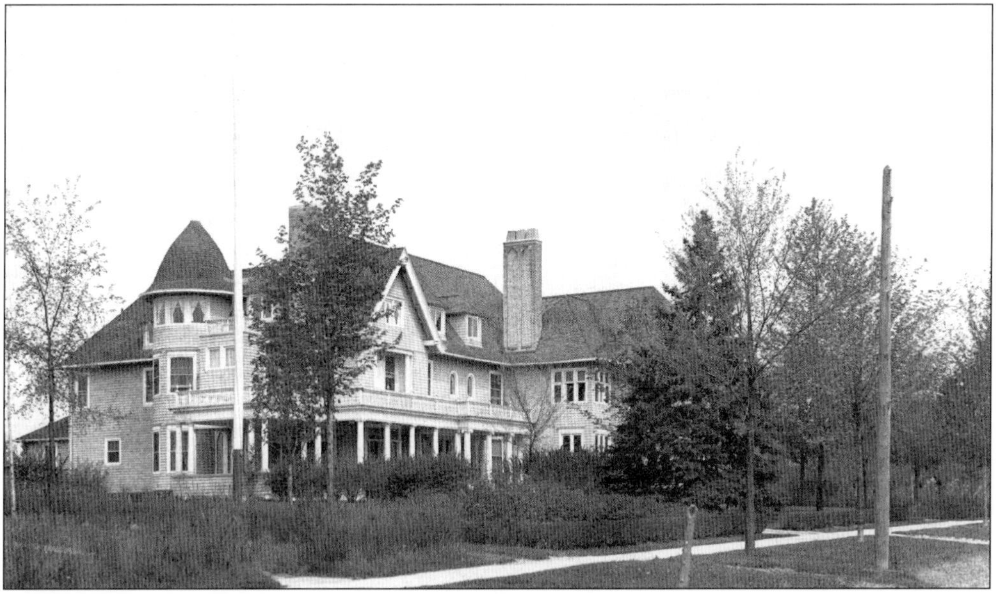

In 1904, Sarah Wright Lancashire added a large addition to Saravilla and included a 40-foot ballroom where she, her husband, Henry, and their friends from Saginaw danced the night away. She also included a billiards room for Henry and two bedrooms upstairs. When the family was in residence, a flag emblazoned with "Saravilla" flew from the pole in the front yard. (Courtesy of the Alma Public Library.)

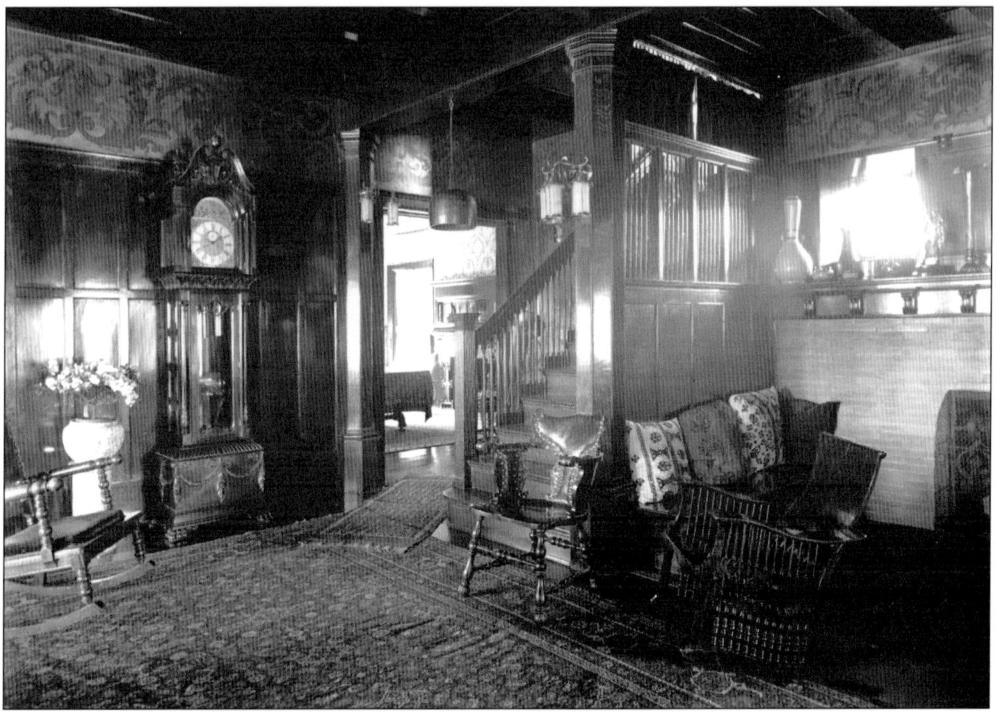

Saravilla was even more sumptuous than Ammi W. Wright's mansion down the street. Sara had long-stemmed roses shipped weekly from Detroit. They were placed in the sterling silver floor vase seen at the left. Maids and handymen saw to the family's needs. (Author's collection.)

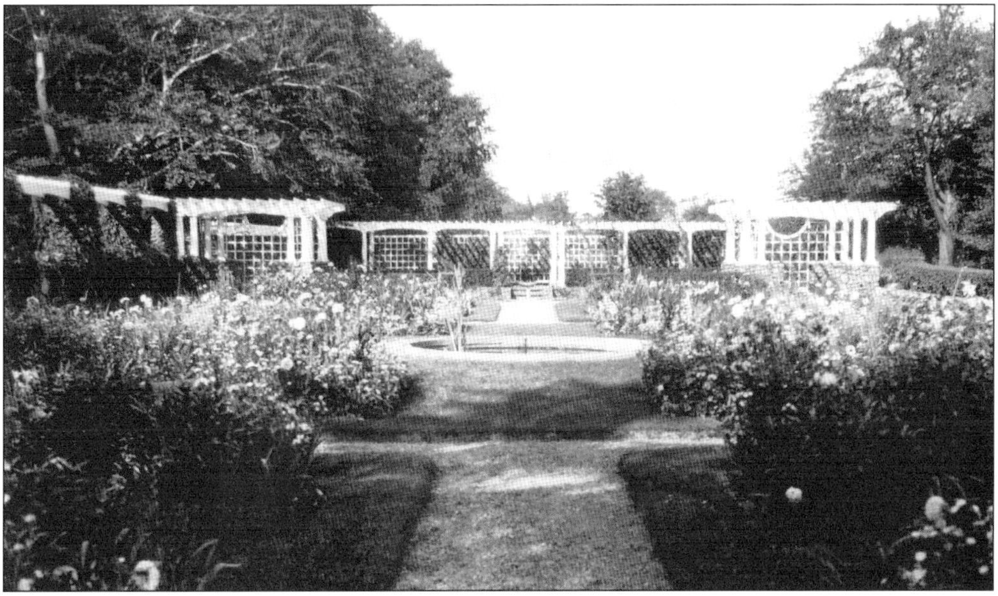

Lancashire's property stretched 600 feet back from State Street and included the house, the carriage house, a large playhouse for the children, tennis courts, and these gardens. After she left Alma, the gardens were maintained by Charles Rhodes, who bought Saravilla, and then by the Gleaners, who used Saravilla as a home for the elderly. The gardens were designed by a landscape architect from Chicago and included a sunken rose garden. (Author's collection.)

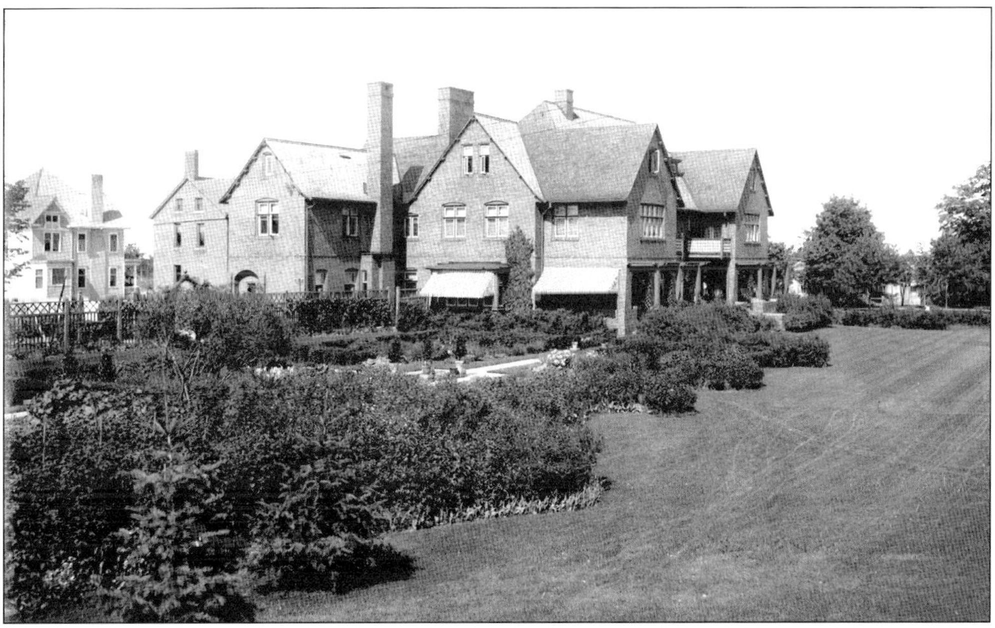

Louisa and Francis King, wealthy Chicagoans, came to Alma in 1901. Francis sought treatment for alcoholism at the Alma Springs Sanitarium. By 1902, the Kings had decided to make Alma their home. They bought a half block on North State Street and built Orchard House, an English Tudor home somewhat in the style of the home they occupied in Elmhurst, Illinois. (Courtesy of Dale Kemler.)

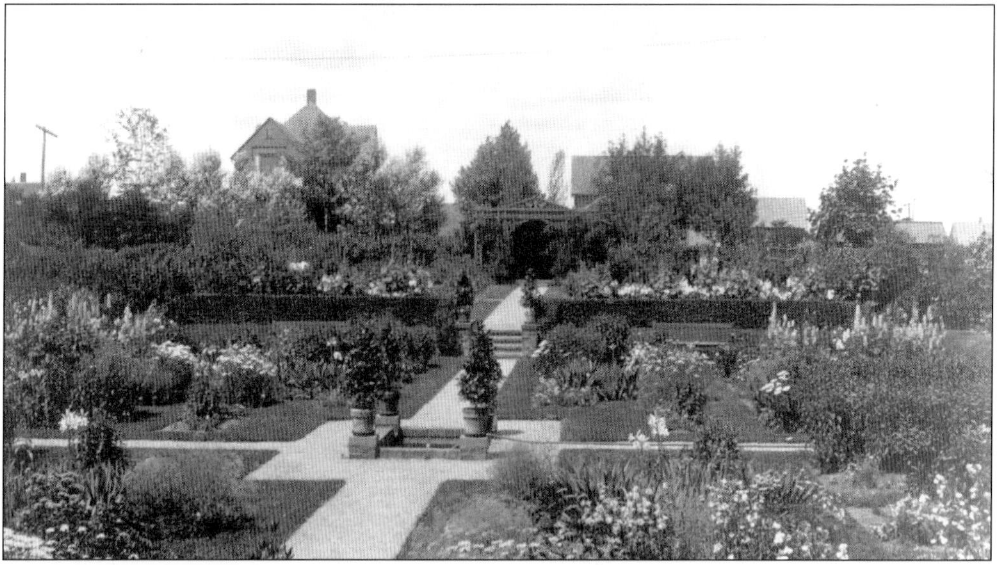

Inspired by her mother-in-law in Chicago, Louisa King began landscaping her spacious yard. Hired gardeners helped her to manage her 32 flower beds, 90 varieties of lilacs, and countless other gardening wonders. From her passion for gardening came nine nationally distributed books, countless magazine articles, and many lecture tours. During the 1920s, she became the most important woman garden writer in the country. (Courtesy of Lucille Behler.)

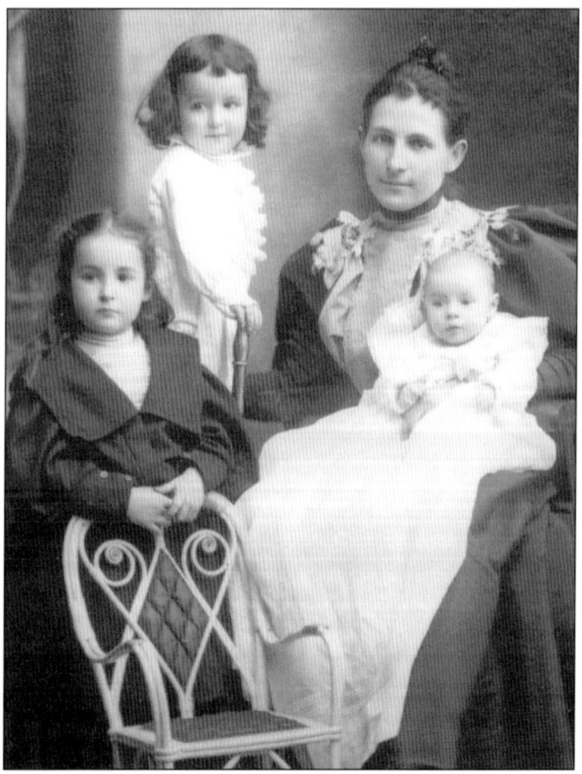

The King's children Elizabeth, Frances, and Henry join their mother in this scene of domesticity. Later the children were sent to preparatory and finishing schools. Maids and nannies assisted with their rearing, and in adulthood, the children hinted that their mother's busyness imbued them with a sense of neglect. (Author's collection.)

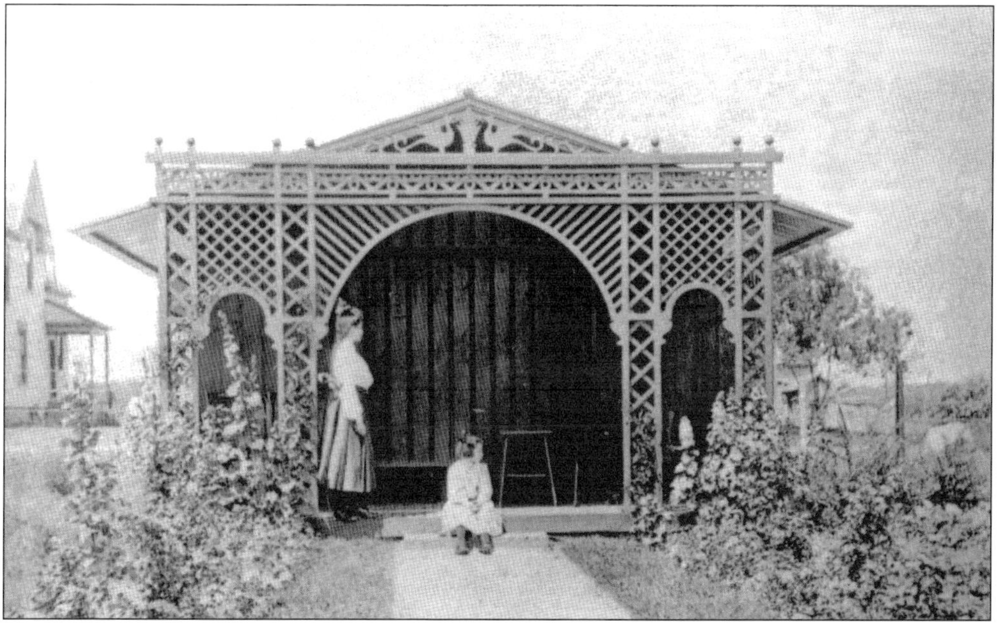

At the end of the path that bisected the gardens sat this picturesque pergola. Here Elizabeth and Frances enjoy the wonders of their yard, with its shady glens, grassy hillocks, teakwood benches, fences, gates, trellises, and never-ending billows of glowing flowers. The grounds were thrown open to the public twice a year, and pilgrims often arrived begging for a tour of the celebrated yard and gardens. (Author's collection.)

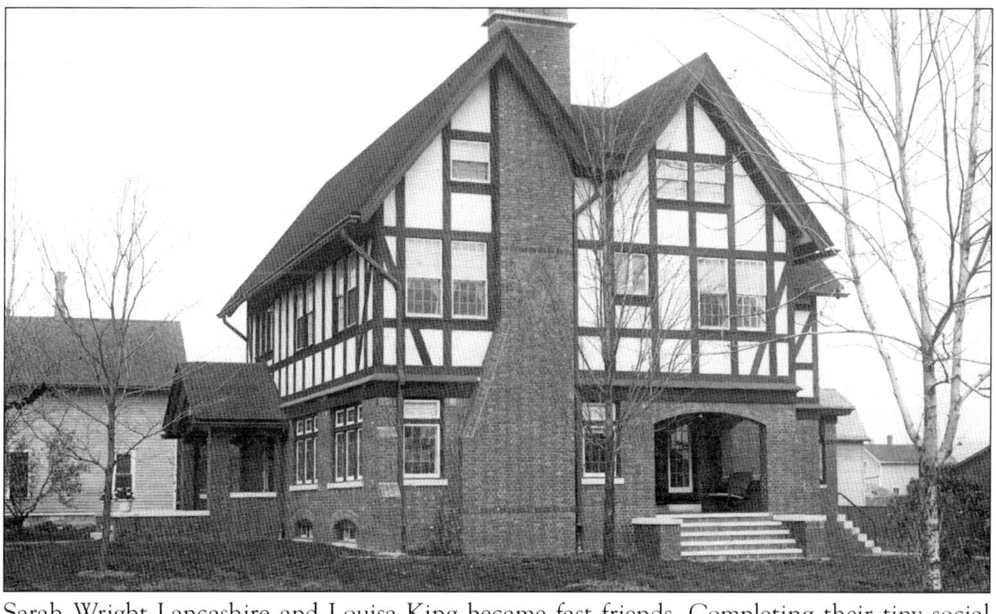

Sarah Wright Lancashire and Louisa King became fast friends. Completing their tiny social circle was Mary Bahlke. She and her husband, businessman William Bahlke, were prominent in Alma society. The Bahlkes built this home on State Street in 1907. Three-time presidential candidate and noted orator William Jennings Bryan was entertained here in 1916. Mary survived William and, upon her death in 1953, gave the house to the city for use as a library. It is now a private home. (Courtesy of Richard Tesman.)

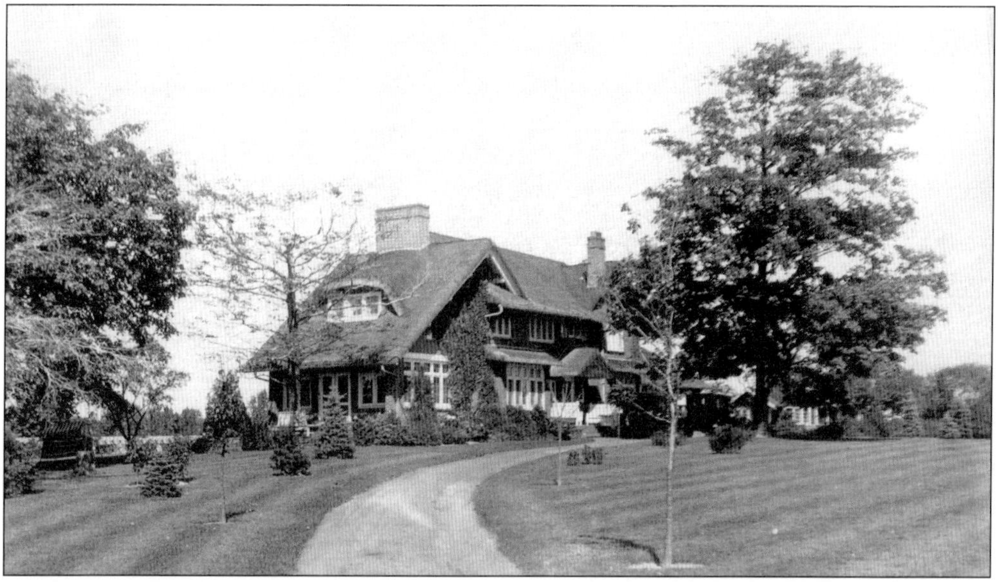

As general manager of Alma's Republic Truck Company, Frank Ruggles made a fortune. On a large parcel of land between Michigan Avenue and the Pine River, he built this house in 1918. Named Roselawn after his wife, Rose, the house was beautifully appointed and was the centerpiece of 14 acres of yards and gardens, including two bridges to islands in the Pine River. Rose had one of the first radios in Alma, and their son Reed kept an alligator in the sunroom. (Courtesy of John Kemler.)

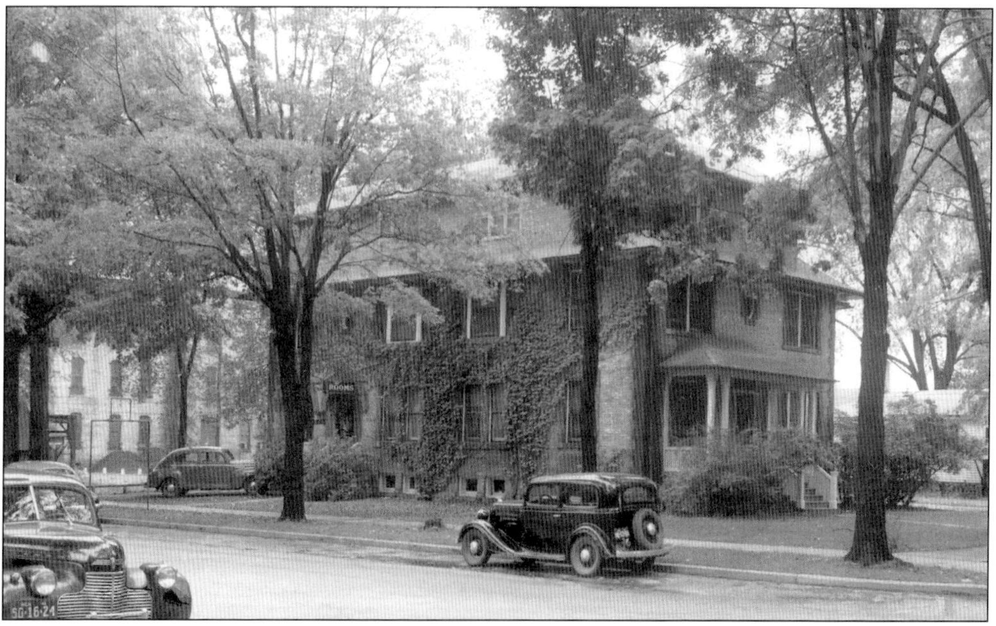

The Maples was Alma's first duplex and a luxurious one at that. It was built on State Street in 1900. The house of Dr. C. L. Downie had occupied the spot but was moved diagonally across the street. On the vacant lot rose this two-apartment building. With its elegant fireplaces, steam heat, and electric lights, it was regarded as one of the finest residences in the city. In 1940, owner Ed Roberts added the third floor. (Courtesy of Richard Tesman.)

# *Three*

# Around the Town

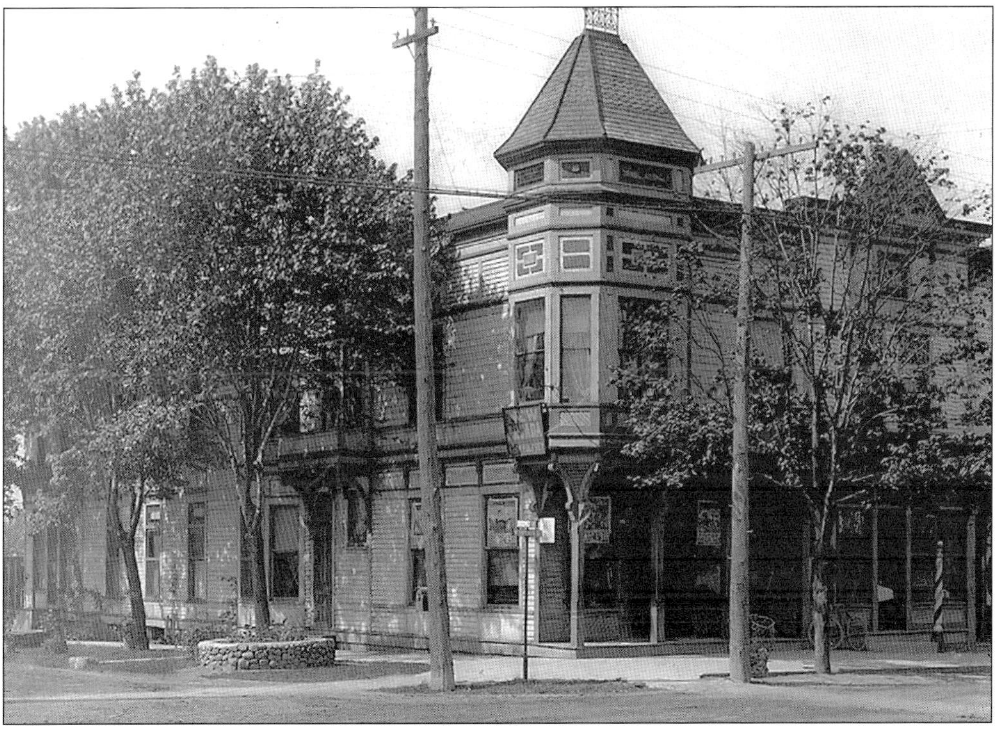

George Pulfrey, longtime proprietor of the Seaman Hotel, later called the Pulfrey House, on State Street, built the Arcada Hotel at Prospect and Superior Streets in 1889. The hotel and its livery attracted a less-well-heeled clientele than did the sumptuous Wright Hotel. The Arcada later became Tildy's Inn, also known as the Wright Hotel Annex, and was demolished in 1958. (Courtesy of the Alma Public Library.)

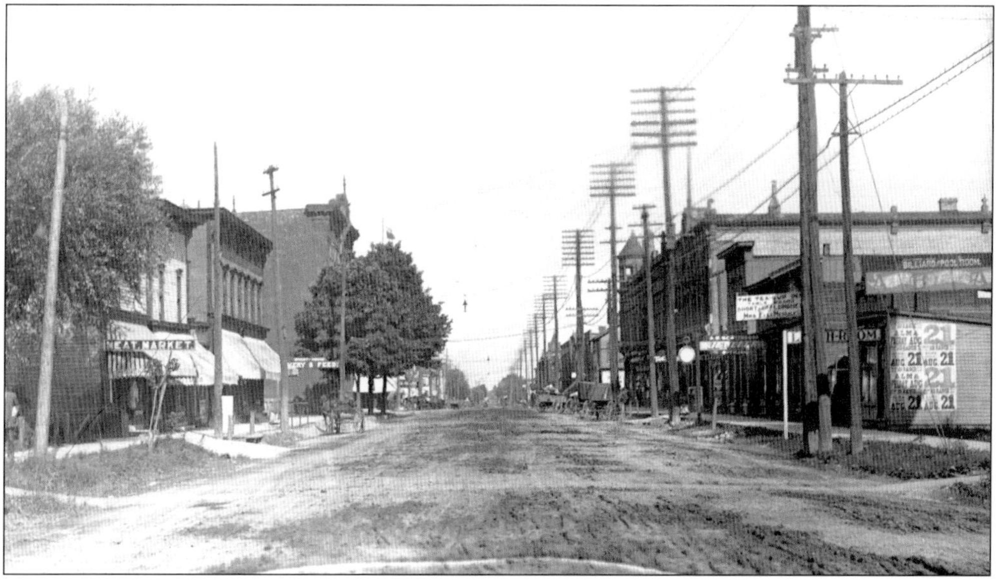

On a bucolic August day in 1908, Superior Street quietly awaits traffic. Excitement is brewing, however, as posters announce that Miller Brothers 101 Ranch Wild West show is scheduled for two performances and a street parade on Friday, August 21. Eila Metcalf's Tea-Cup Inn and Scattergood's Jewelry store are located at the right. (Courtesy of Colleen Boyer.)

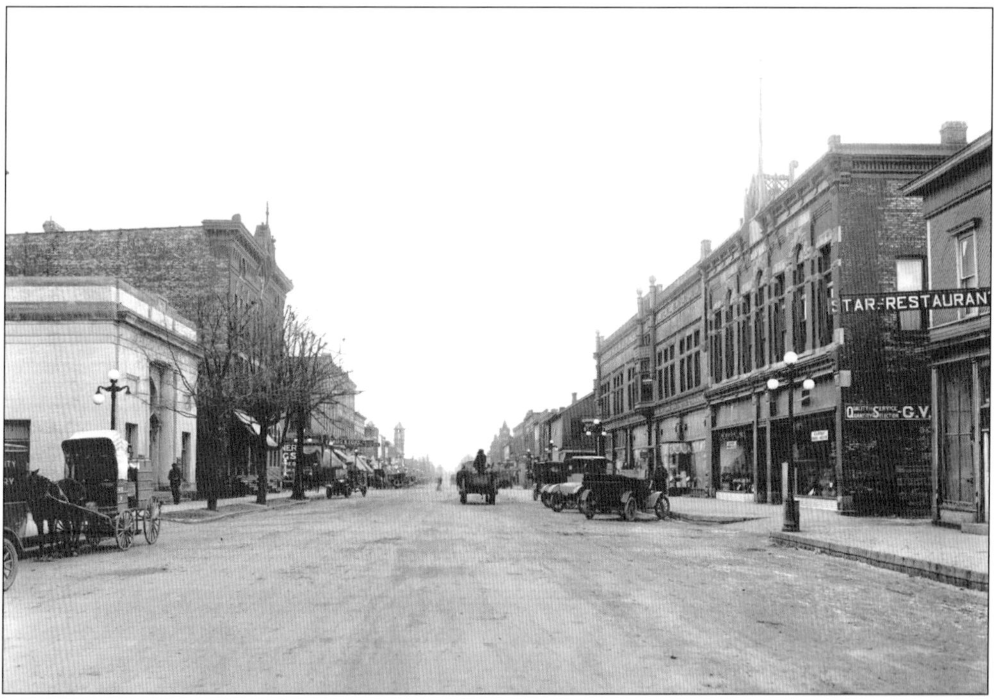


The Alma City Laundry delivery truck and the Union Delivery Wagon No. 6 sit at the left. The new First State Bank and the Wright Hotel are also on the left. On the right is the Merchant's Building, and beyond it the Pollasky Block. This photograph of Superior Street was taken around 1920. (Courtesy of the Alma Public Library.)

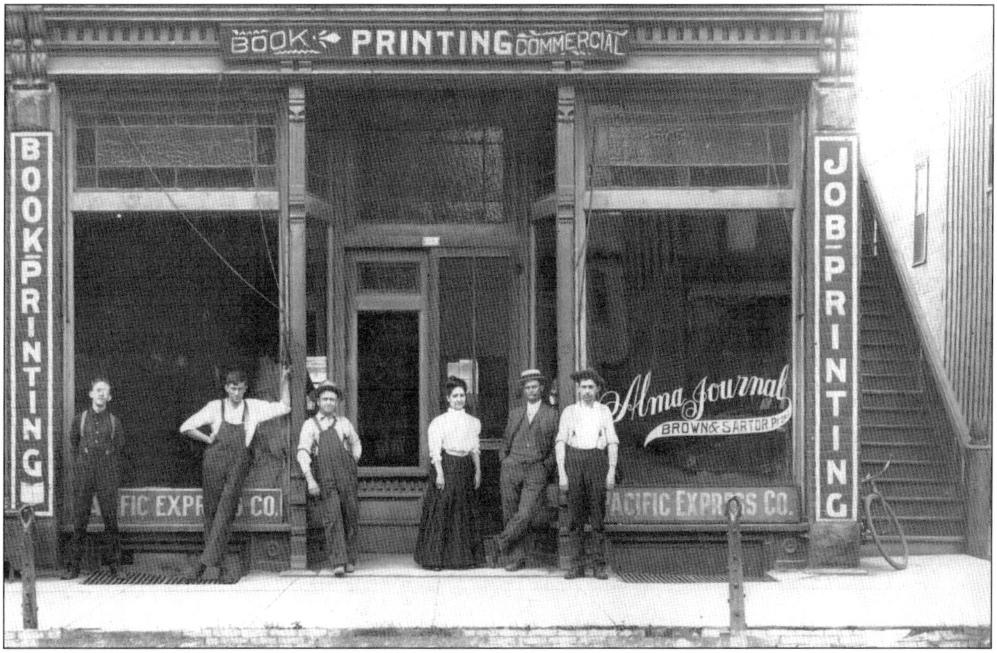


Located in the Merchant's Building on Superior Street, the *Alma Journal* was published by Caris Brown and Joe Sartor. It competed with the *Alma Record* before the two were merged as the *Alma Record and Journal*. Here Sartor stands on the right with his staff and printing crew. (Courtesy of Colleen Boyer.)

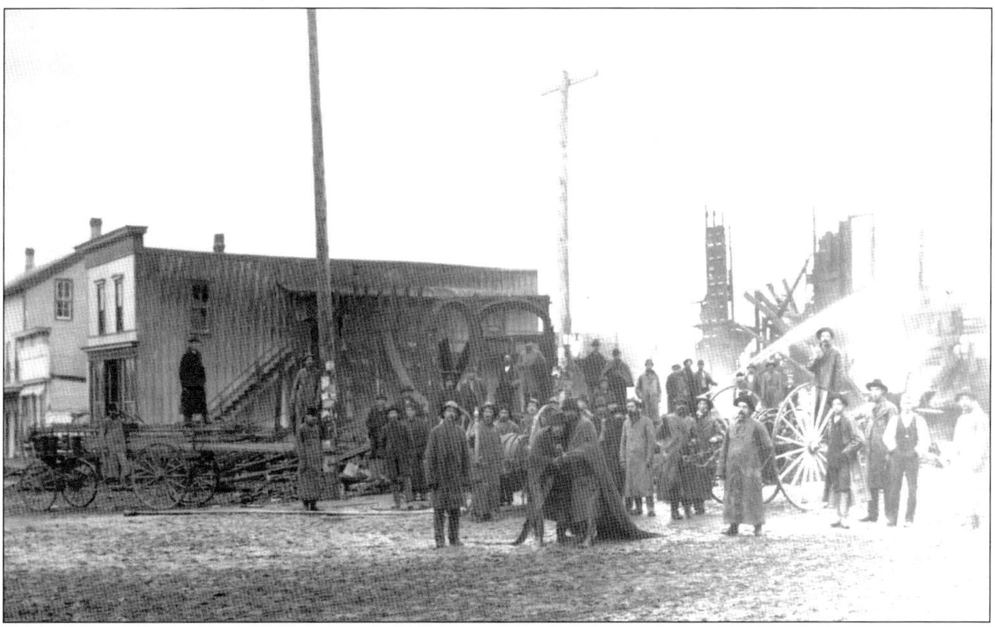

Through a superhuman effort by the Alma Fire Department, neighboring buildings were saved when the Pollasky store burned on October 15, 1893. The scorched building on the left later was moved from State Street to Superior Street, where it has housed, at various times, the *Alma Record*, the Star Restaurant, Baker Photography, Stovall Studio, and the Scripture Palace. (Courtesy of the Alma College Library.)

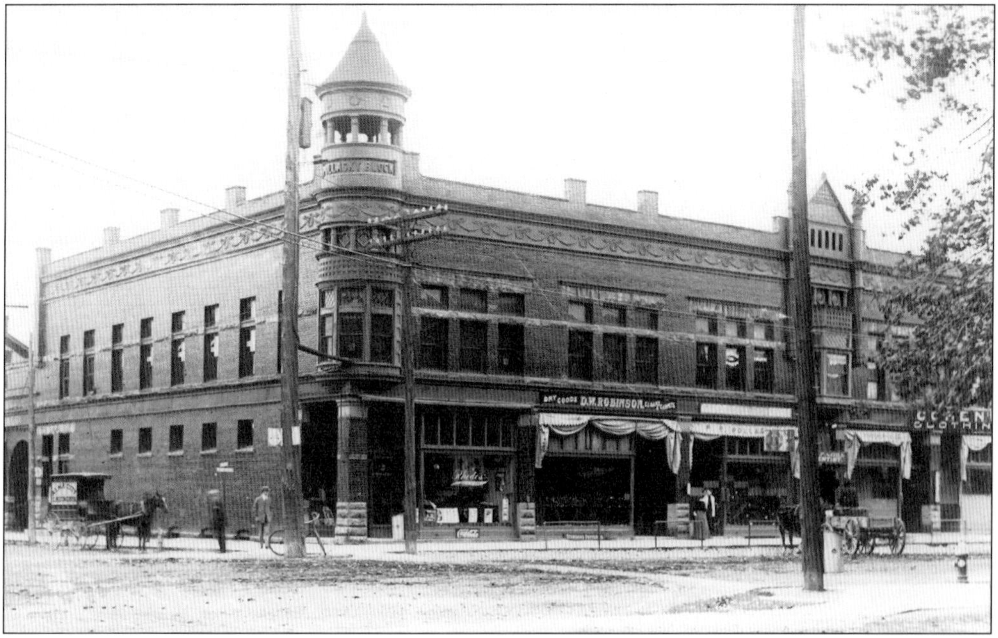

The financial hard times in 1893 prevented Michael Pollasky from replacing his burned building at once. When times improved, however, in 1897 he built this substantial business block with stores on the ground floor and offices upstairs. It enjoyed one of the more advantageous business locations in town. (Courtesy of Richard Tesman.)

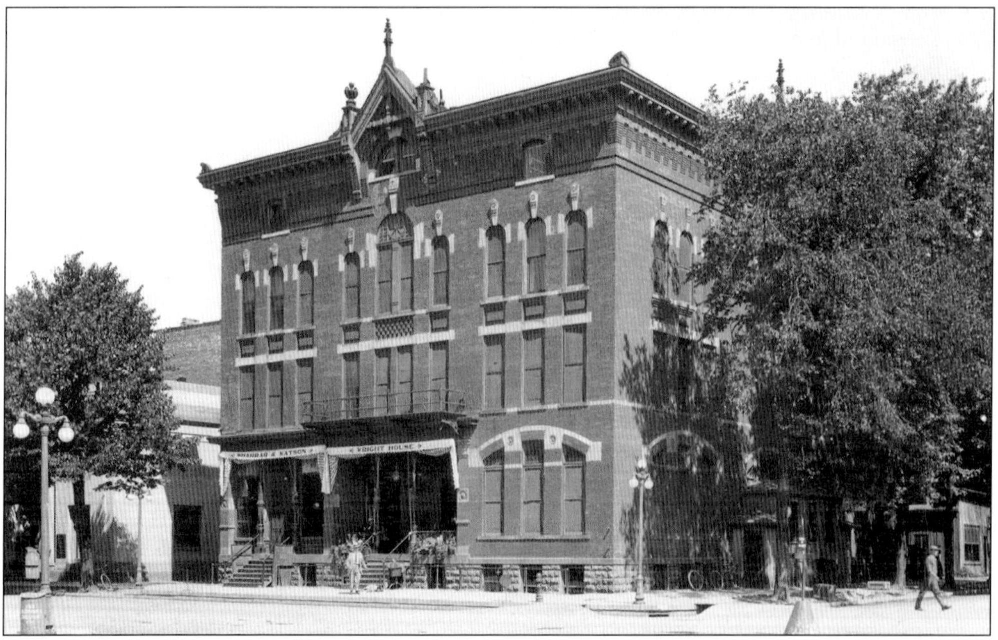

Even before officially moving to Alma, the wealthy Ammi W. Wright was pouring his money into the town. In 1883, he built the Wright House, regarded as one of the finer hotels outside Detroit. Its interior was exquisite, and the service and amenities were superb. Its dining room was the scene of countless social gatherings, and its menu reflected a sophisticated cuisine. (Courtesy of Richard Tesman.)

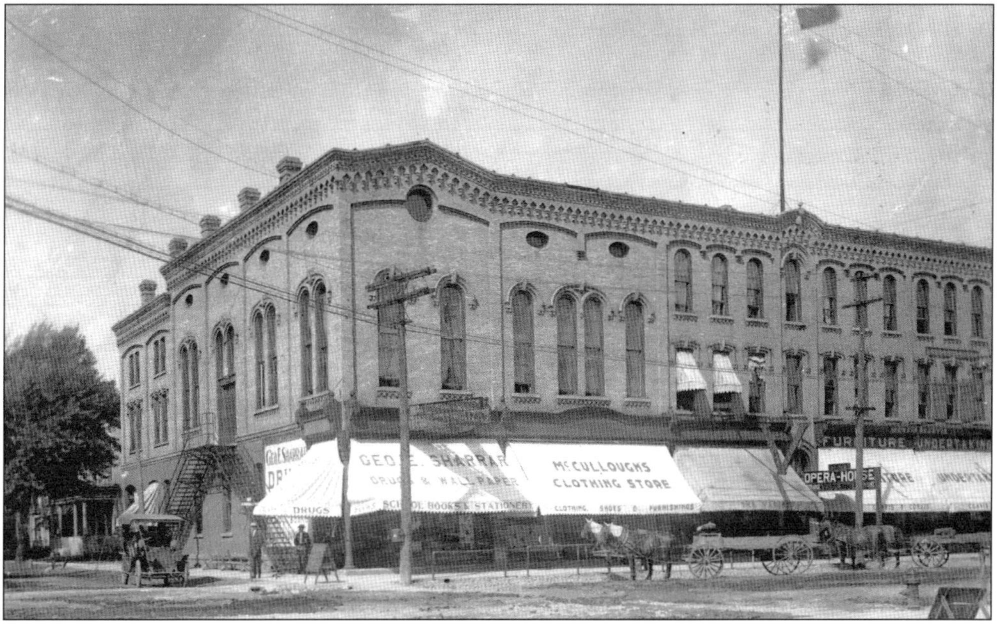


After Wright and Dawson's general store burned in the Hulbert House fire of 1876, the firm moved temporarily to the Pollasky building at the corner of State and Superior Streets. On the opposite corner, Wright built the Opera House Block, shown here. Completed in 1880, it contained an opera house and offices upstairs as well as five storefronts on the ground floor. (Courtesy of the Alma Public Library.)

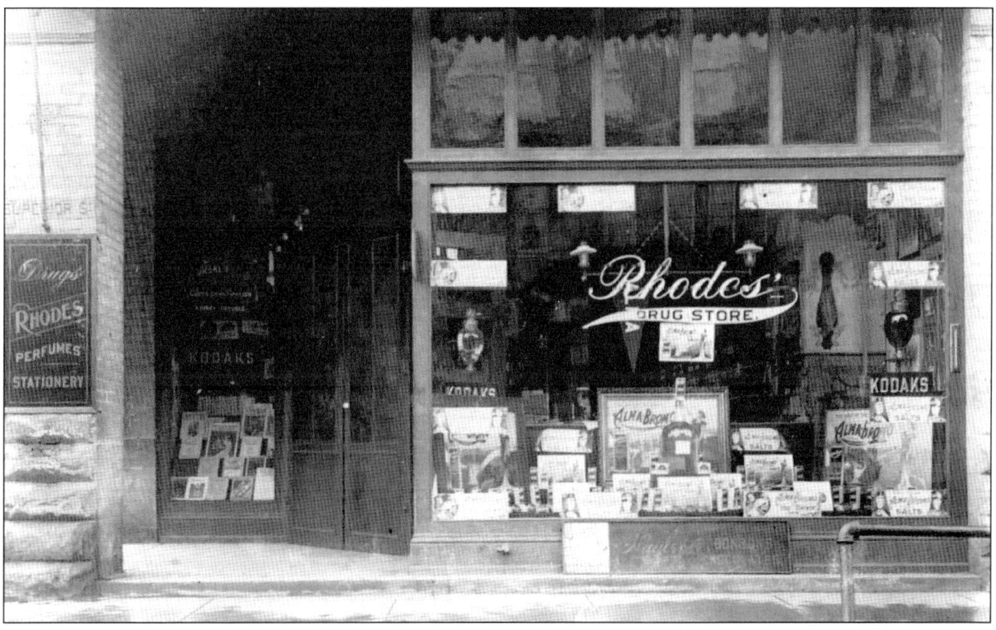


Pharmacist Charles Rhodes conducted this drugstore in the Pollasky Block at the corner of Superior and State Streets. Risking his entire assets, he invested heavily in the new Republic Truck Company. Quickly acquiring a fortune, he bought and occupied the Saravilla mansion. Later when the truck company struggled and his fortunes declined, he joined Celotex Corporation in Chicago, where he once again entered the road to comfort. (Courtesy of the Alma Public Library.)

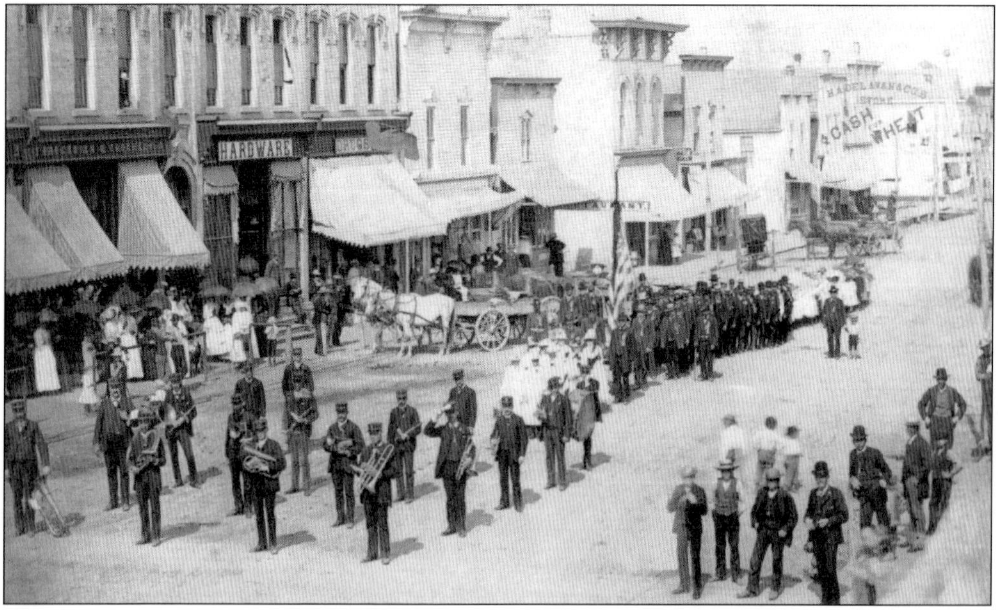


The celebrated Wright's Opera House Band helped the community honor its Civil War veterans during the 1887 Memorial Day parade. Behind the band marched a group of ladies in white. Next came the veterans, most of them in their 40s at the time. At the end of the parade walked children dressed in white. (Author's collection.)

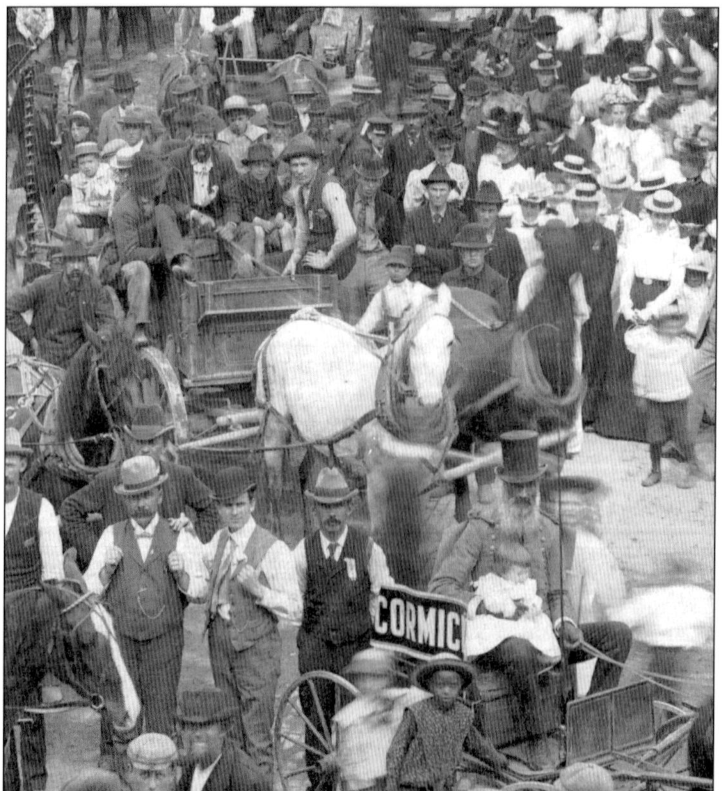


Sponsored by dealer J. W. Holmes, McCormick Day, on Saturday, June 26, 1900, was an event promoting McCormick farm machinery. Superior Street was filled with 40 teams, pulling binders, mowers, and hay rakes. In this picture, wagonloads of celebrants have massed at the Superior Street and State Street intersection. In the foreground, a gentleman wearing a top hat in a buckboard holds his little girl with his wife seated beside him. Many participants pinned on McCormick badges and displayed McCormick banners. (Courtesy of John Kemler.)

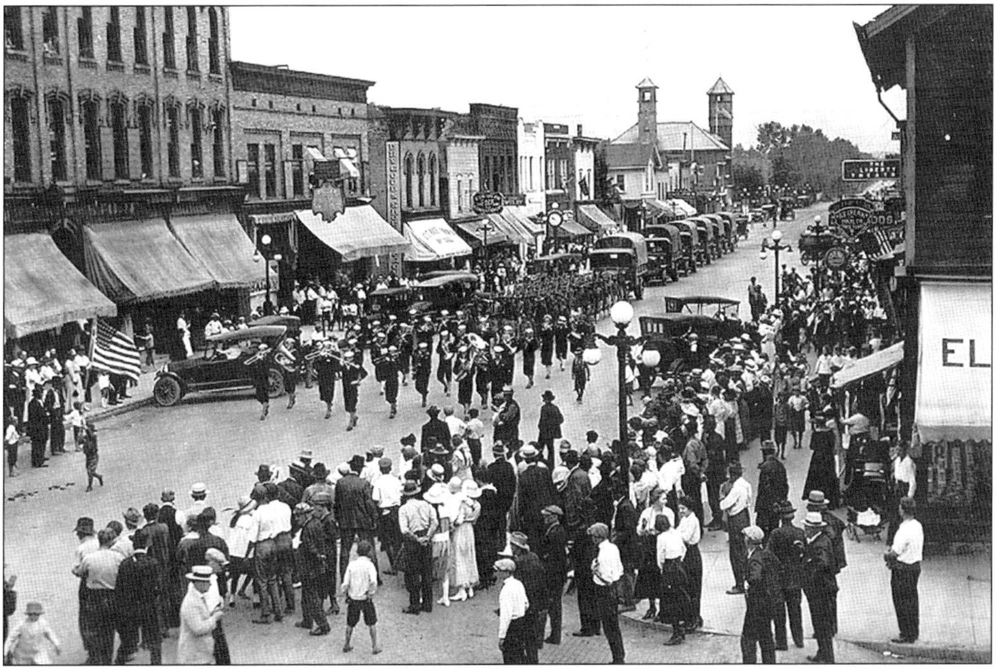


In July 1918, a visit by the navy's Jackie Band from Detroit brought excitement to a city caught up in the drama of the Great War. A parade featuring the band and Alma's Republic Liberty trucks proved inspirational. When bandsman Murphy took the platform in the evening, his ringing Billy Sunday tones resulted in 65 stalwart Alma men shouldering their way to the front of the crowd to volunteer for the armed services. (Courtesy of the Alma Public Library.)

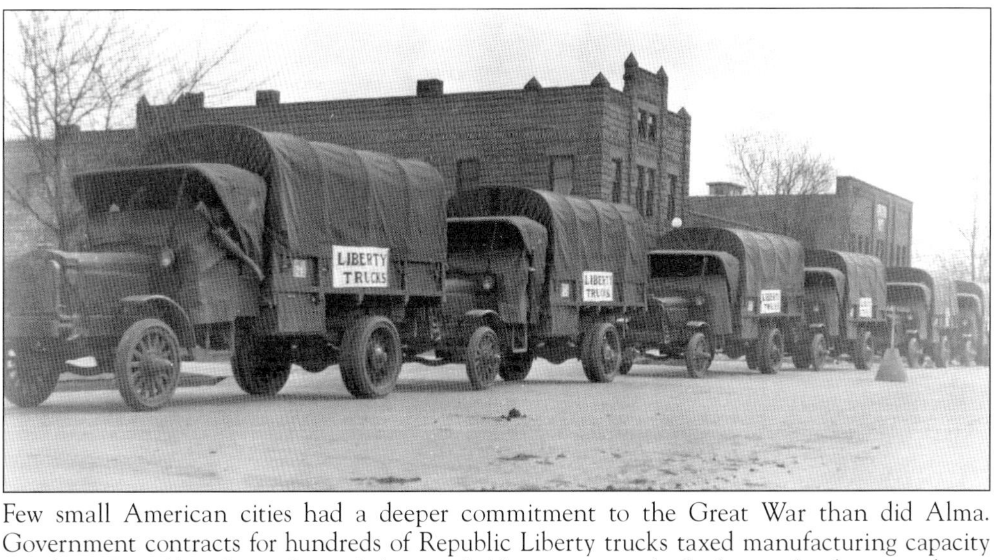


Few small American cities had a deeper commitment to the Great War than did Alma. Government contracts for hundreds of Republic Liberty trucks taxed manufacturing capacity at Alma's Republic plants. Several thousand Alma-area men built the trucks that were being shipped to France. Doughboys from Alma felt a warm glow upon meeting a truck from home on European byways. (Courtesy of John Kemler.)

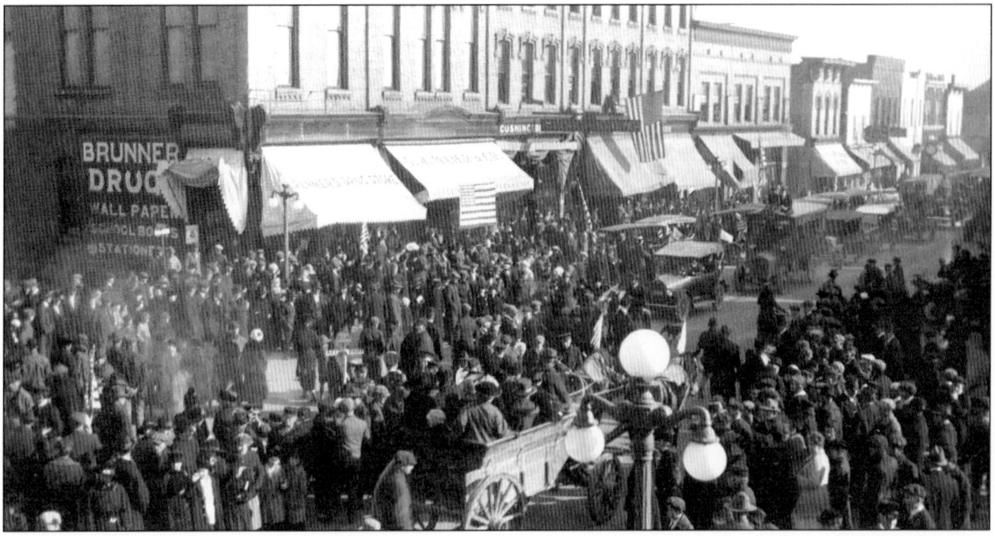


In November 1918, the Great War was nearing an end, and folks were anticipating the announcement of Germany's surrender. A false armistice was announced, creating and then squelching a celebration. When the real armistice was announced, word arrived in Alma by telegraph in the wee hours of the morning, triggering a citywide celebration such as the village had never before experienced. (Courtesy of Richard Tesman.)

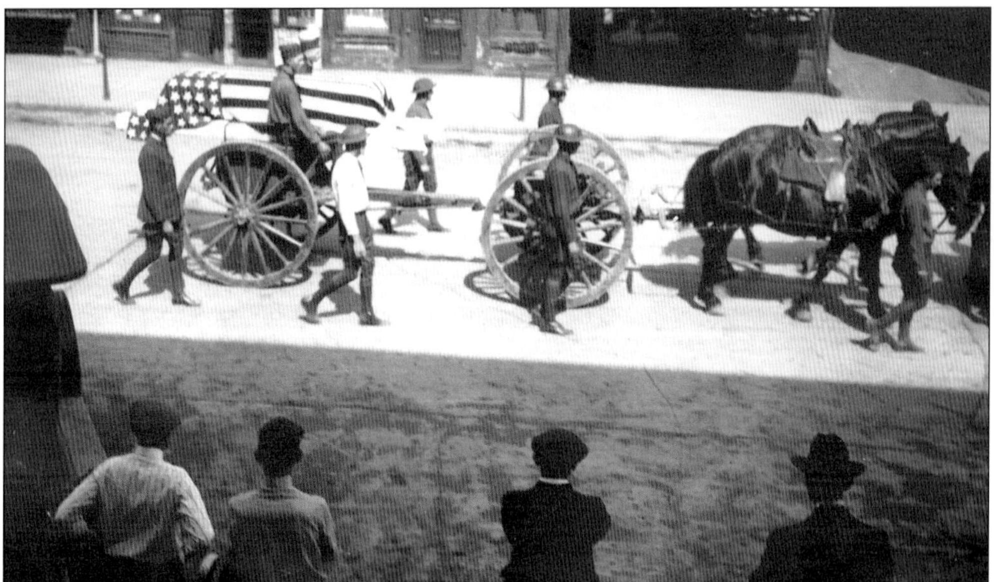

For some families, the war dragged on far beyond the armistice. The first fatality from Alma was Cpl. George Myers, killed in July 1918 in the Battle of the Marne. His body finally arrived in the states, and his funeral in August 1921 was attended by 1,000 people. His remains were conveyed to Riverside Cemetery on a caisson brought from Lansing for the ceremony. His name was already given to the local post of the American Legion. (Courtesy of Richard Tesman.)

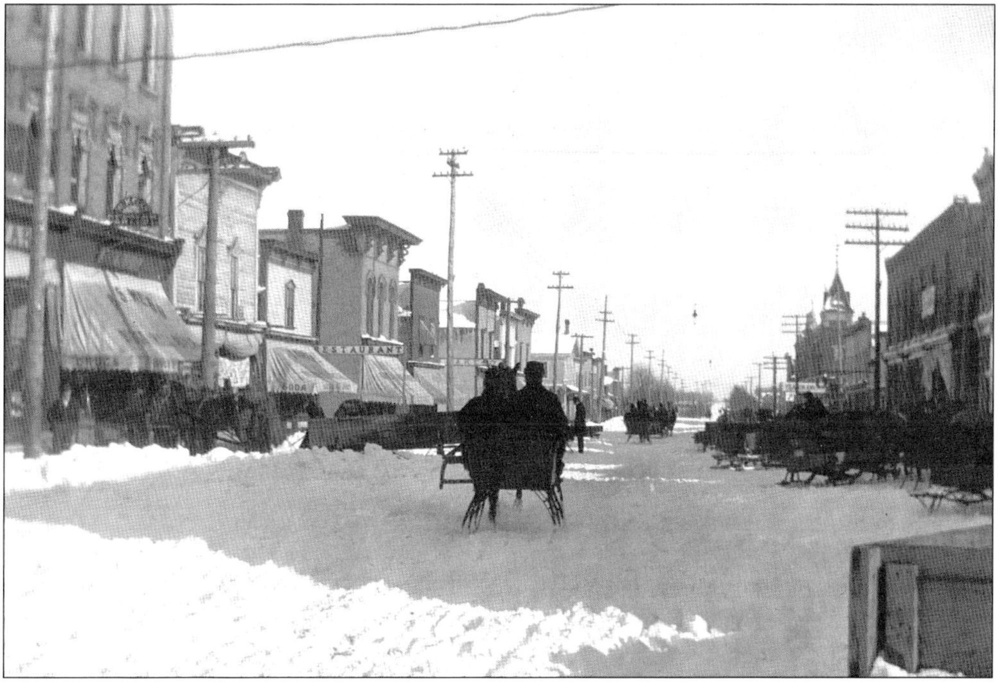


Alma folks were always hoping for good sleighing in winter. Because streets and roads were not plowed, early automobiles often spent the winter sitting on blocks in garages and barns. People still relied on horse-drawn sleighs and cutters to take them through the snow. Here a cutter moves down East Superior Street. (Courtesy of the Alma College Library.)

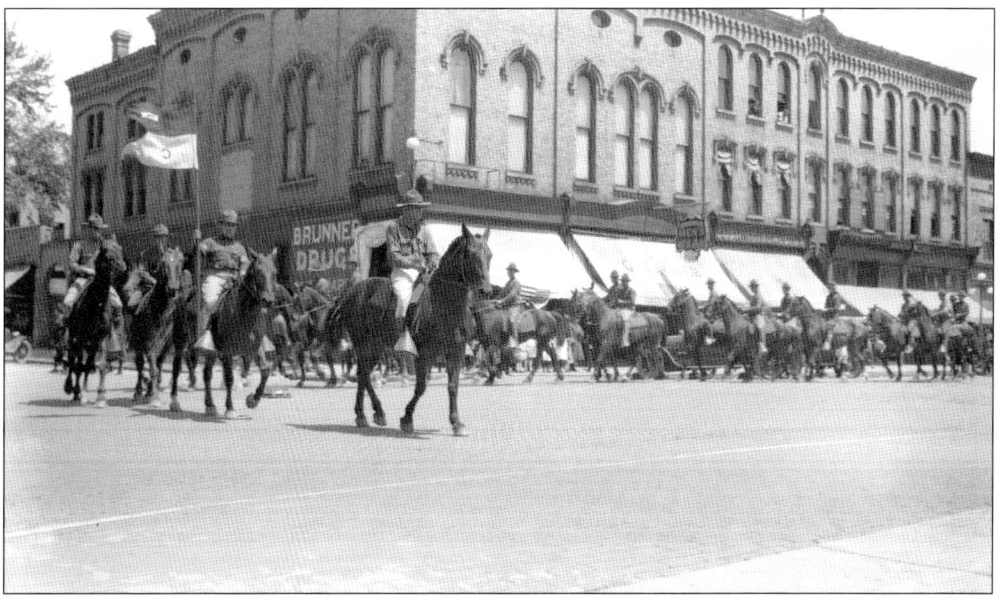


Mounted cavalry was fast becoming a legend when Company C of the 106th Cavalry Regiment, 32nd Infantry Division of the National Guard was formed in Alma in 1921. Traditions die hard, however, and that summer, the cavalry troops rode the 90 miles to Camp Grayling for training and maneuvers. Here the local guardsmen parade on Superior and State Streets. The horses were part of the local scene until 1940. (Photograph by Hubert Elias, courtesy of Dale Kemler.)

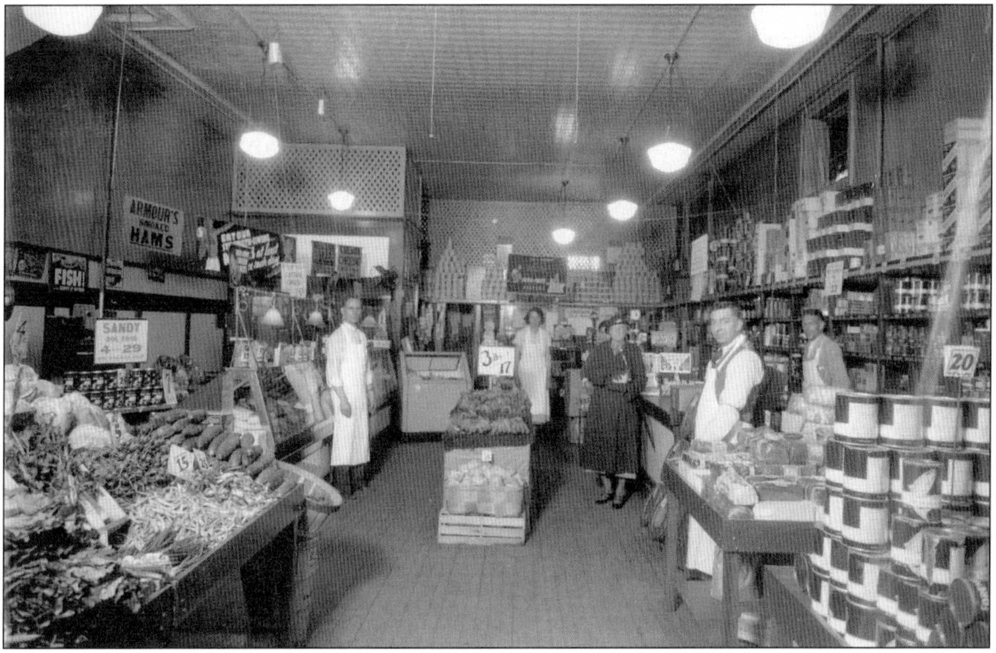


Located in the Lancashire Block, adjoining the Opera House Block on Superior Street, the Kroger Grocery and Baking Company was run by Chester Schultz. In this 1930 view from left to right are Glen Reed; Schultz's wife, Effie; an unidentified lady customer; Schultz; and Dale Richards. The store was selling bananas at three pounds for 17¢. (Courtesy of Teacel Dean.)

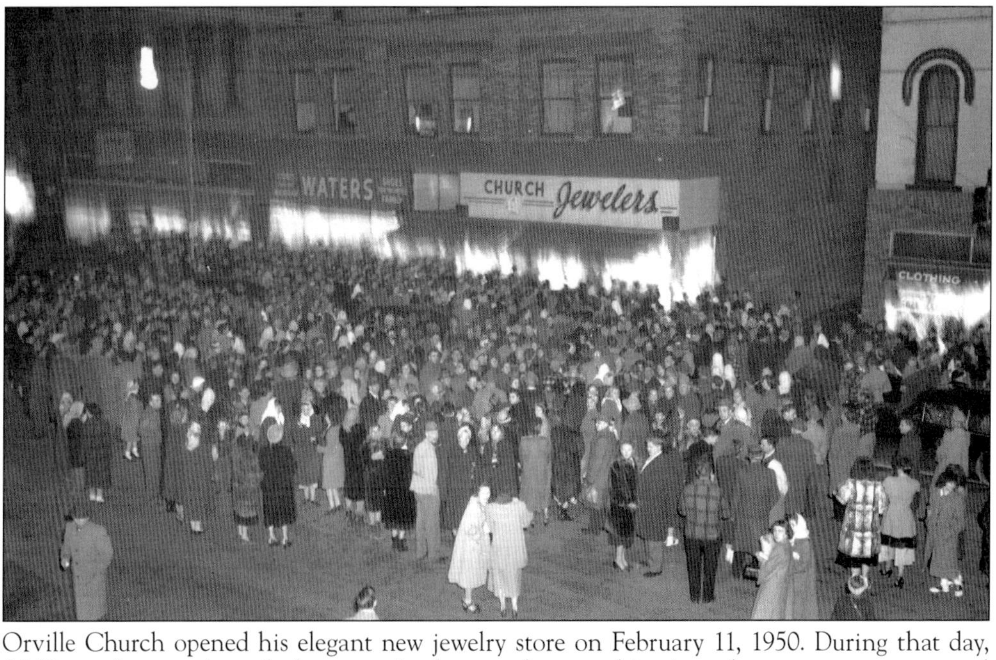


Orville Church opened his elegant new jewelry store on February 11, 1950. During that day, 5,000 people went through the store. As the crowd was pushing into the street, store personnel requested a policeman for crowd control. The police department did not take the call seriously until the mayor went to the store for the ribbon cutting and found the crowd clogging Superior Street. A policeman arrived quickly. (Courtesy of Colleen Boyer.)

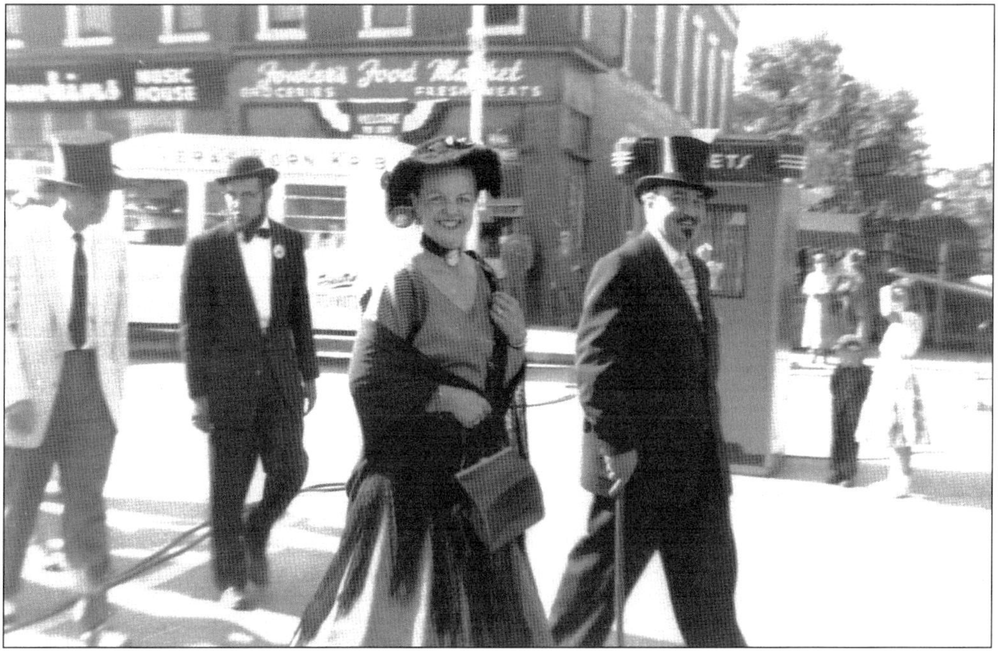


Alma celebrated its centennial in the summer of 1956. The celebration included a carnival, speeches, contests, and a beard-growing contest. In costume, Naoma and Orville Church, prominent business owners, walk up Superior Street on their way to the events. (Courtesy of Colleen Boyer.)

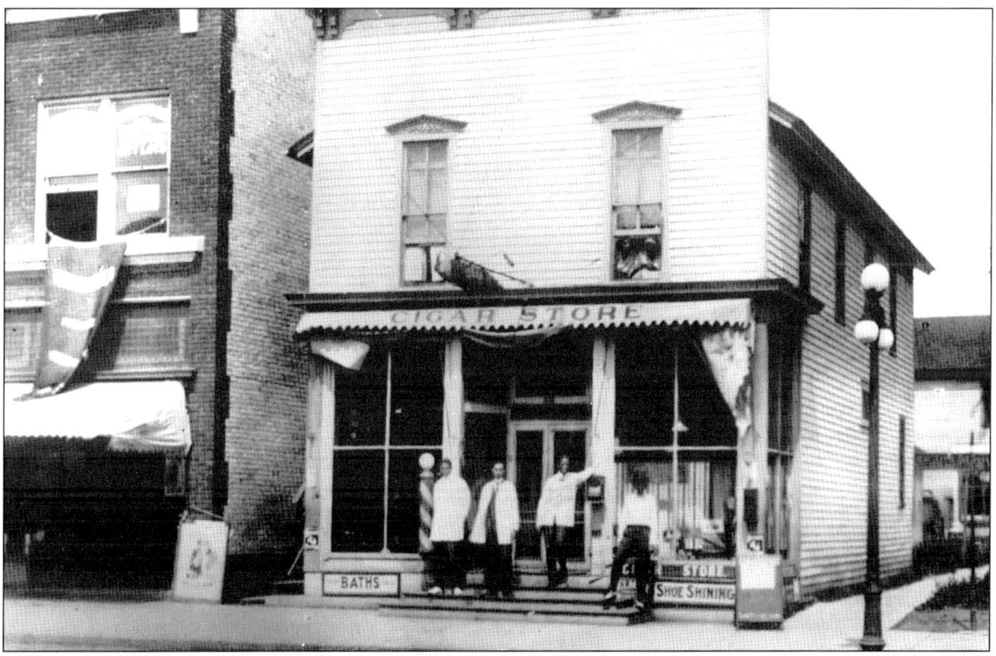


Located on the corner of Superior and Woodworth Streets, the Davis Cigar Store offered much more than cigars. Besides shaves and haircuts, it provided baths as well. Having rented his quarters for years from Ernest Coddington, in 1919 A. W. Davis purchased the building and continued at the location for many years. (Courtesy of the Alma Public Library.)

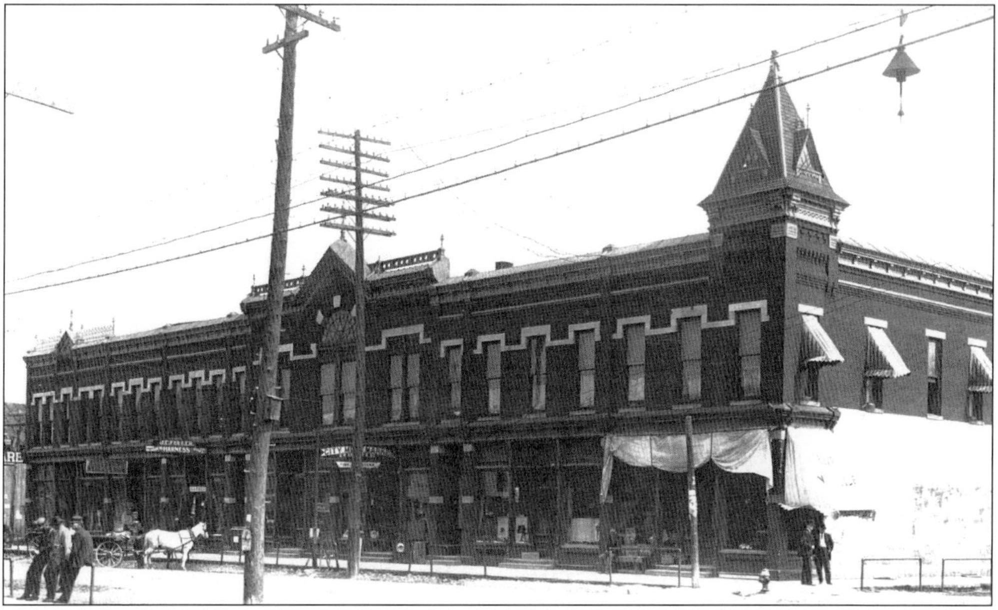

Gen. Nathan Church of Ithaca built the Church Block in Alma in 1886 during a period of prosperity fueled by the activities of Ammi W. Wright. Church was an astute real estate dealer, banker, and business owner whose knack for making money allowed him to move to Paris for a few years so his children could study French. (Courtesy of the Alma Public Library.)

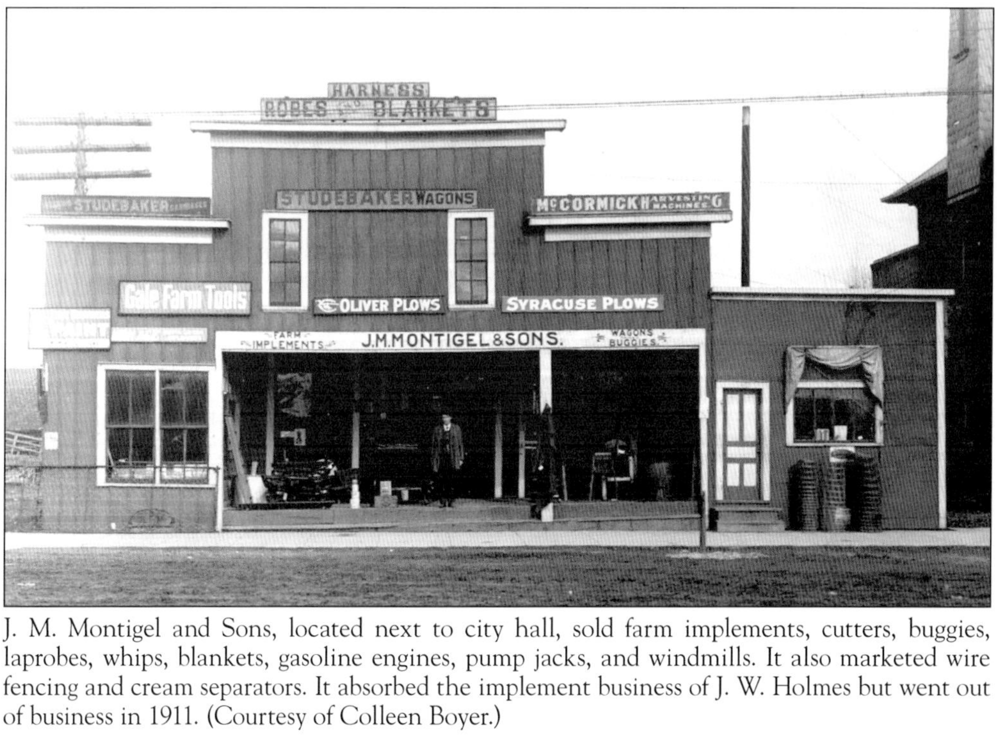


J. M. Montigel and Sons, located next to city hall, sold farm implements, cutters, buggies, laprobes, whips, blankets, gasoline engines, pump jacks, and windmills. It also marketed wire fencing and cream separators. It absorbed the implement business of J. W. Holmes but went out of business in 1911. (Courtesy of Colleen Boyer.)

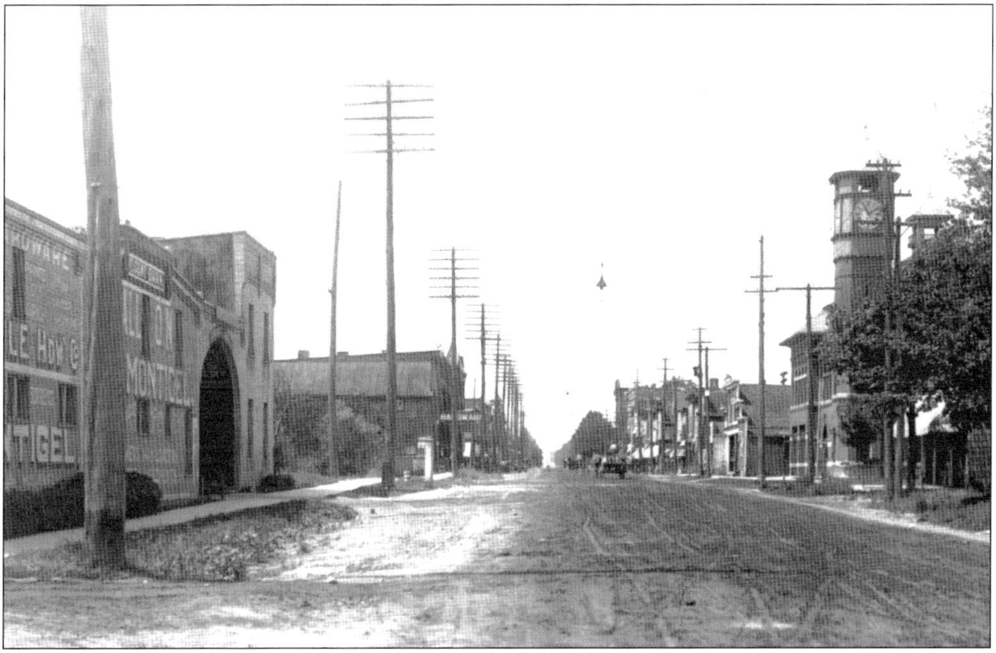

The arched entrance to L. M. Sweet's 10¢ livery stable was a well-known portal to many horses ridden by students coming to high school from the country. The Union School was only a few blocks away. In this view looking west on Superior Street, the new city hall stands on the right. (Courtesy of the Alma Public Library.)

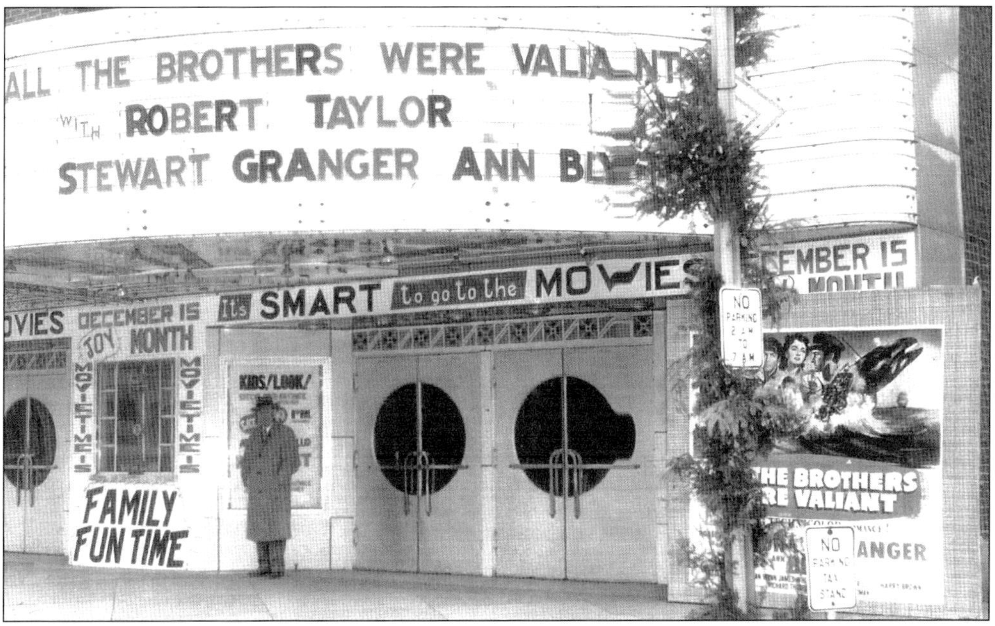


Built as a theater for stage shows, the Strand included the latest in seating, heating, and cooling. Shown here in December 1953, the Strand had long been running motion pictures. It burned in November 1960. Two years later, the debris was removed, and a new movie theater was built. Later the facility was converted to the Gratiot Playhouse, home of the Gratiot County Players. (Courtesy of Colleen Boyer.)

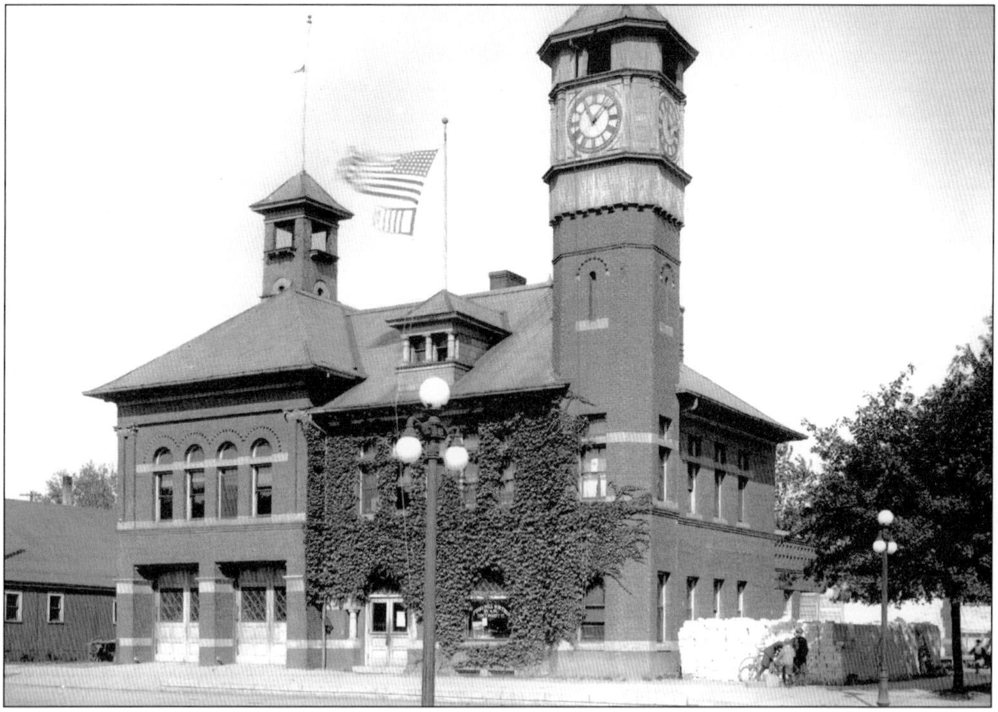

Alma's city hall was built in 1902. With its clock tower and hose-drying tower, it became the most distinctive landmark of the downtown area. It is pictured here in the summer of 1918, as preparations are being made to add a fire barn to the north side of the building. The new fire bays would house Republic fire trucks. The old fire bays in city hall would be remodeled into library facilities. (Courtesy of the Alma Public Library.)

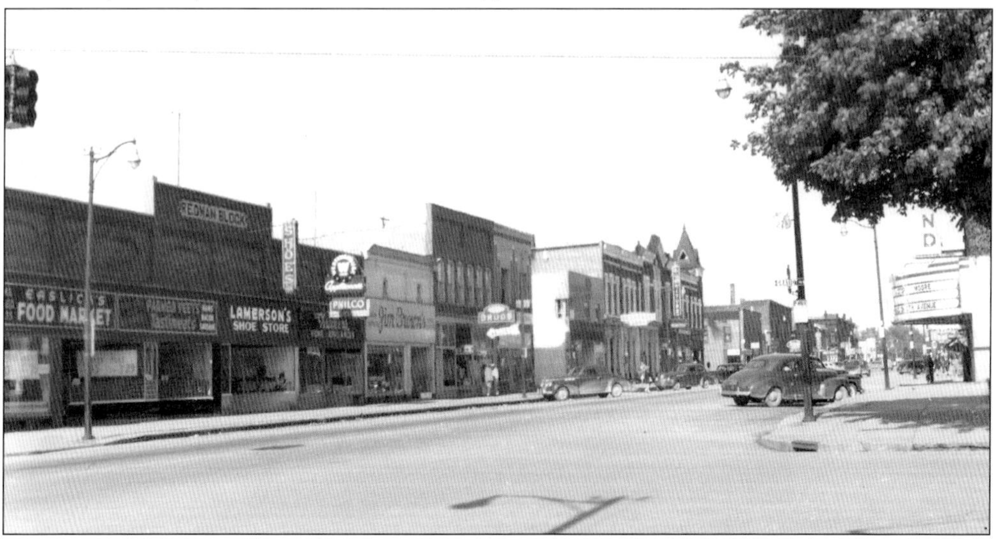


The Redman Block on the left was built by James Redman in 1913 as a meat-processing plant. It was built on a gravel pit, and the blocks for the building were formed on-site. Gradually the business was expanded into Redman Wholesale, a grocery firm run by Bill and Goldie Redman. Through the years, a great many businesses occupied the building's four storefronts. (Courtesy of Richard Tesman.)

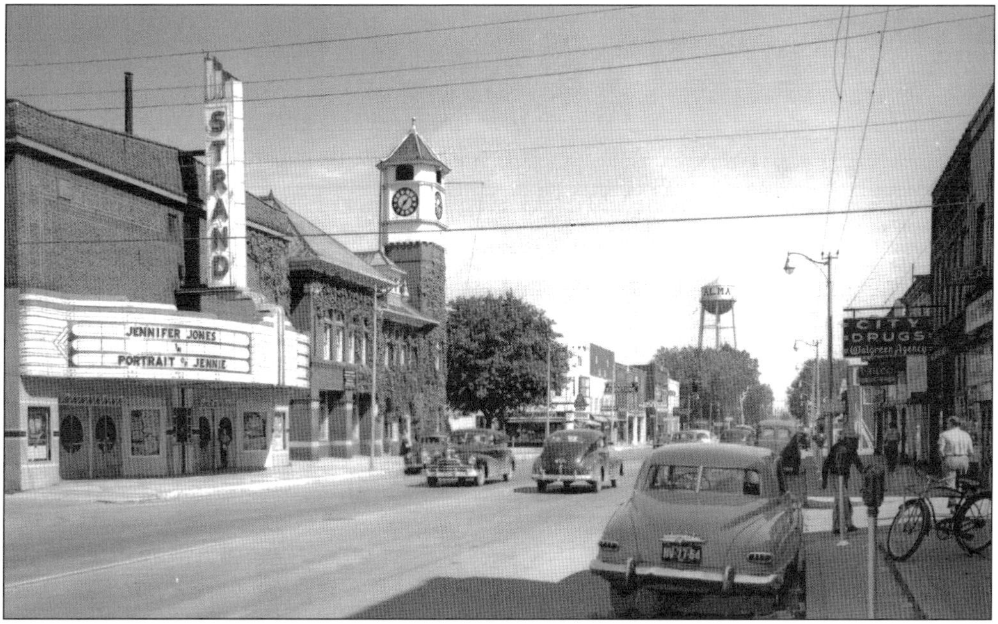


The Strand theater, vine-covered city hall, and an Alma landmark—the water tower in Waterworks Park—reflect a quiet day downtown around 1950. The water tower was dismantled in the mid-1970s to make room for the new city hall. Also shown in this view are Packard's Furniture, the Elks club, City Drug Store, Walther's Home Appliances, and the Alma Tavern. (Courtesy of John Kemler.)

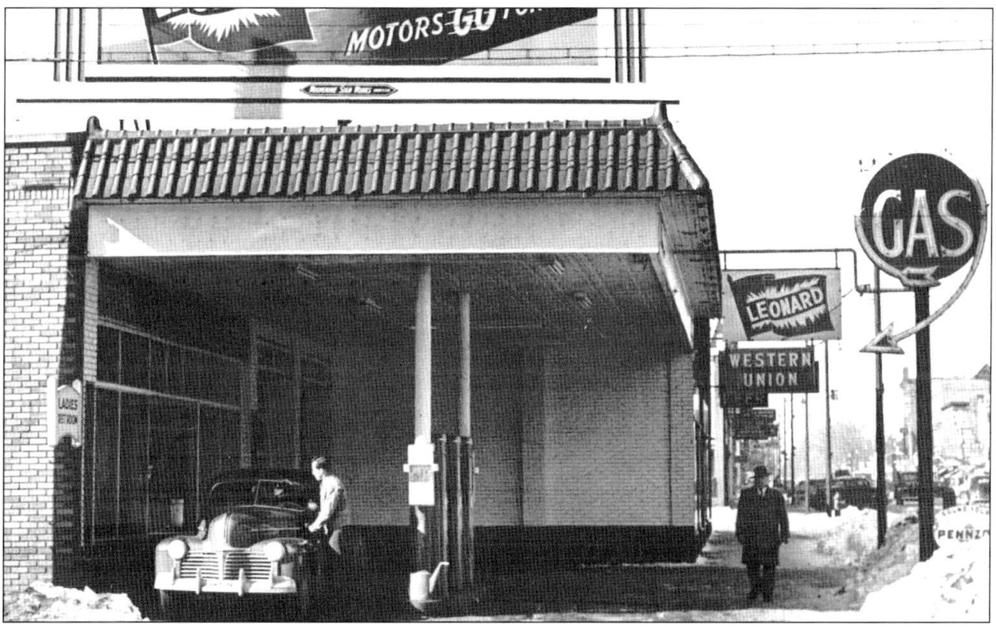


Guy Giles was postmaster in Perrinton when a missent shipment of tire-repair material arrived and set him thinking. Moving to Alma, in 1919 he opened a seasonal tire store, as most people stored their cars during the winter. In 1927, he built this new station west of the roller mills. It offered all filling station services, including a car wash. Later he moved his shop to West Superior Street. (Courtesy of Tom Giles.)

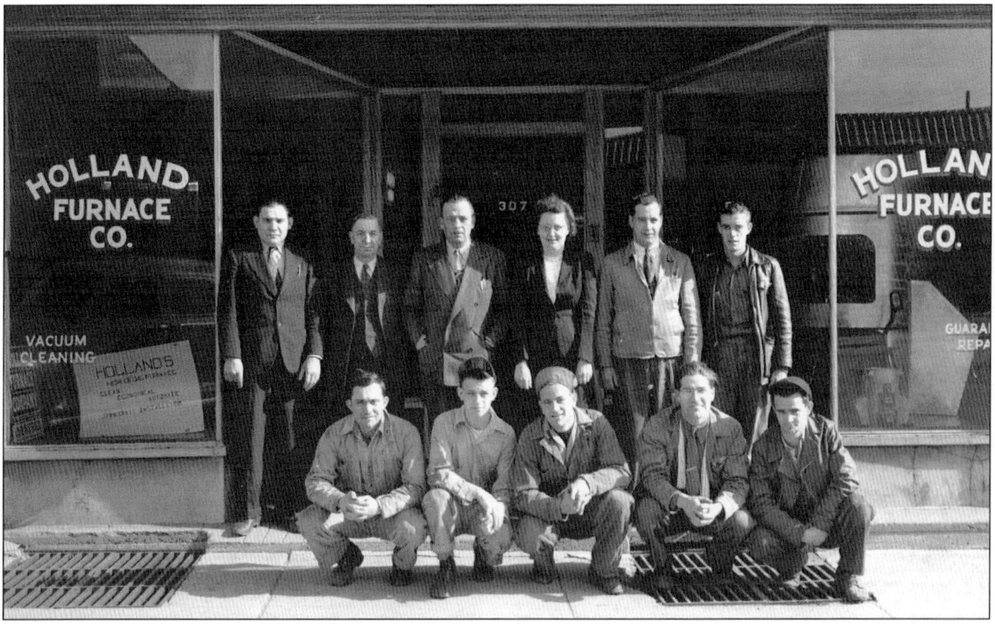


Once people could afford to install furnaces in their homes, businesses like the Holland Furnace Company began to flourish. Located on East Superior Street, this company sold and serviced furnaces that heated entire houses, a far cry from the old kitchen stove that was the main source of heat for most families. In addition, the Holland Furnace Company sent out its roaring suction truck to pull the dust out of heating ducts in homes. (Courtesy of Teacel Dean.)

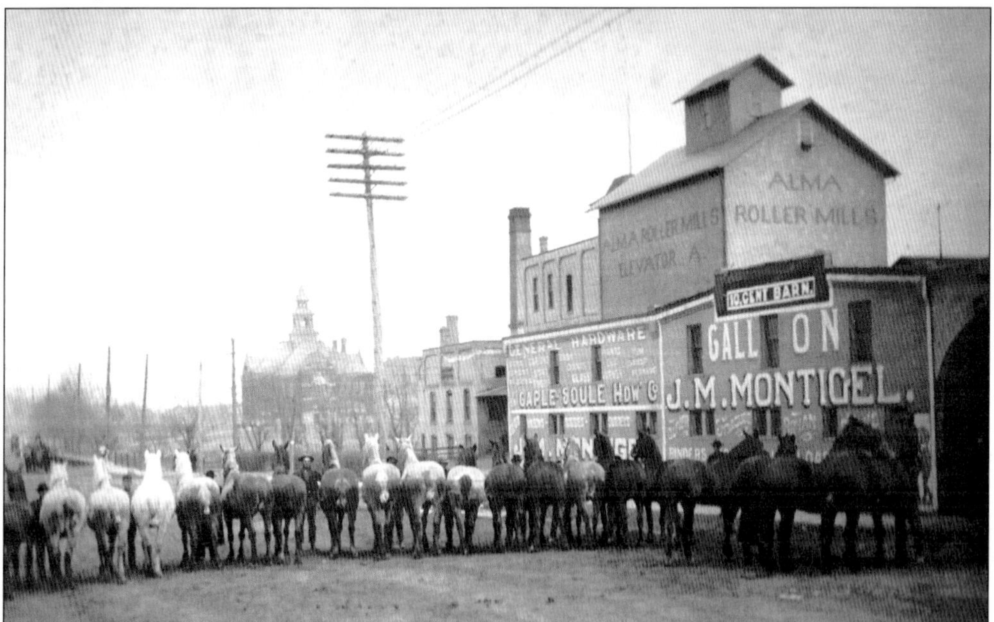


The horse show was a popular annual event in Alma. The show usually featured workhorses with their manes and tails combed and styled to perfection. Sometimes driving horses were shown. Usually the show was conducted at the intersection of Gratiot and Superior Streets, and often it was used for some serious horse trading. (Courtesy of John Kemler.)

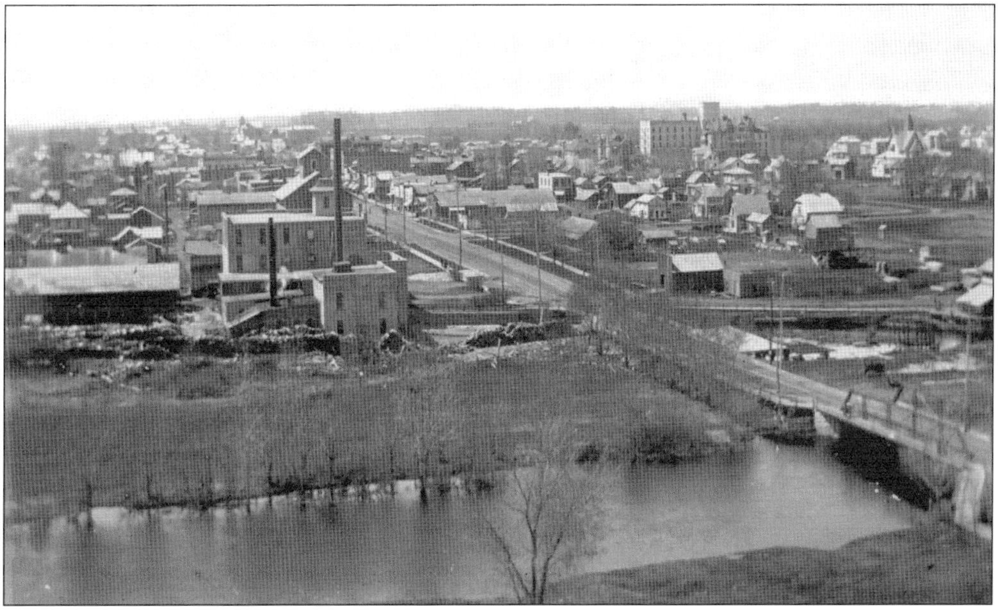

Viewed from the tower of the Union School, Alma sprawls on a pleasant summer day. At the left foreground is the electric plant with its cords of wood needed to fire its boilers. Behind it is the Alma Roller Mills. In the distance on the right is the towering complex of the Alma Springs Sanitarium. The original forest was cleared in the early years of settlement, and many of the trees in this picture were planted along the streets as befitted a growing village. (Courtesy of the Alma Public Library.)

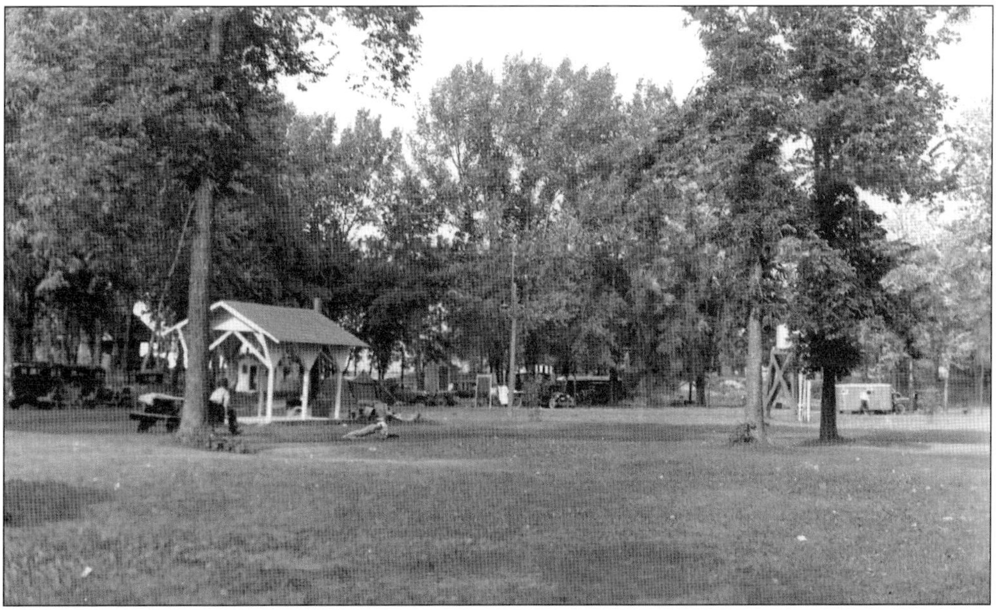

In 1921, the city commission recognized the need for a tourist park. Two state trunk lines ran through Alma, and automobile travel had increased. Tourists who did not wish to pay for hotel accommodations needed a place to pitch their tents. Thus, a tourist park was built on the east bank of the Pine River north of Superior Street. In winter, the park contained a lighted ice-skating rink. (Courtesy of Richard Tesman.)

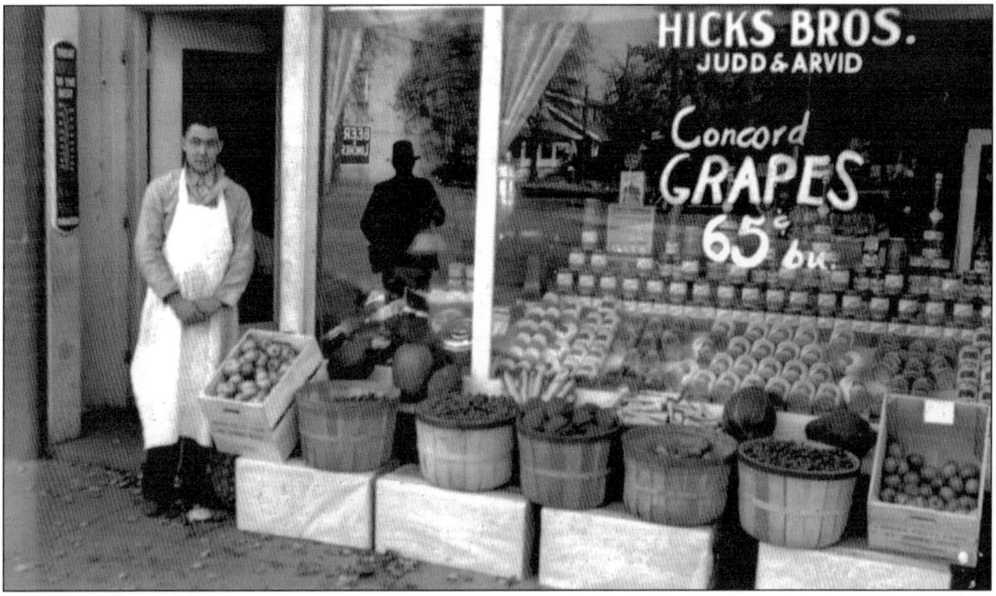


Judd and Arvid Hicks started a grocery store at the corner of Superior and Euclid Streets. It is shown here in 1935. The employee is unidentified. The successful store acquired an addition and became the first IGA store in Alma. Later the Hicks brothers transitioned into the road-construction business and used their former grocery building as headquarters for their new company. (Courtesy of Charles and Diantha Hicks.)

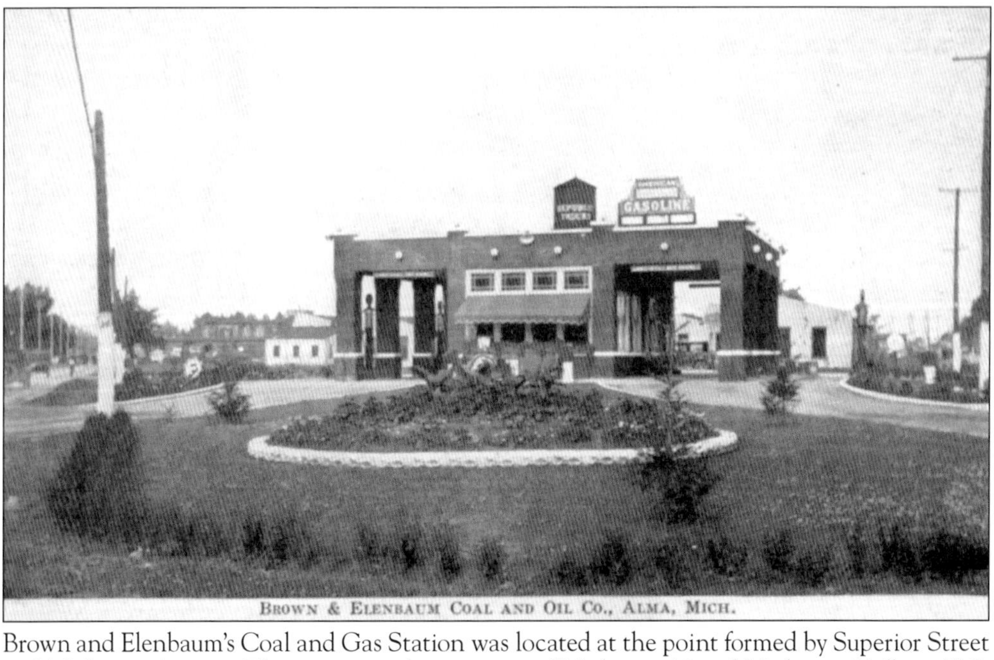


Brown and Elenbaum's Coal and Gas Station was located at the point formed by Superior Street and Michigan Avenue. That spot was the junction of Michigan 46 and Michigan 14 (later U.S. Route 27). The station contained a soda fountain and offered light lunches. It was rare among service stations, as it located its pumps in protective bays and beautifully landscaped its yard. (Courtesy of Richard Tesman.)

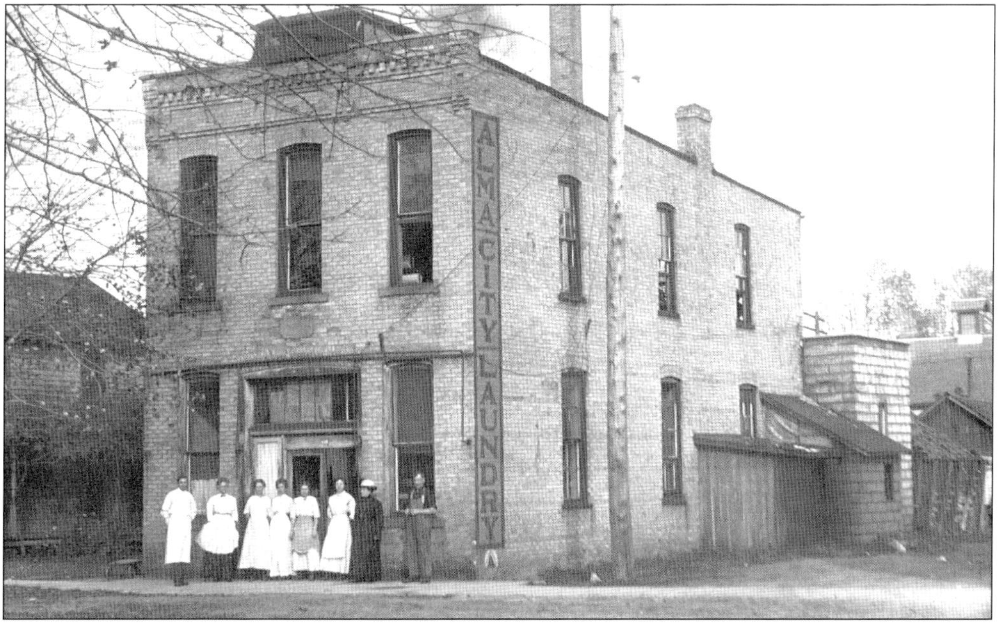


The Alma City Laundry took over the fireman's hall after the new city hall was built in 1902. This building dated from 1884 and housed the fire engines, the fire horses, the harnesses, and the firemen's uniforms. During times when schools were crowded, the second floor was used as classrooms, and students returned home smelling strongly of horses. The building was located on the east side of Woodworth Street north of Superior Street. (Courtesy of Colleen Boyer.)

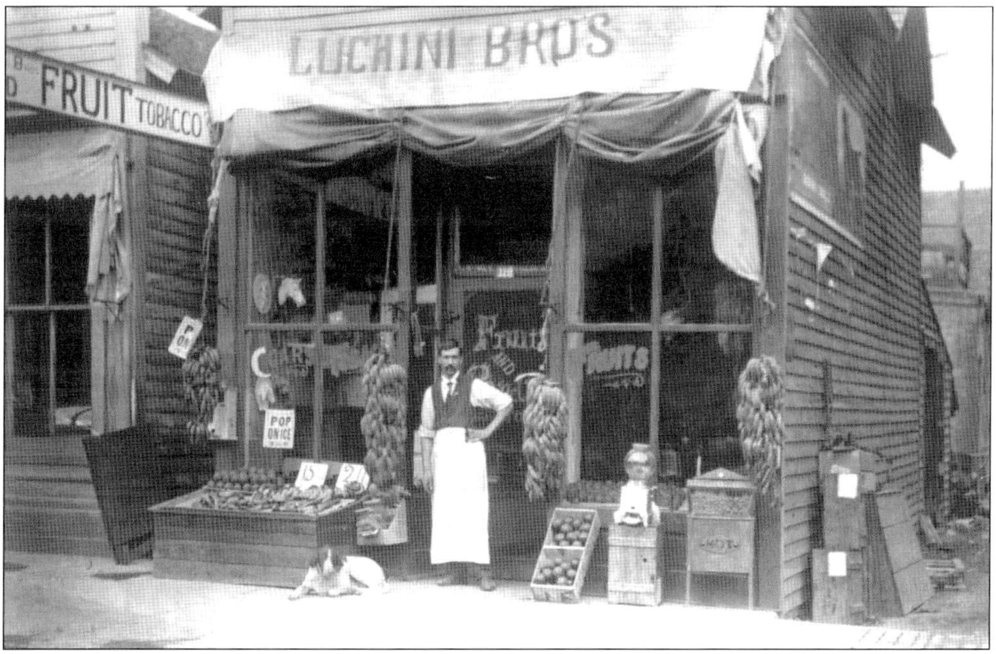


The Luchini brothers, John and Floyd, opened this fruit and candy store on State Street in 1905. John passed through Alma as a traveling salesman and liked the prospects of the town well enough to return as a businessman. In 1911, the Luchinis moved from State Street to Superior Street where they ran a café, poolroom, and bowling alley. (Courtesy of Lucille Behler.)

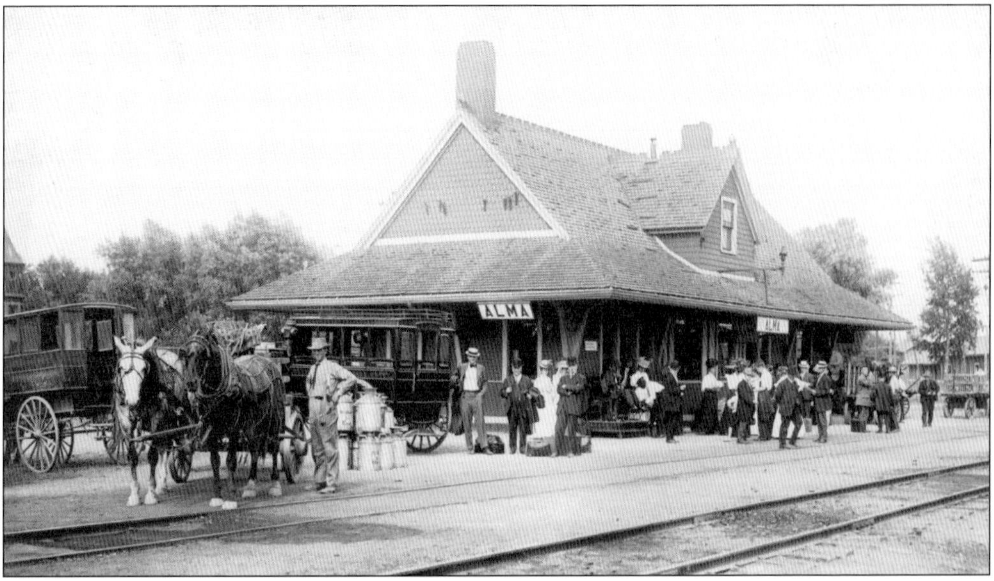


Serving both the Ann Arbor Railroad and Pere Marquette Railway, the union depot, by 1911, saw the arrival and departure of up to 18 passenger trains a day as well as several freight trains. The omnibus on the left is from the Wright Hotel; the one next to it is from the Alma Springs Sanitarium. Both of the posh horse-drawn buses have brought patrons to the depot and await expected arrivals on the next train. (Courtesy of Richard Tesman.)

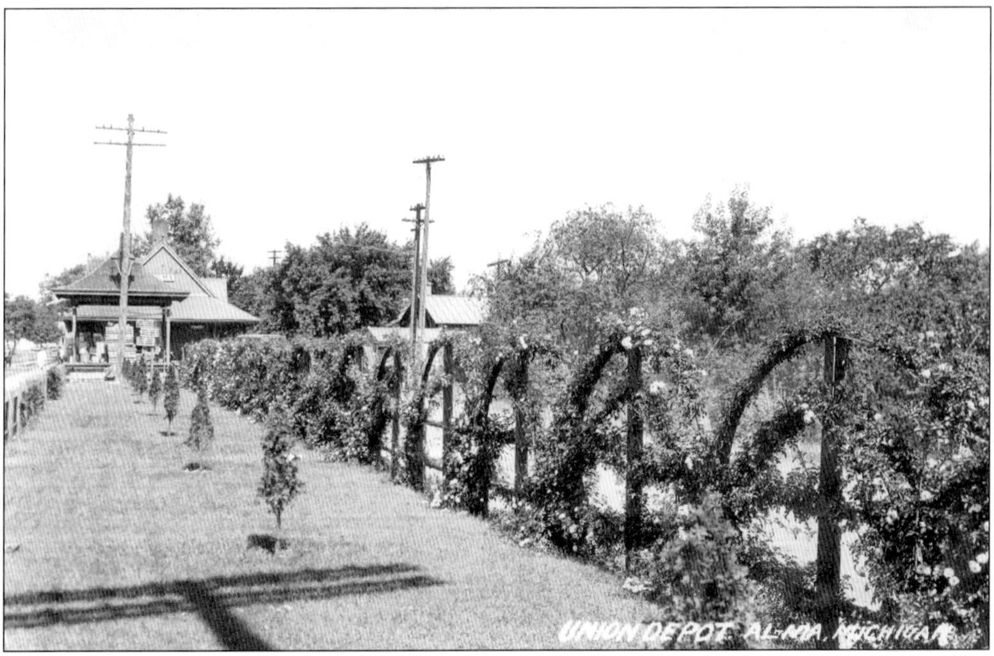


The Civic Improvement League, under the guidance of famed Alma gardener Louisa King, received permission to plant honeysuckle bushes and rambling roses at the union depot in April 1909. Every post on the south side of the lawn received a honeysuckle bush, and at every post on the north fence a pink and fragrant Dorothy Perkins rambler was planted. Once the roses matured, their effect when in full bloom was breathtaking. (Courtesy of Richard Tesman.)

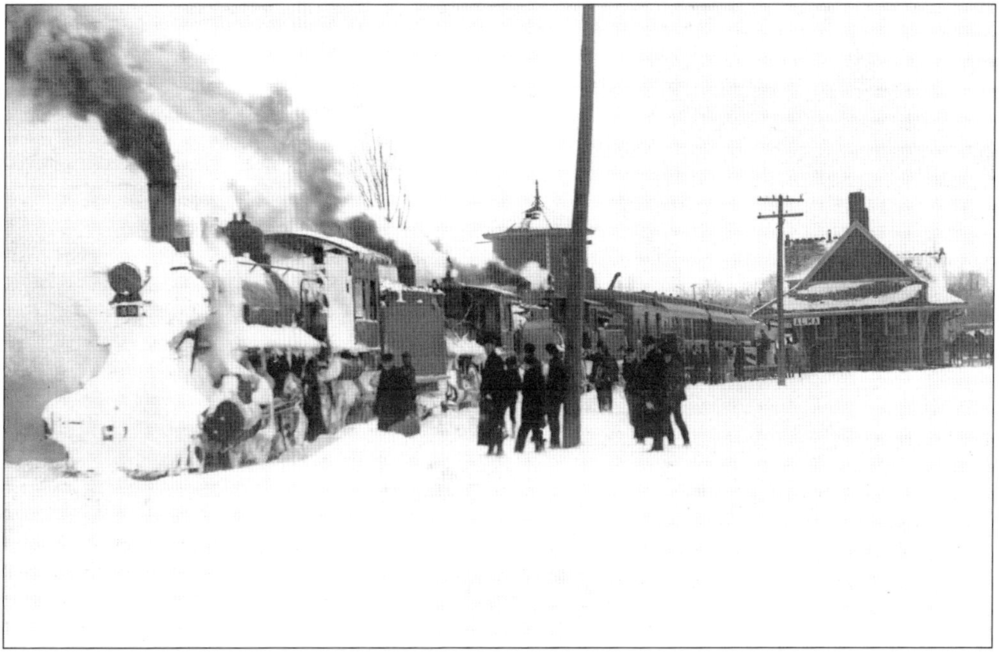


A blizzard in late February 1908 brought all of central Michigan to a halt, including traffic on the Ann Arbor and Grand Trunk Railroads. No passenger trains moved from Tuesday through Friday, and, as shown here, it took three locomotives to bring the first passenger train into Alma following the storm. (Courtesy of Richard Tesman.)

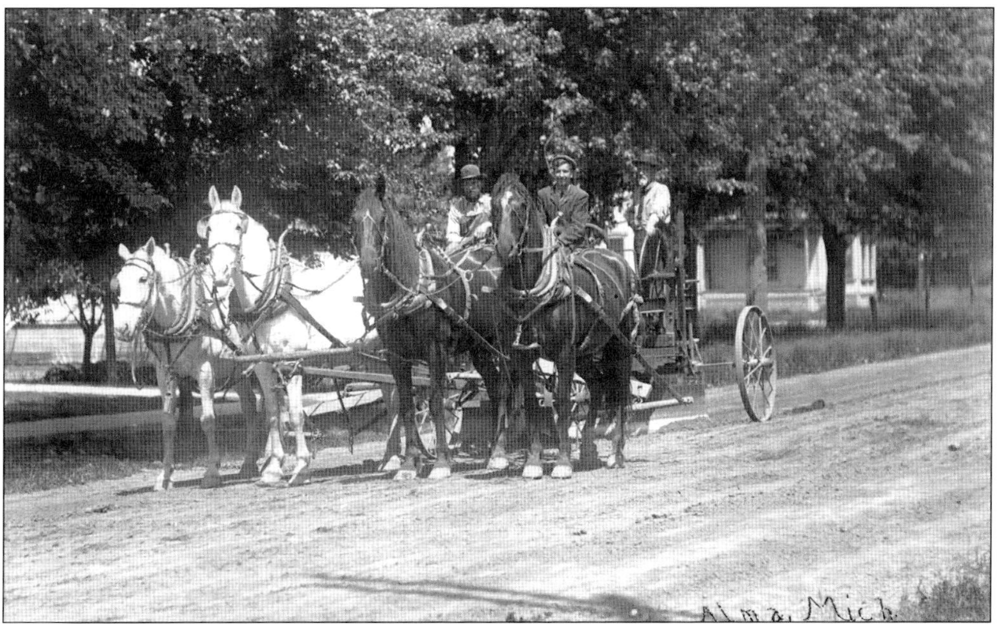


For years the streets of Alma were dirt or mud. Finally bricks and stones offered new stability, then paving arrived. Here a horse-drawn grader smooths the gravel streets, making travel easier for buggies, carriages, wagons, and passengers. (Courtesy of Richard Tesman.)

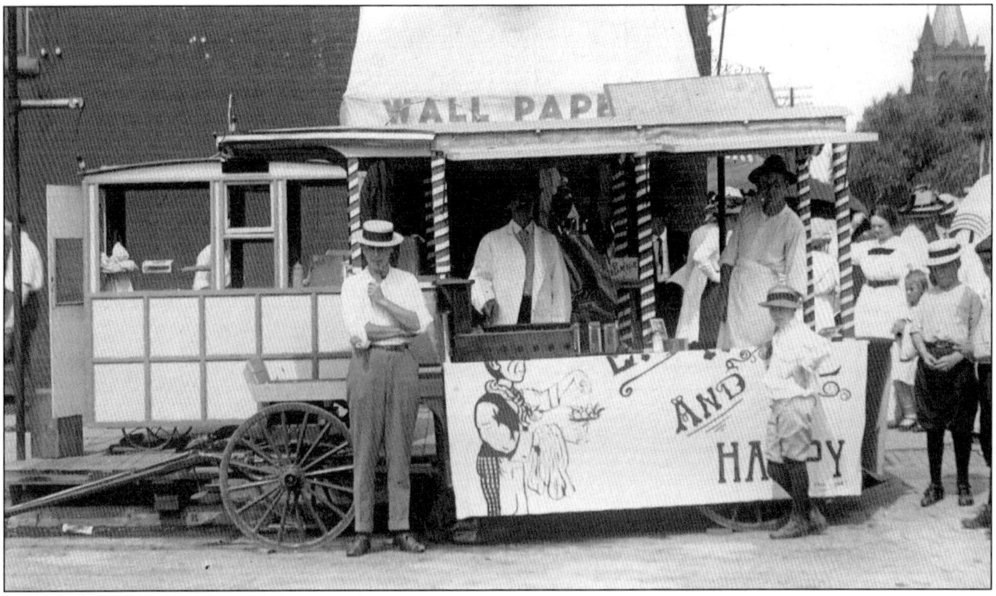


Downtown celebrations brought this concessions wagon to the corner of Superior and State Streets. This intersection was the focal point of many celebrations, including Fourth of July activities and the annual circus parade. The prospects of popcorn and frankfurters have drawn young and old alike on this pleasant summer day. (Courtesy of Colleen Boyer.)

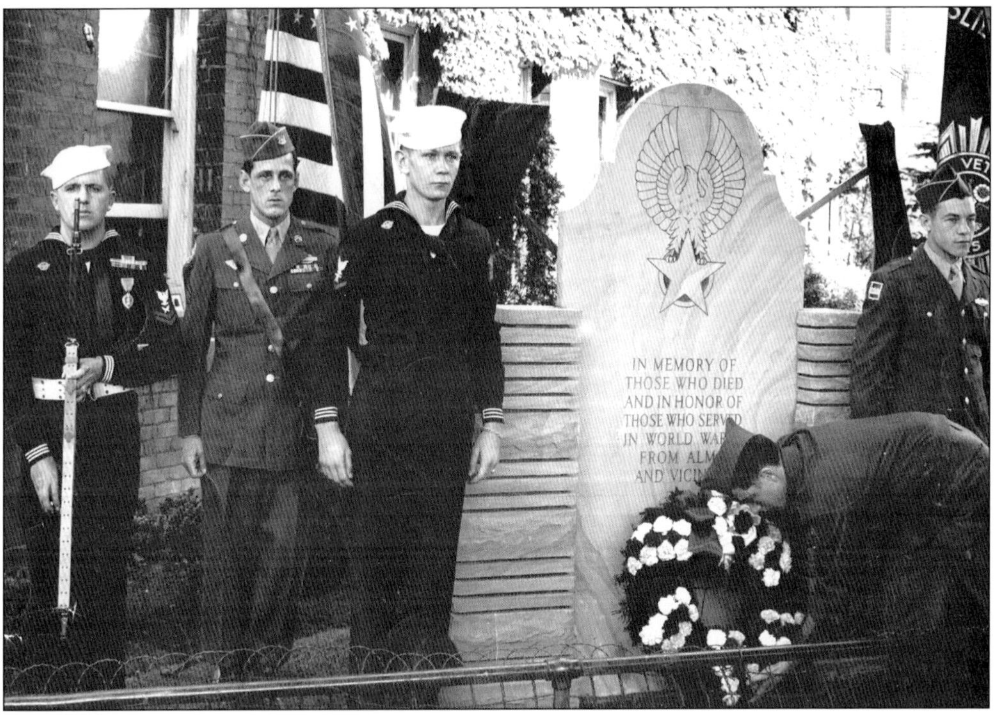


Honoring area World War II veterans, this monument was located at Alma's old city hall. Shown here from left to right are Myron Humphrey, Bryant Betts, Bill Brown, Mercer Cook, and VFW representative Dave Parker. After Alma's new city hall was built and the old city hall became privately owned, this memorial was moved to Riverside Cemetery. (Author's collection.)

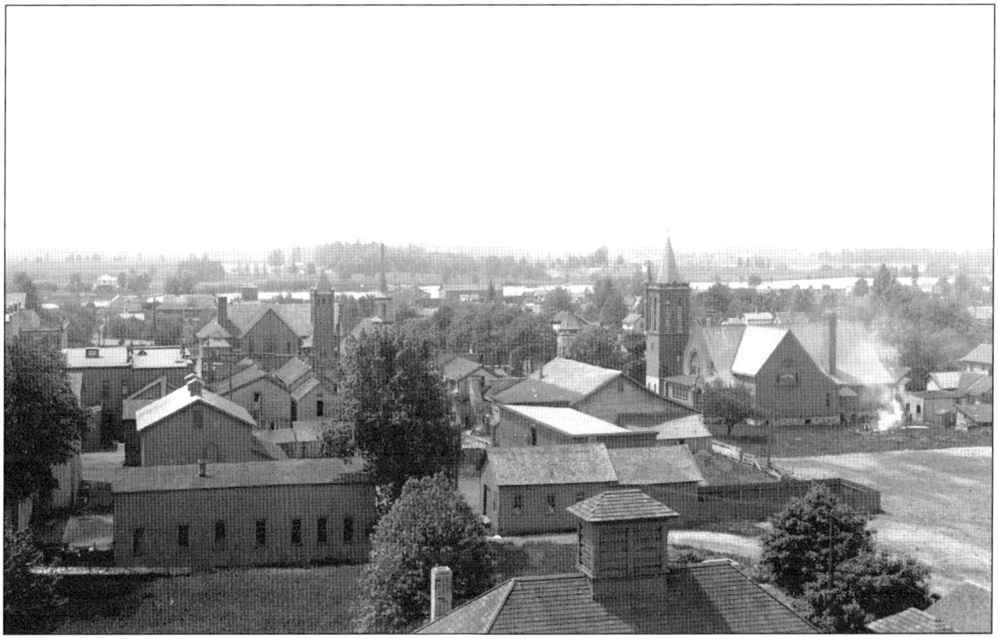

Taken from the tower of the Alma Springs Sanitarium around 1906, this view depicts the roof of Ammi W. Wright's carriage barn in the foreground, the Presbyterian church at the right, and the old and new Methodist churches in the center. In the distance are the Pine River and Turck's woods, later to become Conservation Park. (Photograph by Hubert Elias, courtesy of Dale Kemler.)

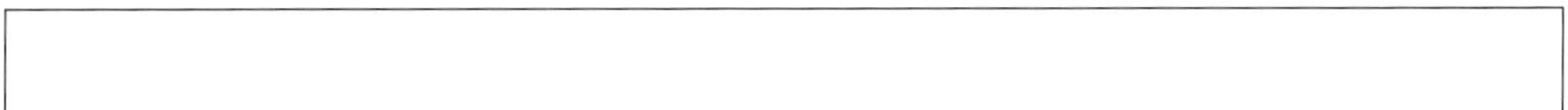

The tower of the sanitarium provided a fine view north up State Street. The light brick house was built in 1880 by Henry Delavan. It was the first brick house in Alma and reflected the prosperity generated by Delavan's businesses downtown. In the distance lies the imposing Saravilla mansion. Beyond it stands Orchard House, the newly constructed mansion of Francis and Louisa King. (Courtesy of John Kemler.)

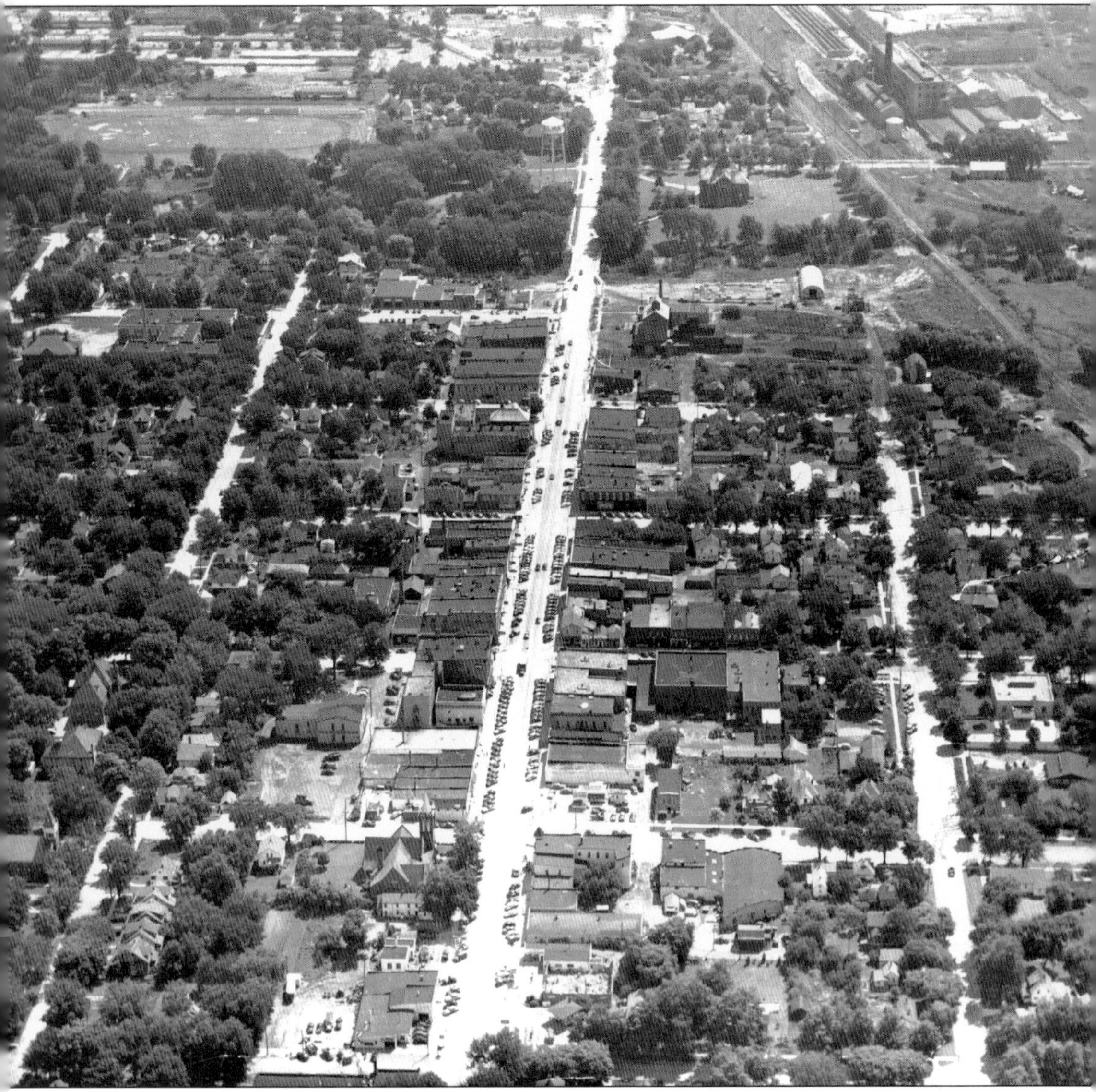

This view of Alma from the air looks east down Superior Street. Taken in 1950, the view preserves the memory of many buildings that have since been removed: the Alma Roller Mills, the Alma Sugar Company, Swift and Company duck farm, Republic Truck Company, Alma High School, the Ward School, the Union School, Stilwell Junior High School, the Wright Hotel, the Wright Livery, the Salvation Army building, the city water tower, the Messinger home, and the city garage. (Courtesy of the Alma Public Library.)

# Four

# MAKING A LIVING

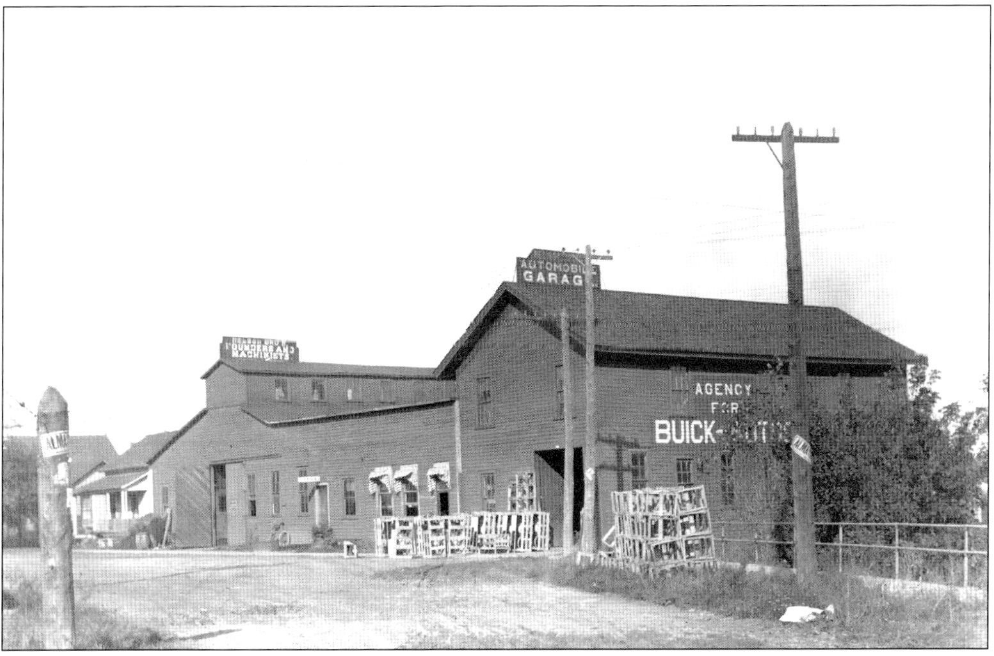


In 1907, Montigel's machine shop and implement business was sold to Nelson brothers Harry and Clare. So successful was their management that their business boomed. Harry designed a pump jack, and within 30 months, 30,000 of them were built. Their Little Jumbo gasoline engine was in such demand that they had to find new manufacturing space and moved to Saginaw in 1911. As shown here, they also took on the Buick dealership before their move. (Courtesy of Richard Tesman.)

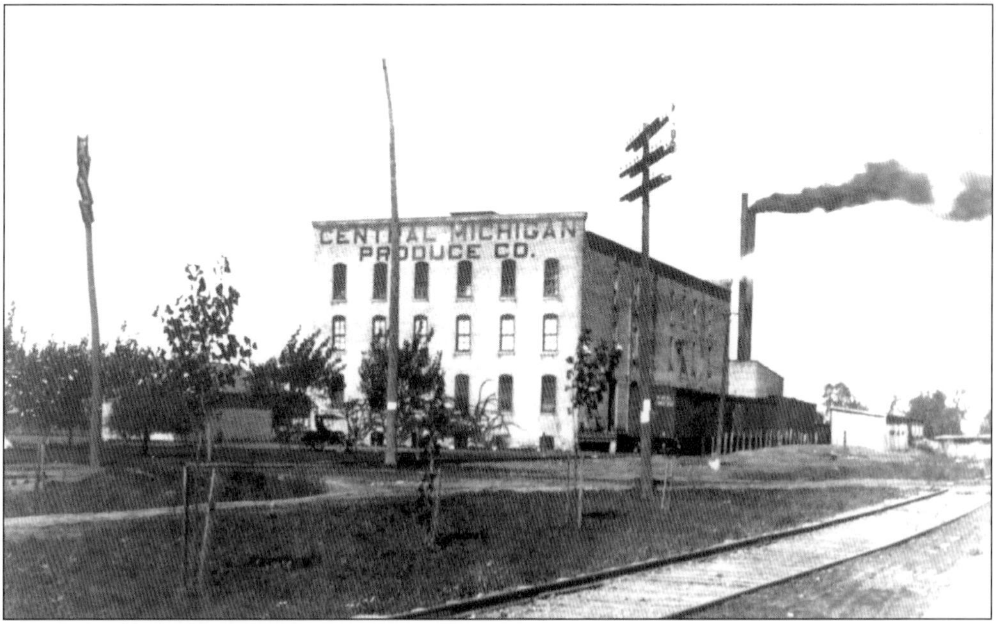

After cream separators became common, the Central Michigan Produce Company was formed in 1903 to manufacture large quantities of prime butter. The company had 10 branch houses and 21 receiving stations in central Michigan. After being purchased by the Swift Packing Company of Chicago, Central Michigan Produce Company began raising and marketing thousands of ducklings. (Courtesy of Lucille Behler.)

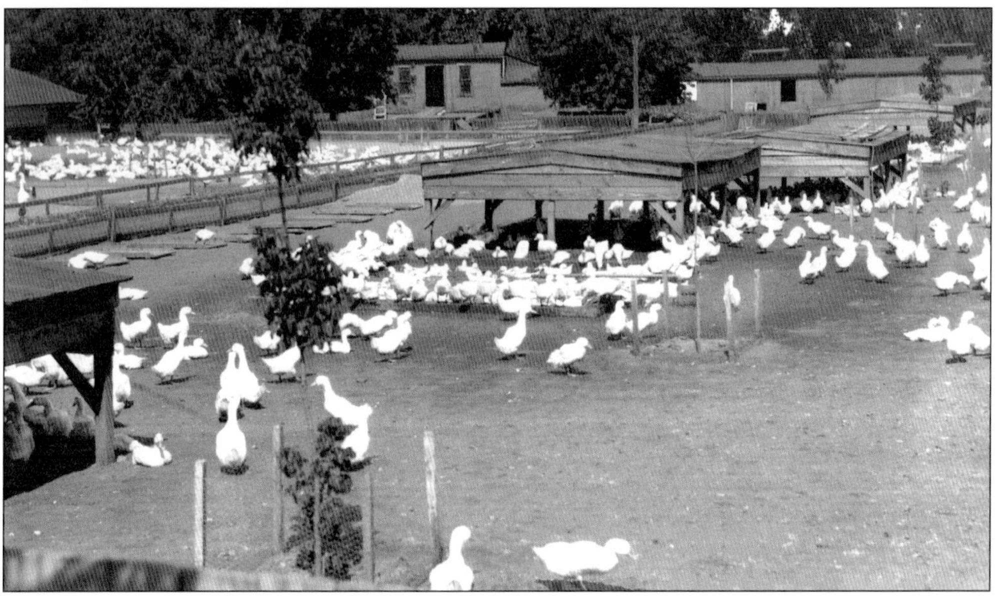
Swift and Company bought the Central Michigan Produce Company and increased its production of poultry. By 1916, the company, on three and a half acres, was raising 10,000 ducks and 30,000 chickens a year. Incubators had a combined capacity of 15,000 eggs. The process, from hatching to butchering, required only 9 to 11 weeks. For many years, Swift and Company ran its fragrant business next to plant No. 1 of the Republic Truck Company. (Courtesy of Richard Tesman.)

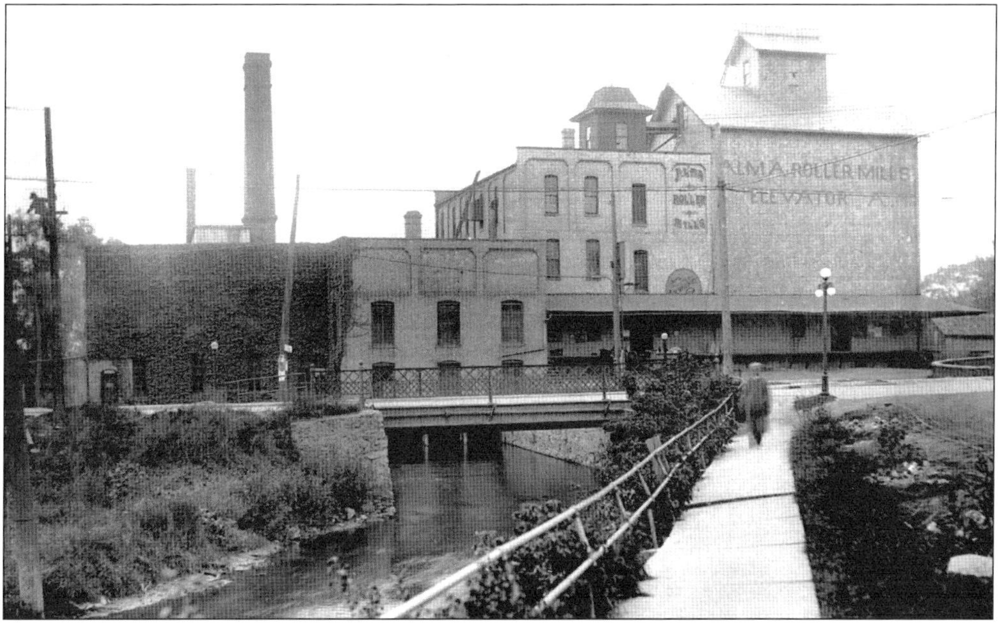


Ralph Ely's small steam-powered gristmill was replaced in 1869 by James Gargett's large Empire Mills. His imposing mill burned in 1880. The site was purchased by W. S. Turck who was joined by Ammi W. Wright in building the Alma Roller Mills—the smaller section with windows pictured here. The adjoining elevator had a capacity of 60,000 bushels. A cooper shop on the premises turned out barrels for shipping flour. (Courtesy of Colleen Boyer.)

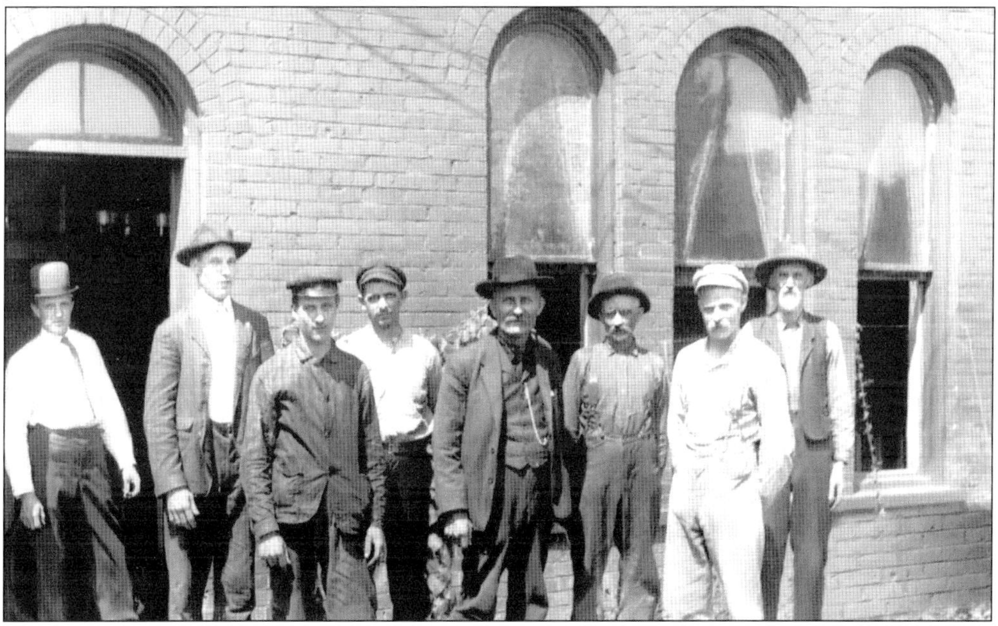

The roller mills crew, shown here around 1900, was led by Lewis John Striggow, the well-dressed man in the center. These men were skilled laborers, having learned the processes used in the manufacture of several brands of flour, including Arcada Straight, Alma Patent, and Baker's. Grain for milling arrived by rail, and most of the mill's product was exported to other parts of the country. (Courtesy of the Alma Public Library.)

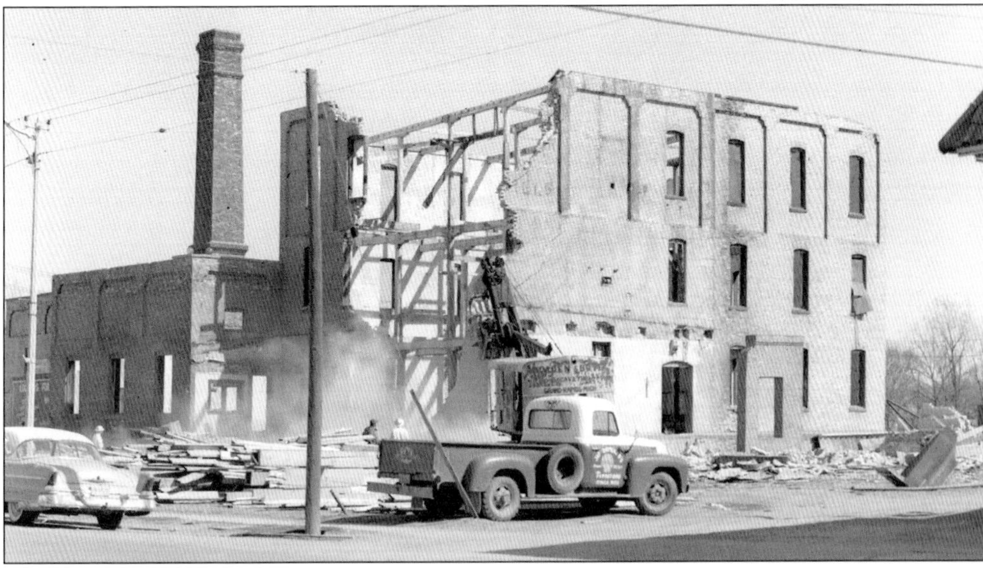

The Alma Roller Mills were bought by Harris Milling Company of Mount Pleasant. Then Harris sold the mills to the city, which planned to demolish them for a parking lot. When the General Telephone Company was looking for a site for its large, new communications center, the city offered to sell it the mills property. In the spring of 1958, Capitol Wrecking of Lansing razed the mills in preparation for construction of the communications center. Once the mills were gone, Pine Avenue was extended to Center Street. (Photograph by Hubert Elias, courtesy of Dale Kemler.)

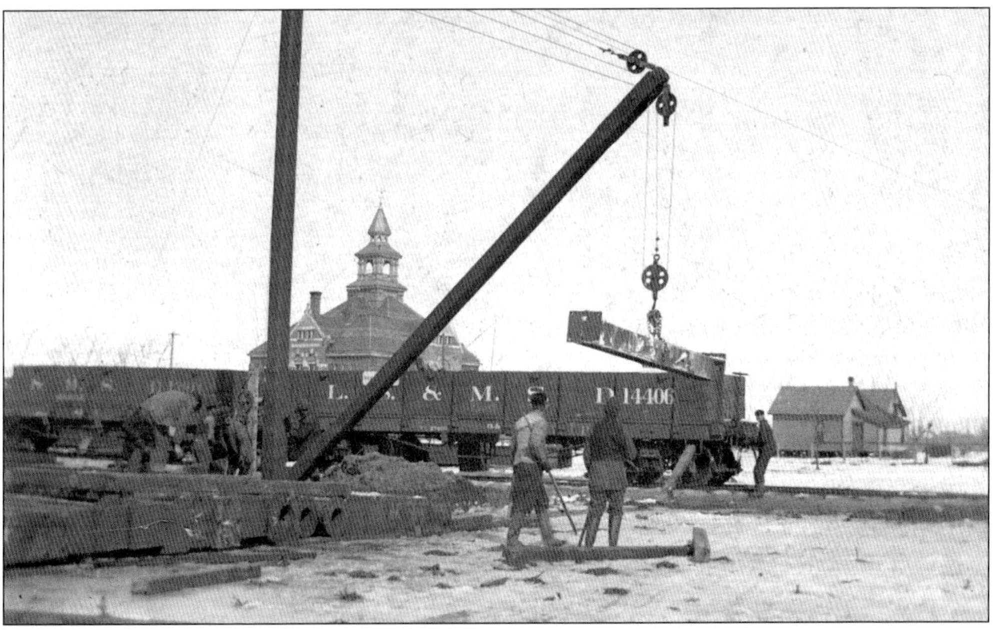

In the 1890s, Ammi W. Wright introduced the growing of sugar beets to the farmers of Gratiot County by raising beets on several of his own farms. Beet raising was a labor-intensive enterprise, and at harvest, beets had to be hauled by team and wagon to the railhead for shipment to a sugar plant in Bay City. Consequently, Wright organized the Alma Sugar Company in 1899. Here steel is being unloaded for construction of the huge factory. (Courtesy of the Alma Public Library.)

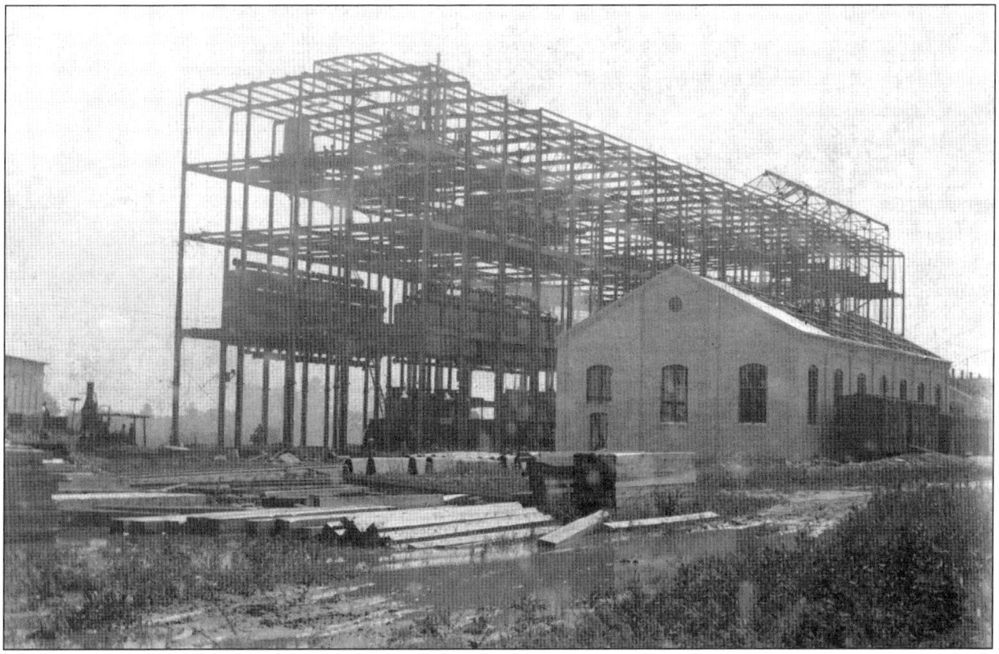

The Kelby Manufacturing Company constructed the large 300-foot-by-90-foot, five-story building. The sugar plant required 10 boilers, a lime kiln, beet sheds, flumes to float beets into the plant, and a cooper shop that produced 30,000 sugar barrels a year. The plant began processing beets in the fall of 1899. (Courtesy of the Alma Public Library.)

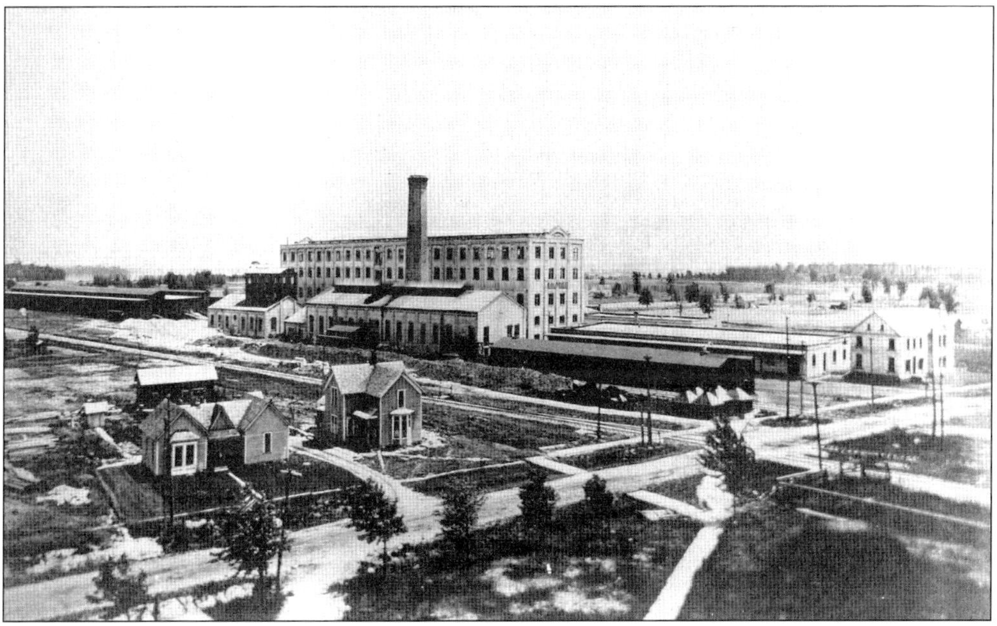

Although the sugar company was in operation only three months of the year, once under way, it ran 24 hours a day, seven days a week. In all, it ran the equivalent of eight months of regular manufacturing hours. Farmers and other laborers counted on this seasonal employment during November, December, and January. Wages to the 275 employees put holiday gifts under the Christmas tree and helped pay off many farm mortgages. (Courtesy of John Kemler.)

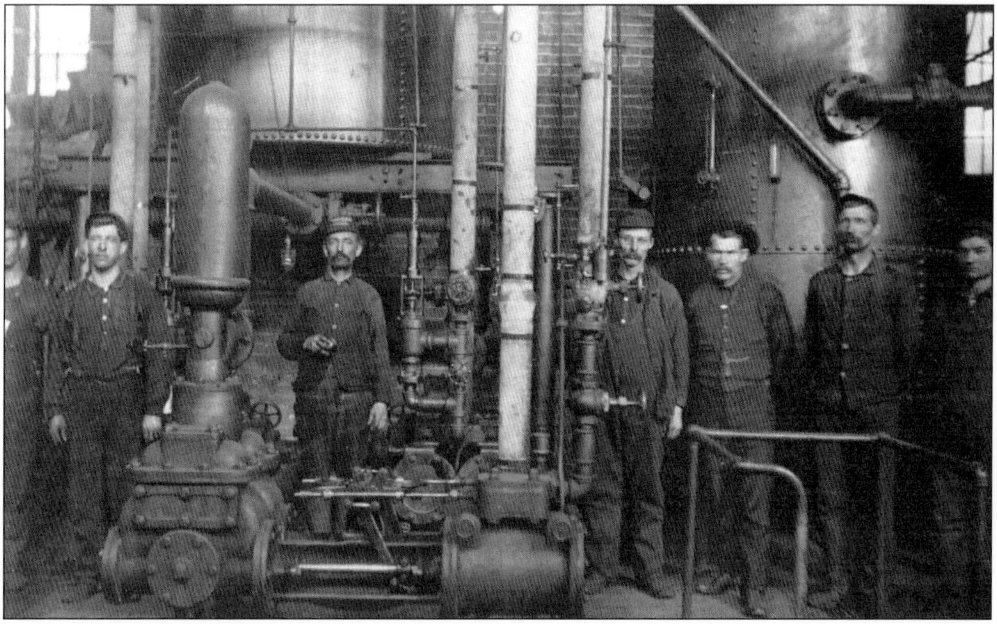

Even though it produced an offensive "burnt fudge" odor, the sugar company also produced a great deal of money for local farmers and businessmen. In its first six seasons, area farmers received $1.3 million for beets, laborers earned $303,000, and the company produced 53 million pounds of sugar. Consolidated with other companies, it ran until 1953, and the main building was razed in 1962. (Courtesy of John Kemler.)

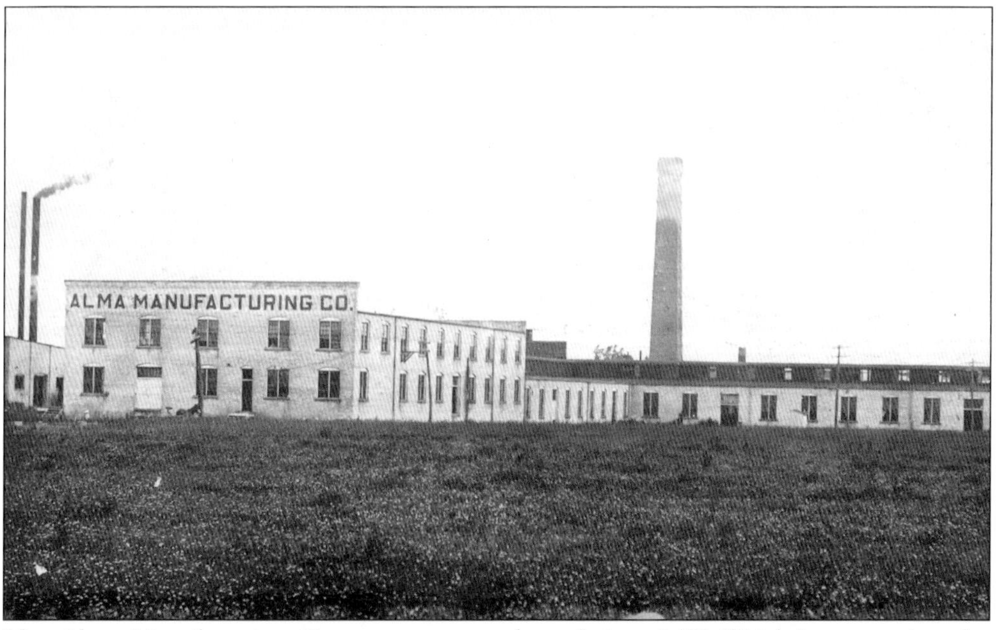


The Alma Manufacturing Company was another of Ammi W. Wright's companies, the amalgamation of two firms from Lansing. The new company produced the very successful McVickers one-cylinder gasoline engine, renowned for its simple design. The factory stood on Michigan Avenue, and in 1912, it housed the Alma Truck Company that was soon transformed into the Republic Truck Company. (Courtesy of Richard Tesman.)

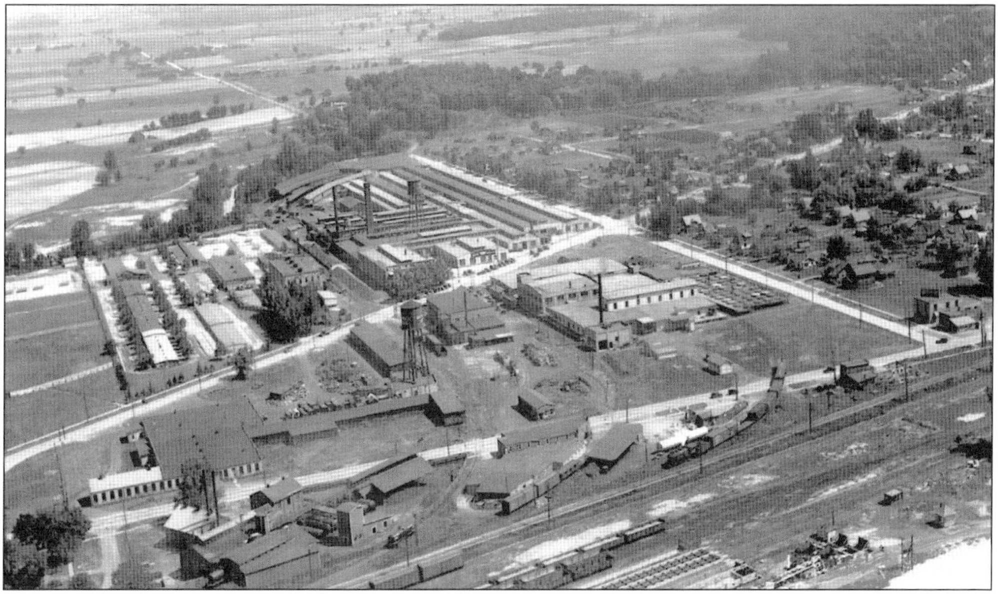

By 1920, Alma's manufacturing district covered many acres along Superior Street (bottom of picture), Michigan Avenue (angling toward the top right), and Bridge Street (angling toward the left). At top center is the main plant of the Republic Truck Company. Below it is the Libby, McNeill, and Libby vegetable processing plant. To the left of Republic Truck is Swift and Company's sprawling poultry farm. At lower left is Republic's plant No. 2. (Courtesy of the Alma Public Library.)

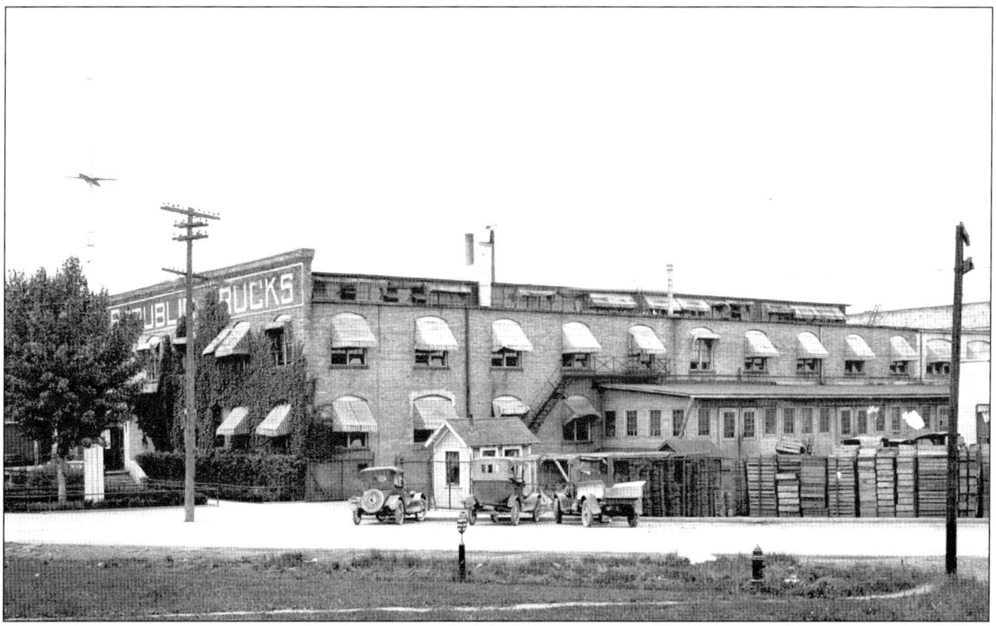

The Republic Truck Company came out of the short-lived Alma Truck Company. Republic was an assembly company, building trucks from components produced by other companies. Its tough and winning design, however, soon marked it as a popular brand, and from its inception in 1913 to its peak in 1920, it grew into the largest exclusive truck manufacturer in the world. (Courtesy of John Kemler.)

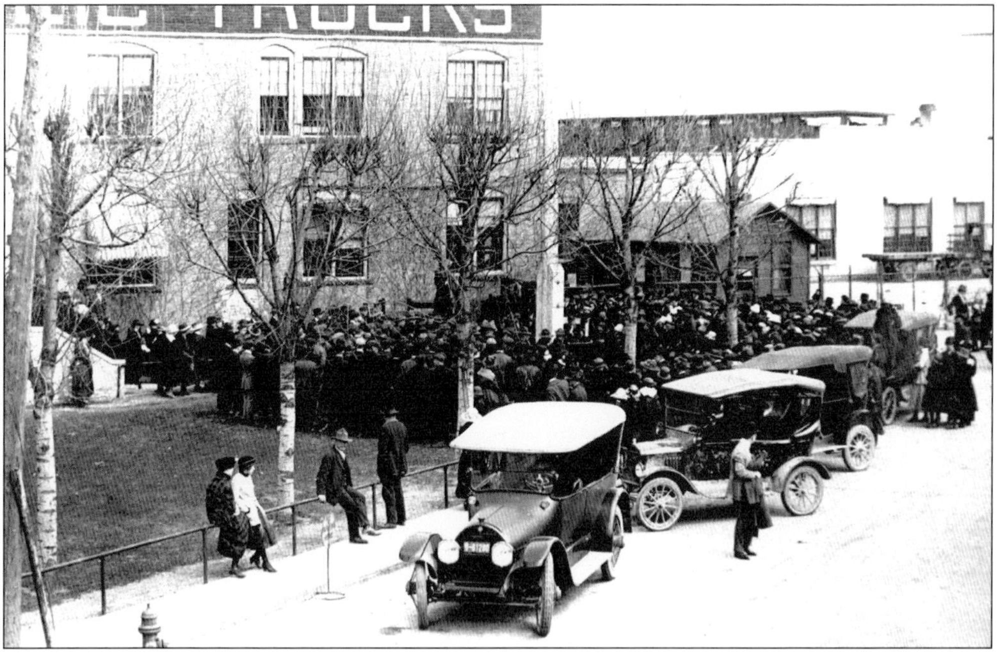

The truck company's main office, formerly the Alma Manufacturing plant, housed executives of the company, chief among them Supt. Frank Ruggles. Here a group of citizens and employees has gathered to hear an inspirational speech during World War I. At the time, the company was producing large numbers of Liberty trucks for the war effort. (Courtesy of Colleen Boyer.)

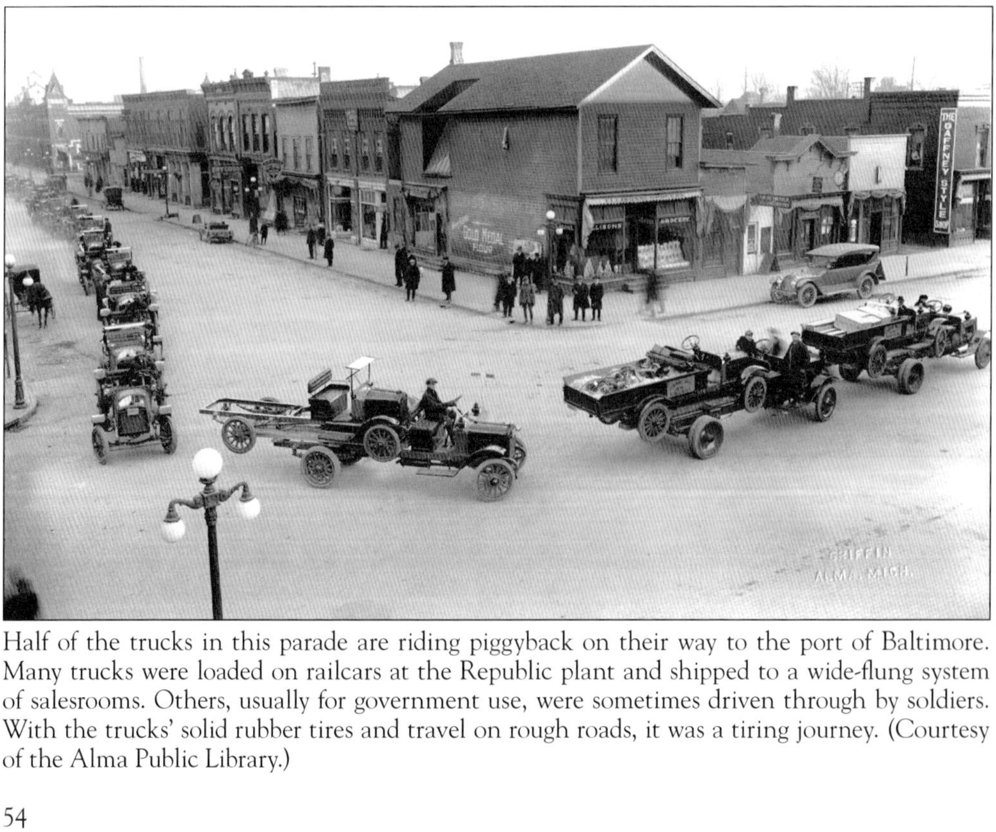


Half of the trucks in this parade are riding piggyback on their way to the port of Baltimore. Many trucks were loaded on railcars at the Republic plant and shipped to a wide-flung system of salesrooms. Others, usually for government use, were sometimes driven through by soldiers. With the trucks' solid rubber tires and travel on rough roads, it was a tiring journey. (Courtesy of the Alma Public Library.)

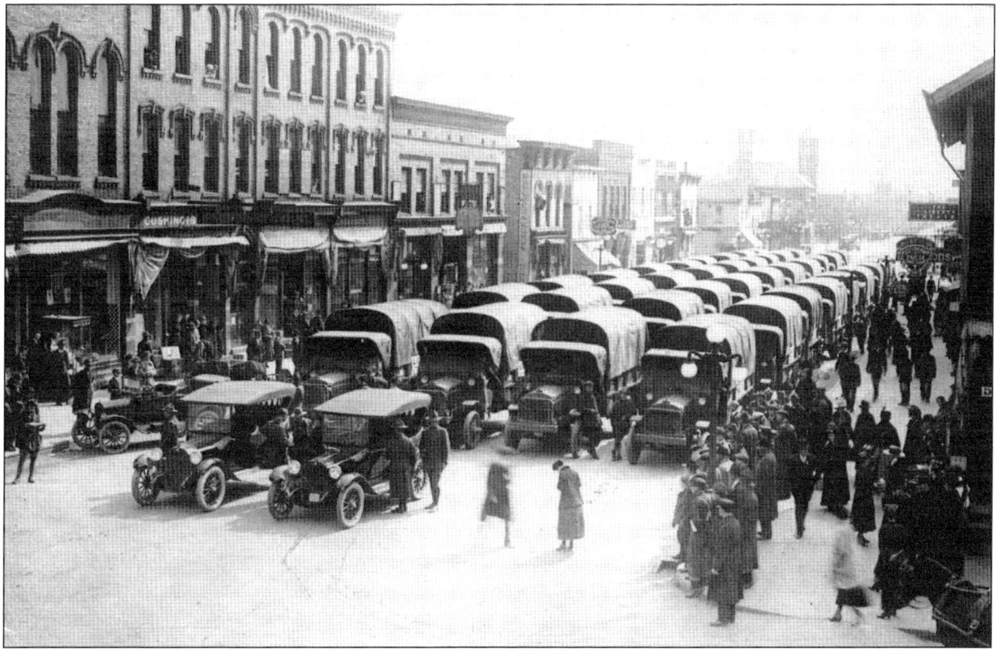

Bringing pride to Alma people, the Liberty trucks, here lined four abreast on Superior Street, symbolized the city's contribution to the war effort during World War I. Trucks were driven in caravans to East Coast ports. Many a homesick doughboy from Gratiot County, plodding the roads of France, would feel a glow when meeting a Republic truck from home. (Courtesy of Richard Tesman.)

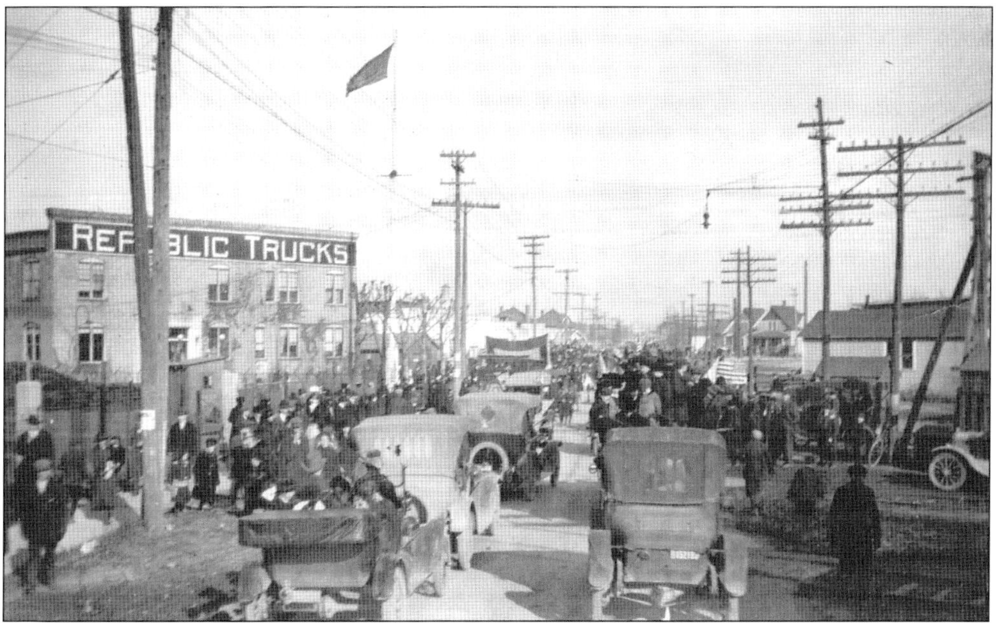


Word of Germany's surrender unleashed a wild celebration in Alma. Here the crowds descend upon the Republic Truck Company factory, rejoicing that the Great War is over and that Alma's trucks played a significant role in ending it. (Courtesy of John Kemler.)

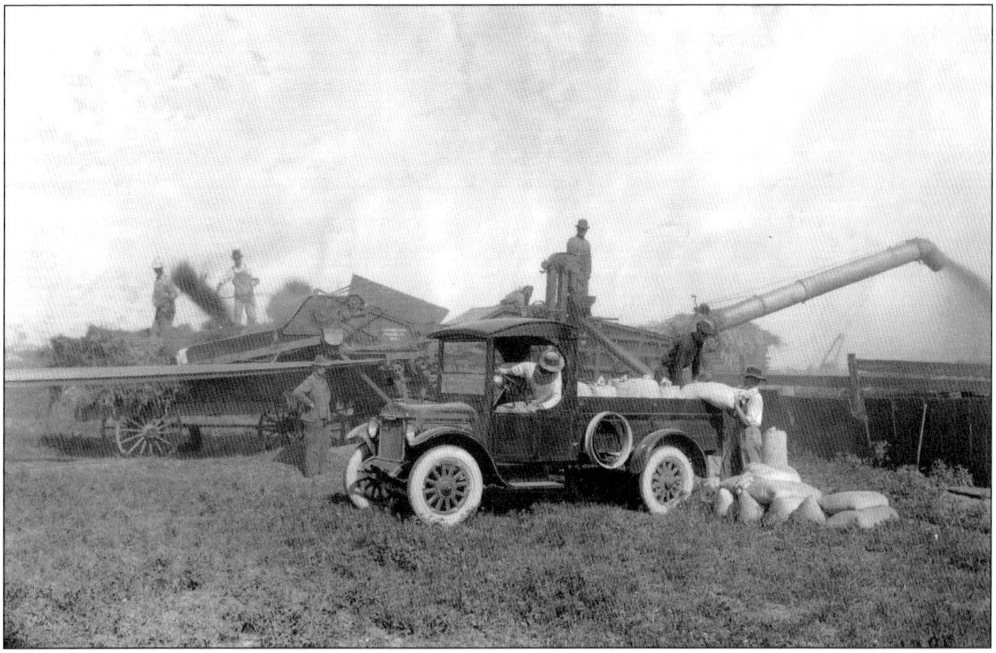

A popular Republic model was the Rapid Transit, a small delivery truck. Here the sharp, little Republic pickup, with white-sidewall tires, hauls away bagged grain from a threshing machine. This truck was one of the models that had its prices reduced in 1921 during a downturn in truck sales. (Courtesy of the Alma Public Library.)

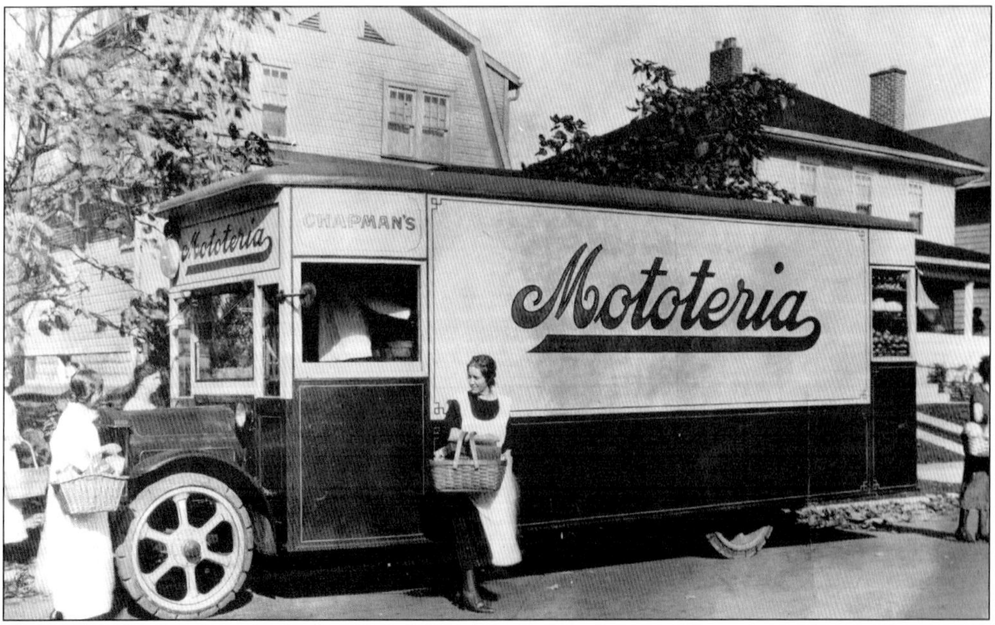


The Republic Truck Company filled all kinds of special orders through the 1920s. Dump trucks, road graders, delivery vans, passenger buses, fire trucks, snowplows, wreckers, and trucks for every kind of job left the factory in Alma. This Mototeria, used in some unnamed city, was a rolling grocery. Ladies, with their baskets on their arms, could shop for tinned goods, boxed food, and fresh fruit. (Courtesy of the Alma Public Library.)

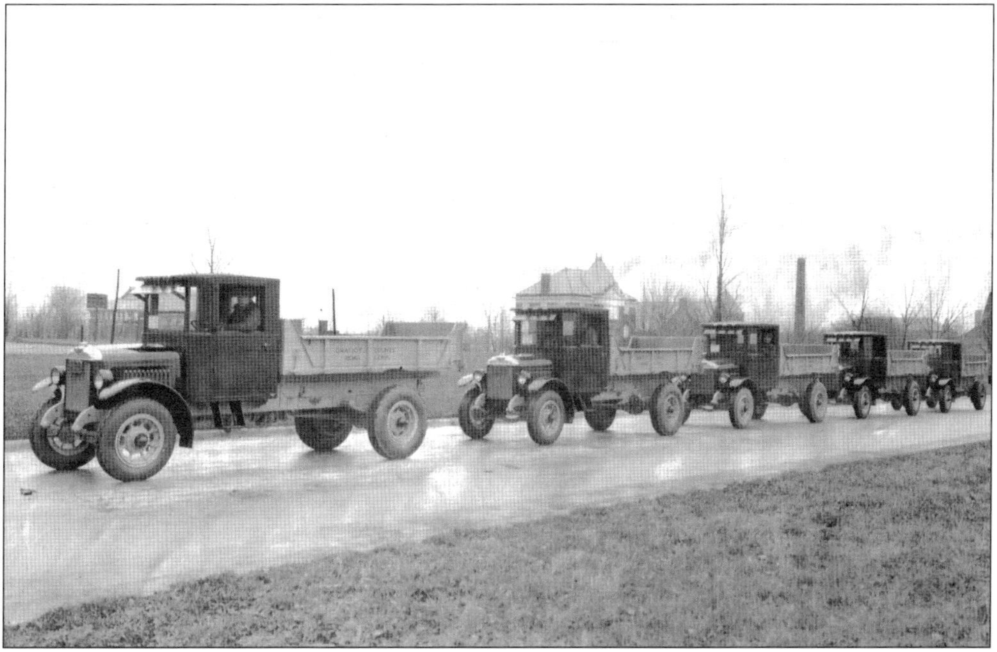

The Gratiot County Road Commission bought this fleet of Republic trucks for road maintenance and general hauling. Many counties in Michigan used Republic trucks exclusively for their grading and road-building projects. The reputation of the trucks for toughness and ease of repair promoted confidence and sales. (Courtesy of the Alma Public Library.)

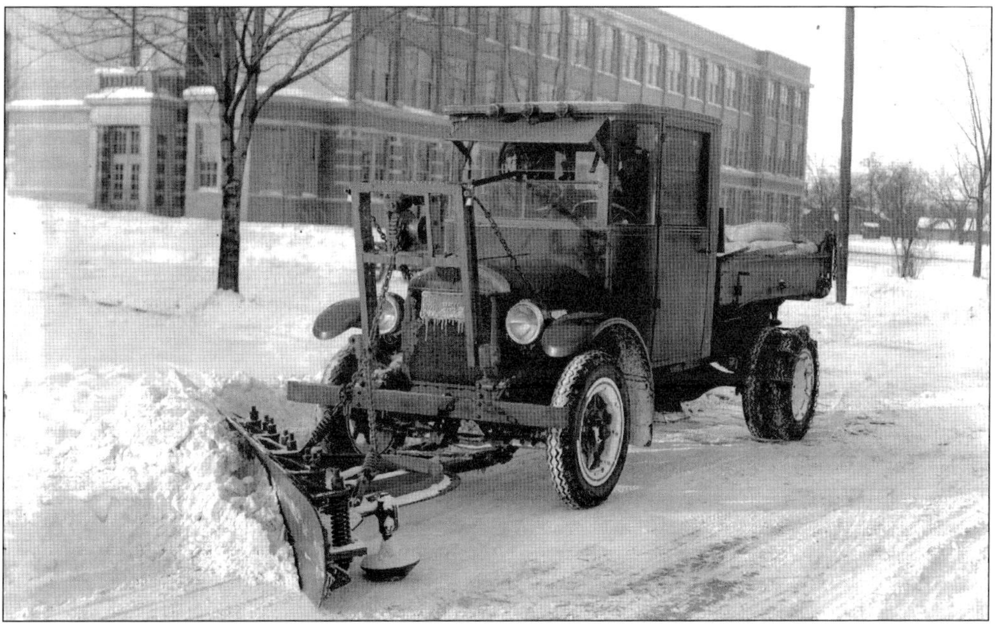

This snowplow, clearing Alma's Pine Avenue near the Stilwell Junior High School, was but one of the many styles and designs of Republic road trucks. Despite the popularity of its product, the company struggled through a sharp economic depression in 1921 and experienced intense competition from large companies like Chevrolet and Ford during the 1920s. (Courtesy of the Alma Public Library.)

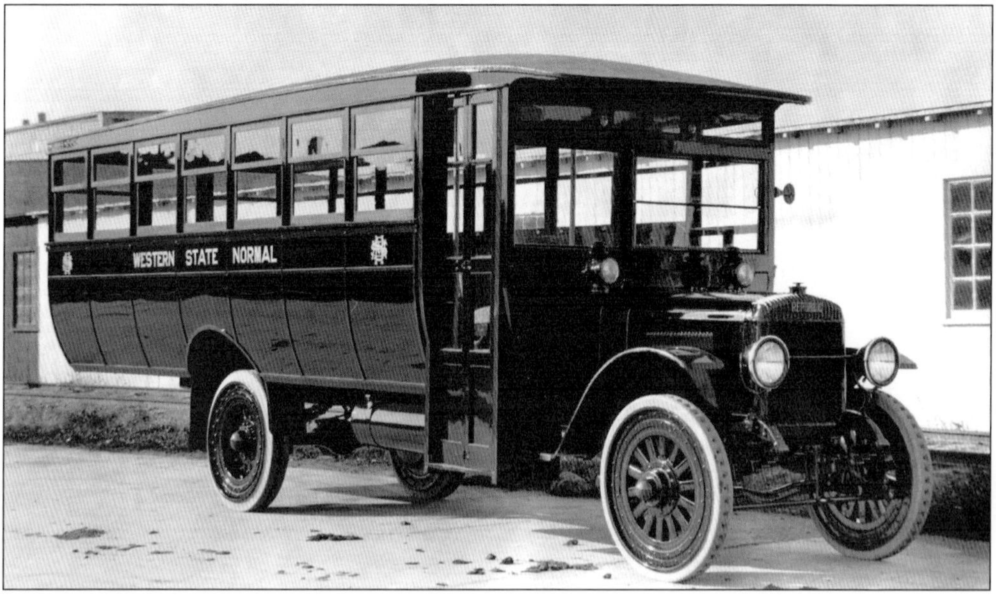


Made for Western State Normal College in Kalamazoo, this bus was used to transport students and supplies. The Hansen Bus Company of Alma also ran a fleet of Republic buses on its local routes. Once the world's largest truck company, Republic was bought by LaFrance Motor Company in 1929. Later that company became part of Sterling Motors, and Republic ceased to exist, its vacant Alma factories being occupied by other companies. (Courtesy of the Alma Public Library.)

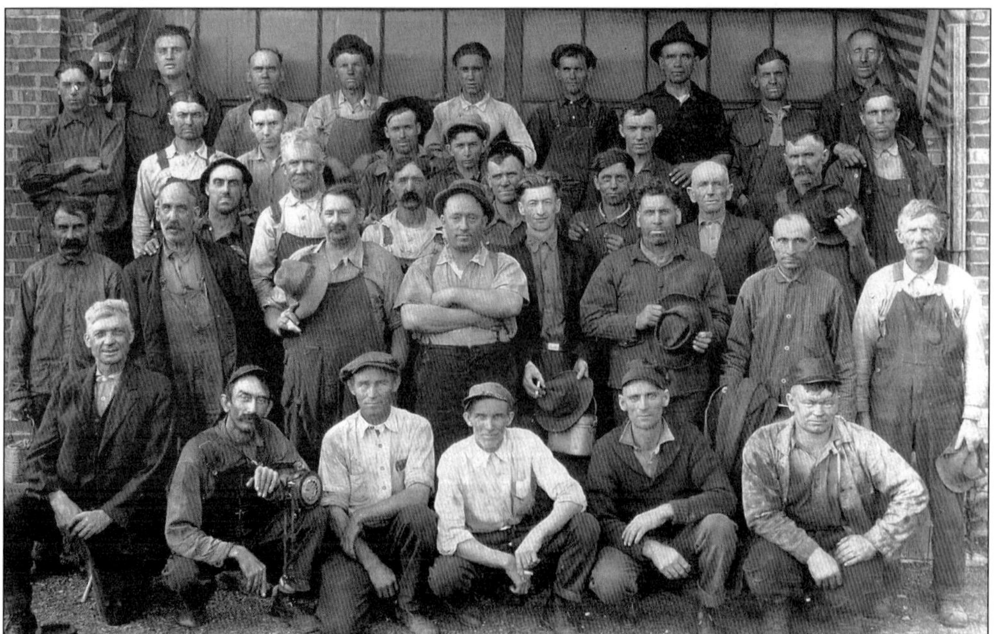

The Northern Wheel Company was begun in 1920 and weathered the recession of 1921 in full production. In 1921, it built 135,000 wheels, including a large number of replacement wheels for Ford and Dodge automobiles. Pictured here are the production workers of the company in 1920. (Courtesy of John Kemler.)

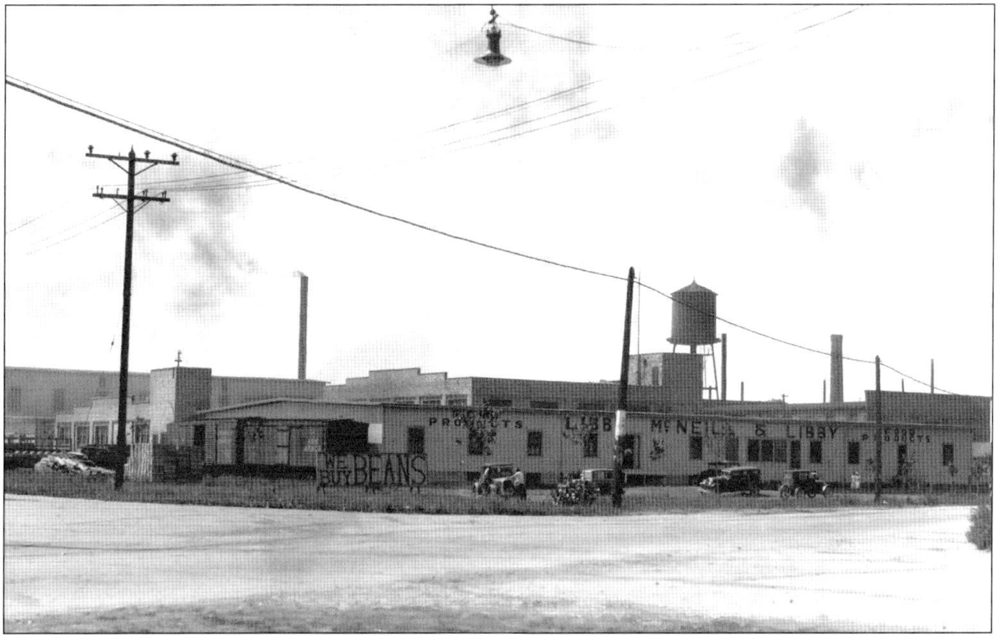


Established in 1914 as a pickle plant, Libby, McNeill, and Libby grew rapidly and soon occupied six buildings along Michigan Avenue and Bridge Street. Hundreds of pickle barrels and rows of pickle vats symbolized the company, which also processed other vegetables, including beans, cauliflower, and tomatoes. It employed 200 people during the busy season. (Courtesy of Richard Tesman.)

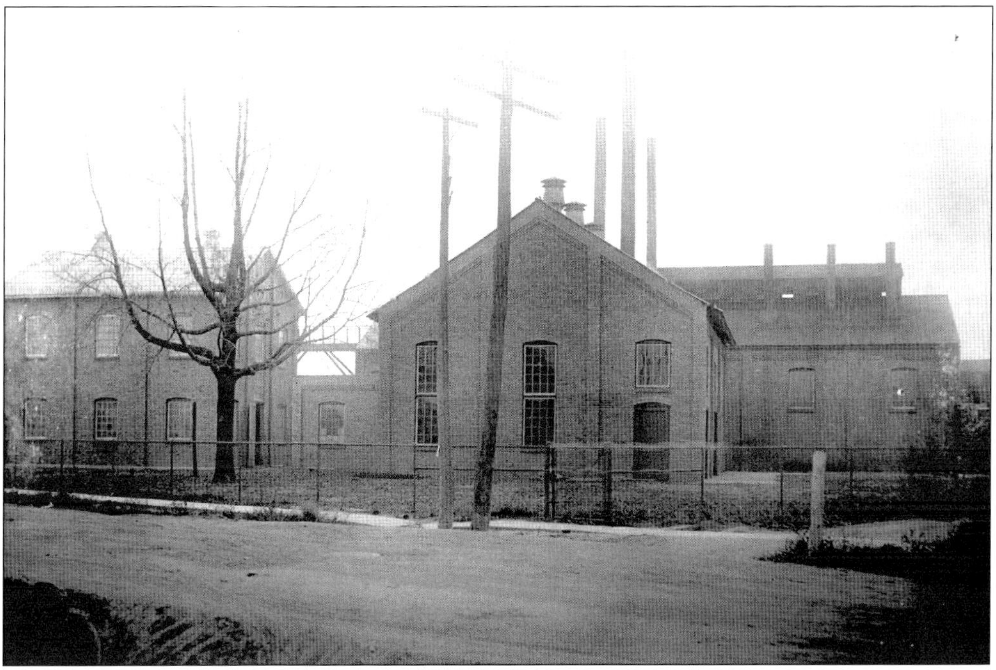

Michigan Federated Utilities operated this gas plant on the south side of Superior Street. It processed coal into coke to burn in manufacturing gas that was piped to Alma businesses and homes. Its business office was located on State Street behind the Opera House Block. (Courtesy of Colleen Boyer.)

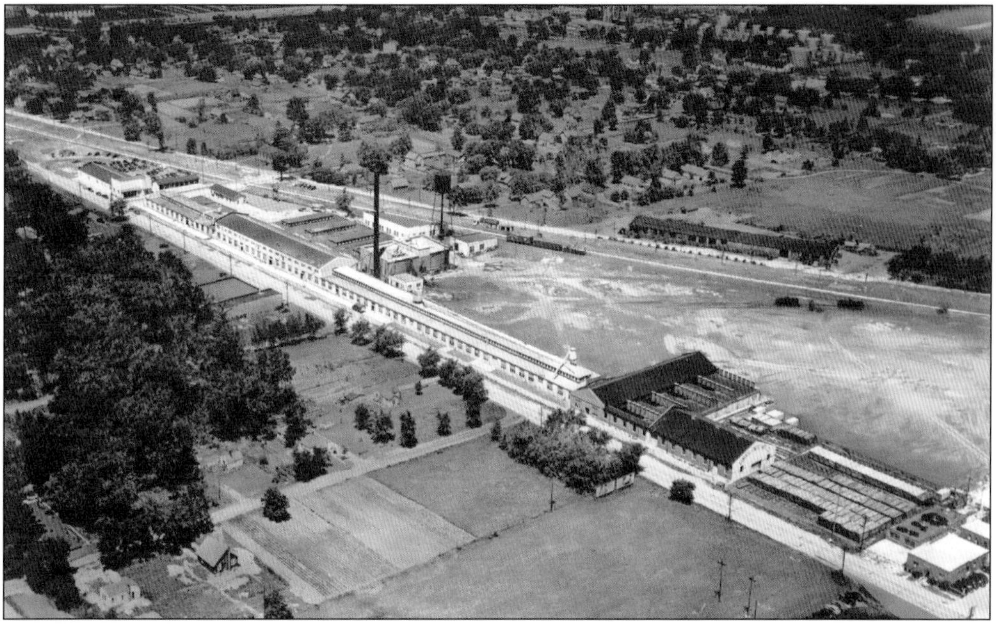

The Lobdell-Emery Manufacturing Company is shown here stretching along Superior Street. In 1926, its factory in Onaway burned in a spectacular fire. The company was making 80 percent of the steering wheels used in the automobile industry. Fearful of bringing U.S. automobile manufacturing to a halt, the company quickly looked for available quarters and chose the empty Republic Truck Company Plant No. 3 in Alma. (Courtesy of Tom McCreery.)

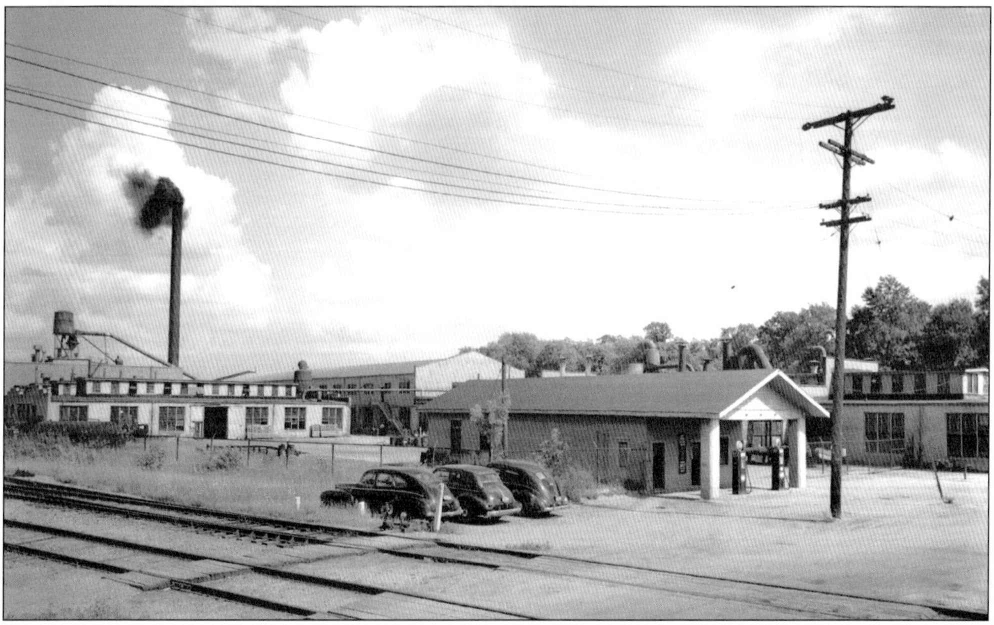

The company began to grow by adapting. It substituted steel bicycle rims for its famous wooden rims. It stopped making wooden steering wheels. It struggled through the Depression but survived because its skilled workforce enabled the company to meet market demands. Pictured about 1940 is the workers' entrance building that contained a small dining room. (Courtesy of Tom McCreery.)

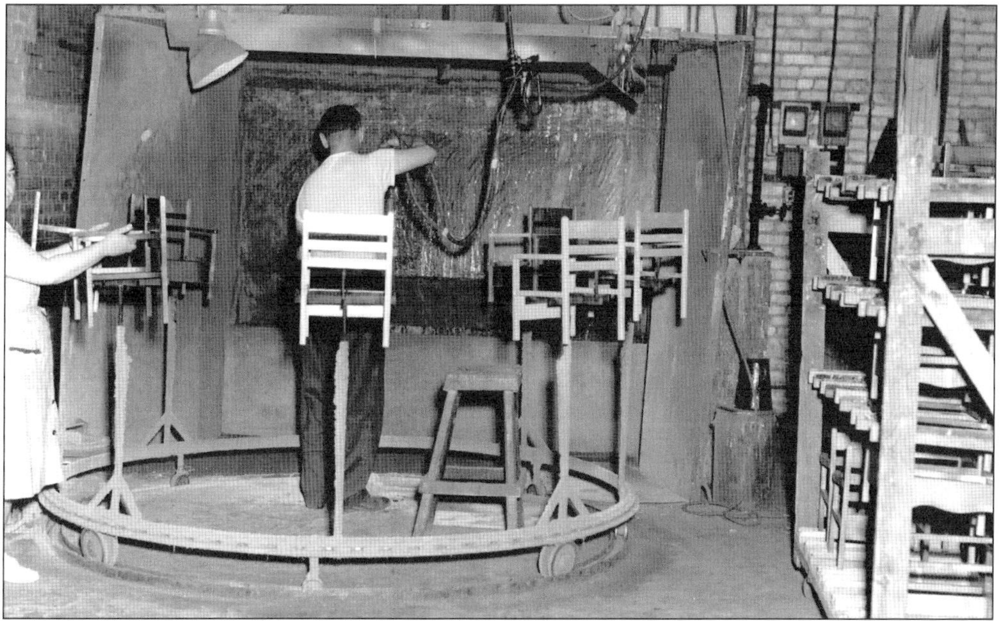

Among the company's wooden products were several models of furniture for children. Here potty-chairs are being painted in a water curtain spray booth. For years, the company thrived because of employees who were skilled woodworkers. Exquisite joining of wooden components in bicycle rims and wooden steering wheels reflected the talent of the workforce. (Courtesy of Tom McCreery.)

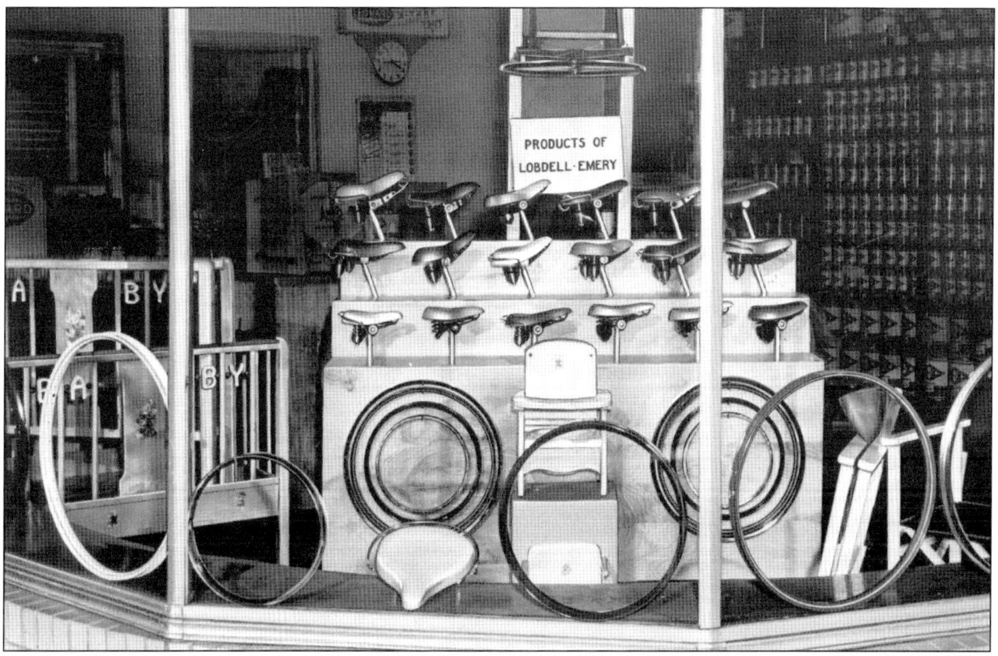


A display in a downtown window showcases products produced by the Lobdell company in the 1940s. Steel bicycle rims, bicycle seats (saddles), children's cribs and potty chairs, and canvas director's chairs were some of the products of the company. It also made gun stocks and baseball bats. (Courtesy of Tom McCreery.)

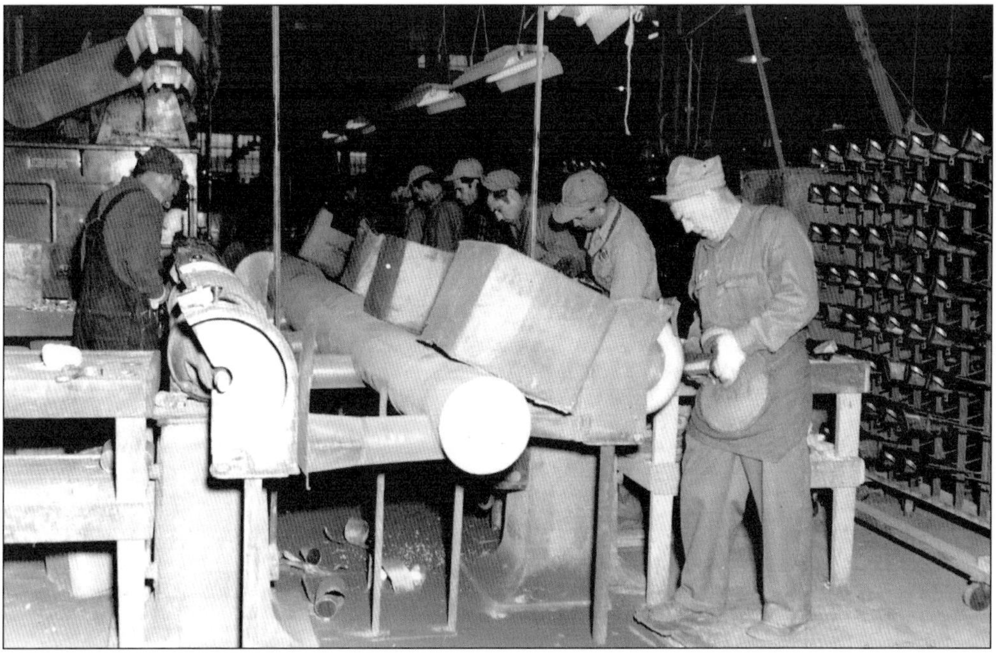

Lobdell-Emery Manufacturing Company struggled until it was reorganized around 1950 and received contracts from the Ford Motor Company for wooden seat backs and wooden floorboards. Thus began a long association with Ford, which set the company on the road to prosperity. Pictured is the buffing and polishing department. (Courtesy of Tom McCreery.)

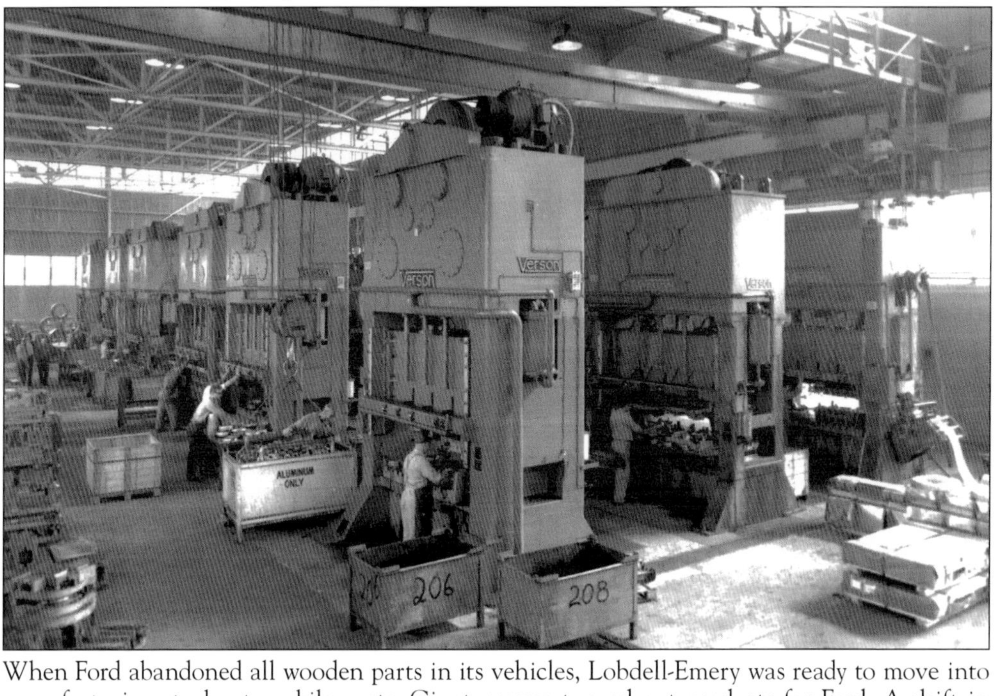


When Ford abandoned all wooden parts in its vehicles, Lobdell-Emery was ready to move into manufacturing steel automobile parts. Giant presses turned out products for Ford. A shift in the automobile supply business hurt the company in the 1990s, and in 2005, the company, now Oxford Automotive, closed it factory in Alma. (Courtesy of Tom McCreery.)

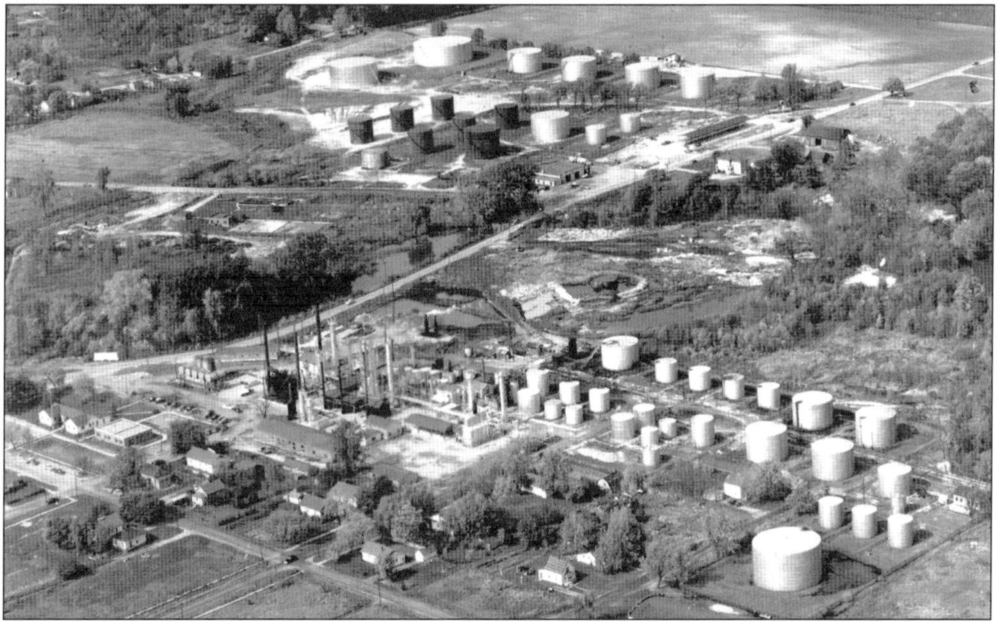

The oil boom of the 1930s in central Michigan had a powerful impact on Alma. The discovery in 1933 of the Porter Oil Field prompted the construction of the Mid-West Refinery on Bridge Street in Alma. The plant began operations in the summer of 1934, and after the Crystal Oil Field was opened in March 1935, Mid-West began a steady expansion that resulted in this refinery, as shown around 1950. (Courtesy of the Breckenridge and Wheeler Area Historical Society.)

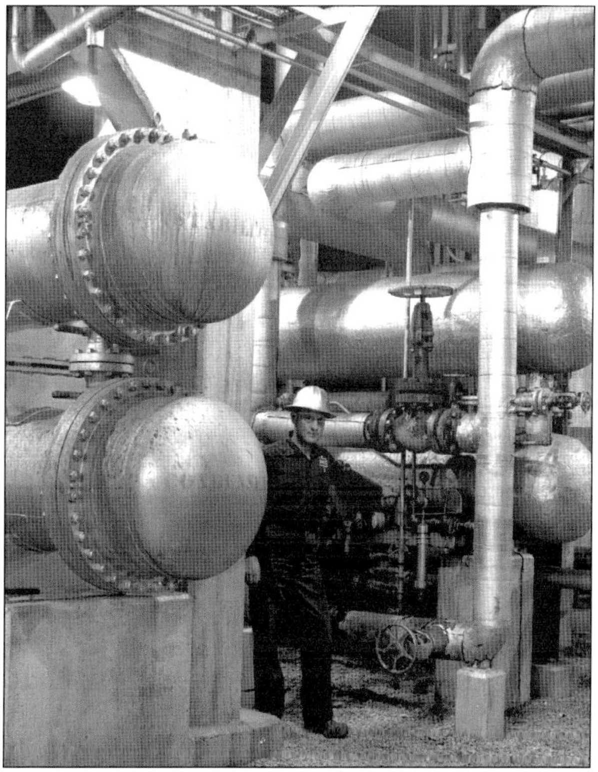

Mid-West Refinery ran a pipeline to the Crystal Oil Field 20 miles away. The refinery hummed 24 hours a day, producing gasoline, naphtha, kerosene, and fuel oils. Working among the giant pipes of the plant is John McBride. Mid-West later was absorbed by Leonard Refinery. It was closed, and the entire plant was dismantled and hauled away. (Courtesy of the Breckenridge and Wheeler Area Historical Society.)

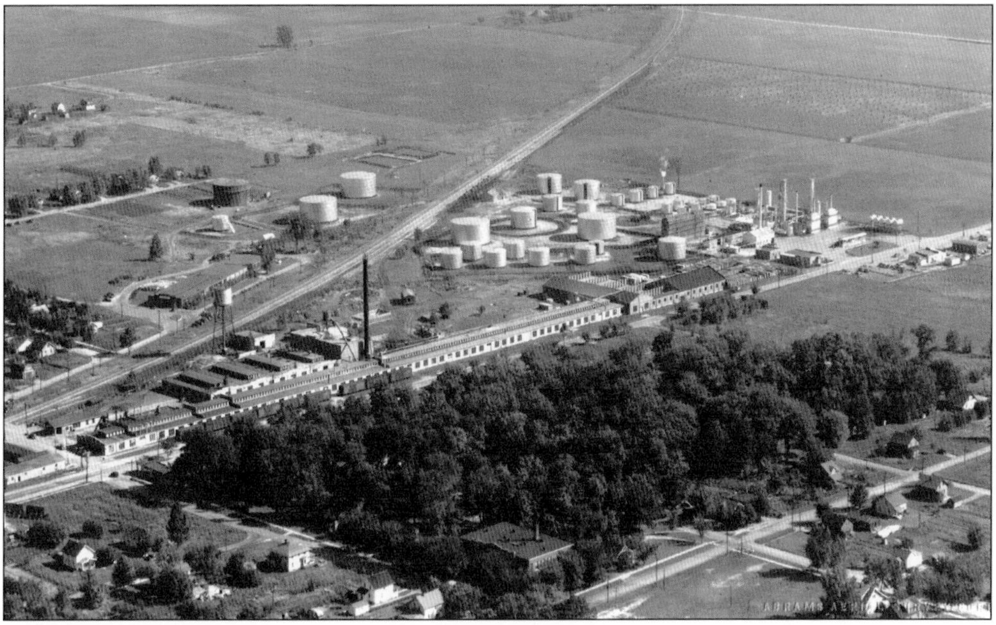

This 1940s-era photograph shows the Republic School nestled in the woods in the foreground, the lengthy Lobdell-Emery Manufacturing Company plant stretching beside Superior Street, the county garage behind the Lobdell water tower, and Leonard at the right. Leonard Refinery began in 1936 by absorbing the Acme Refinery and adding a revolutionary Dubbs Cracking Unit. (Courtesy of Robert Smith.)

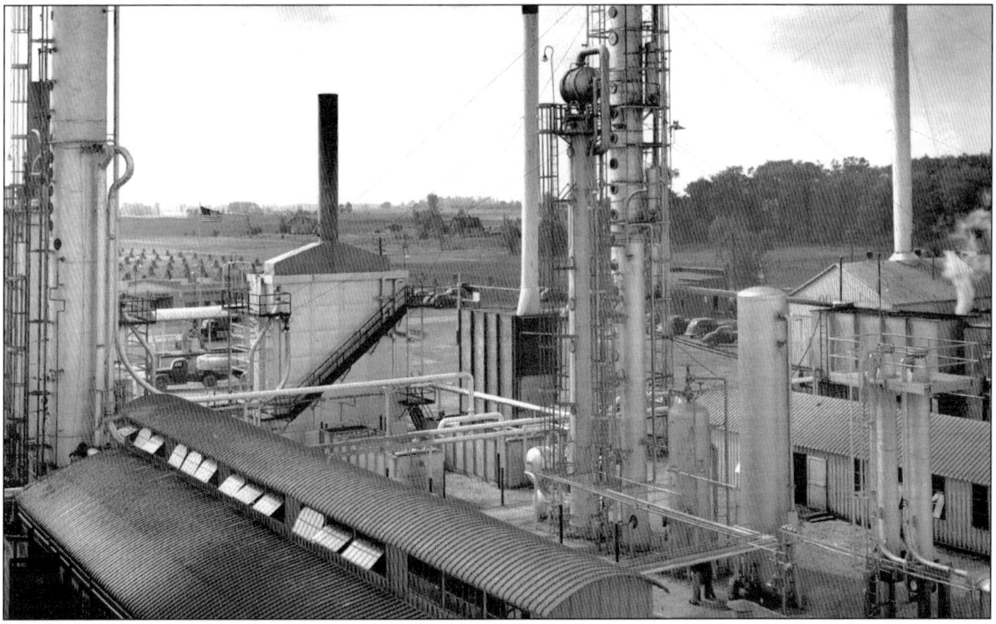

This view of Leonard Refinery, expanding along Superior Street in the late 1930s, reflects the sharp contrast between the towering processing units and shocked corn on the south side of Superior Street. Alma was experiencing unexpected growth through this new industry that helped the town prosper for years. (Photograph by Maurine Stovall, courtesy of the Breckenridge and Wheeler Area Historical Society.)

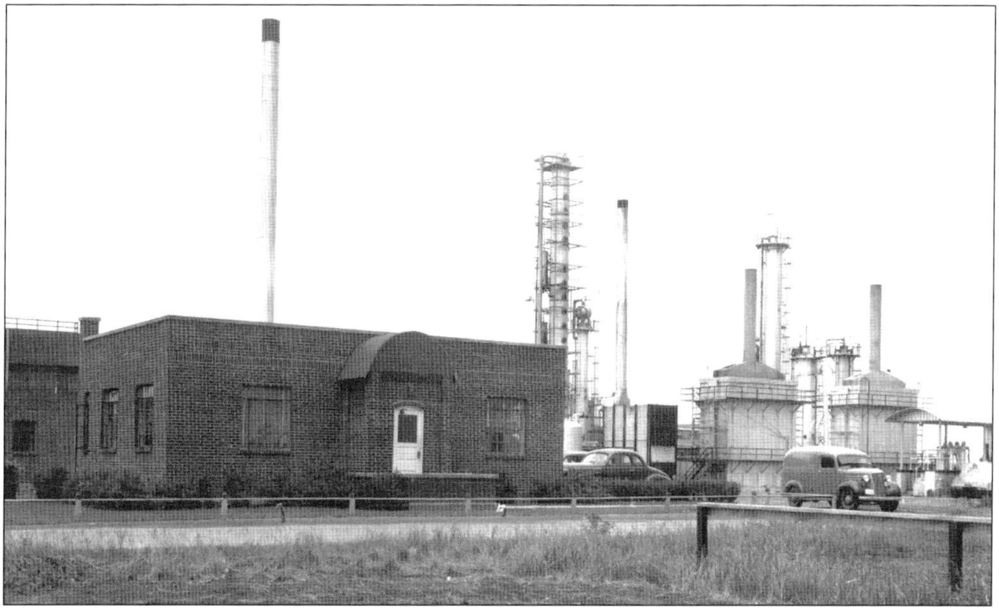

Using a combination of railcars and pipelines, Leonard Refinery obtained enough crude oil to continue operations after local oil fields played out. Transportation advantages of Michigan routes 46 and 27 as well as two main rail lines benefitted Alma during the oil boom. (Courtesy of the Alma Public Library.)

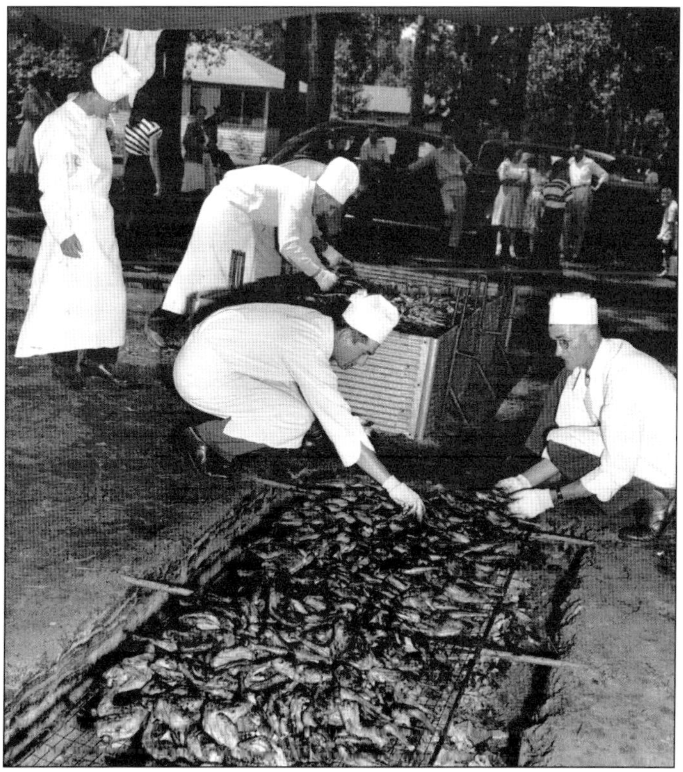

The annual Leonard picnic was often held at Lake Lansing. Chefs drove down early to dig the pit and place the charcoal before barbecuing enough chicken to feed several hundred people. The company bussed employees and families who did not wish to drive. These chefs included Mike Patterson at left and Jack Cawrse in back. (Photograph by W. Nelson, courtesy of Robert Smith.)

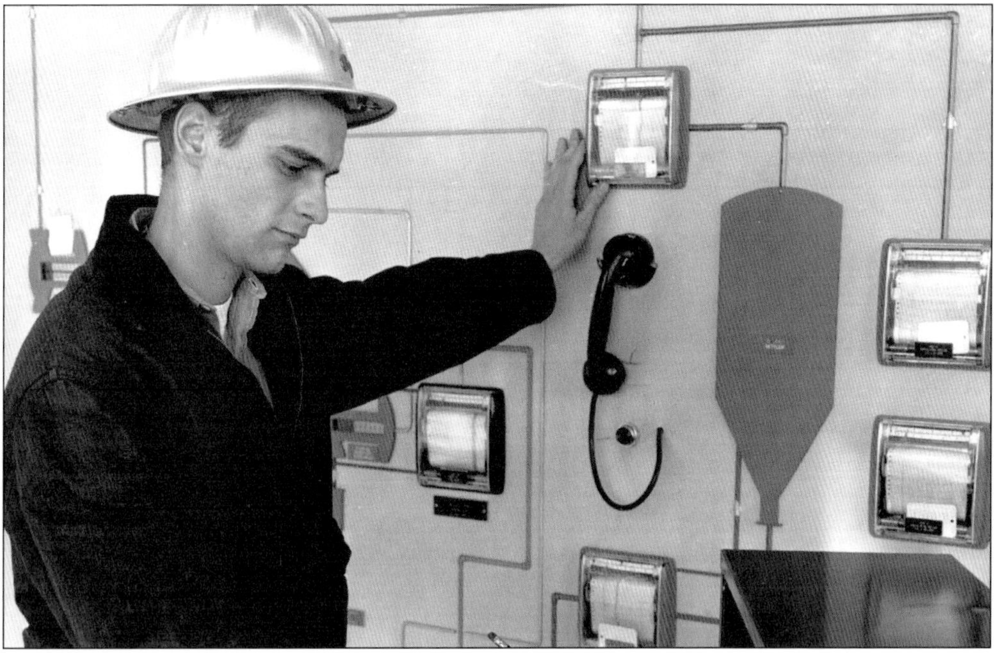

Keeping a refinery running without a glitch or shutdown required constant monitoring of the refining processes that were under way. Here Lyle Patterson reads temperature meters on a Fluid-Catalytic Cracker at the refinery. It reported temperature every minute, and the readings were recorded. (Courtesy of Robert Smith.)

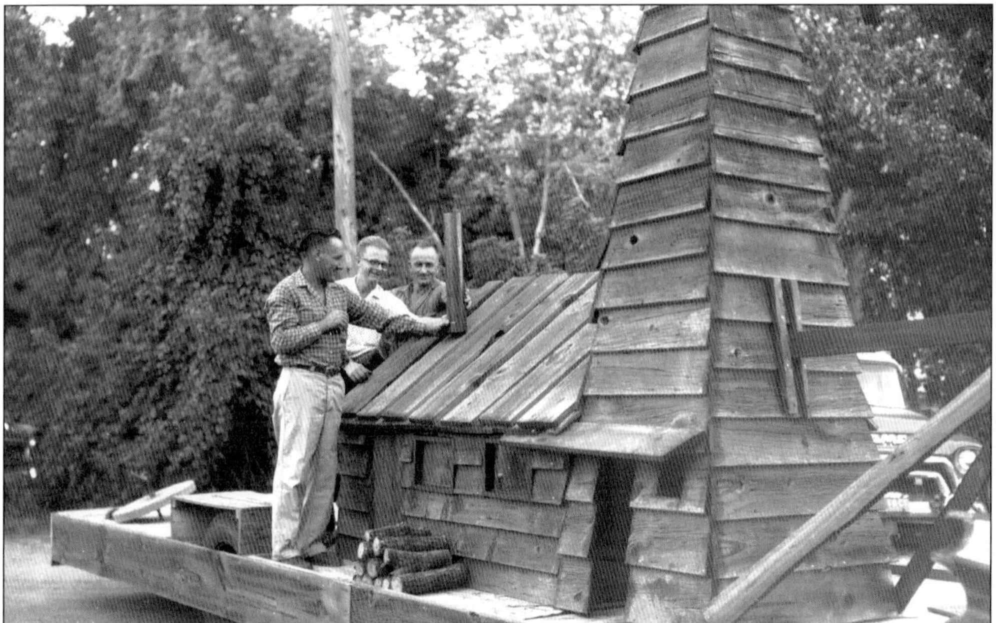

The Leonard Refinery's entry in Alma's centennial parade in 1956 was this reproduction of Colonel Drake's first oil well in Titusville, Pennsylvania. Here, from left to right, Art Crispin, Frank Chapman, and Lloyd Johnson ponder where to add the smokestack to the pump house. (Courtesy Robert Smith.)

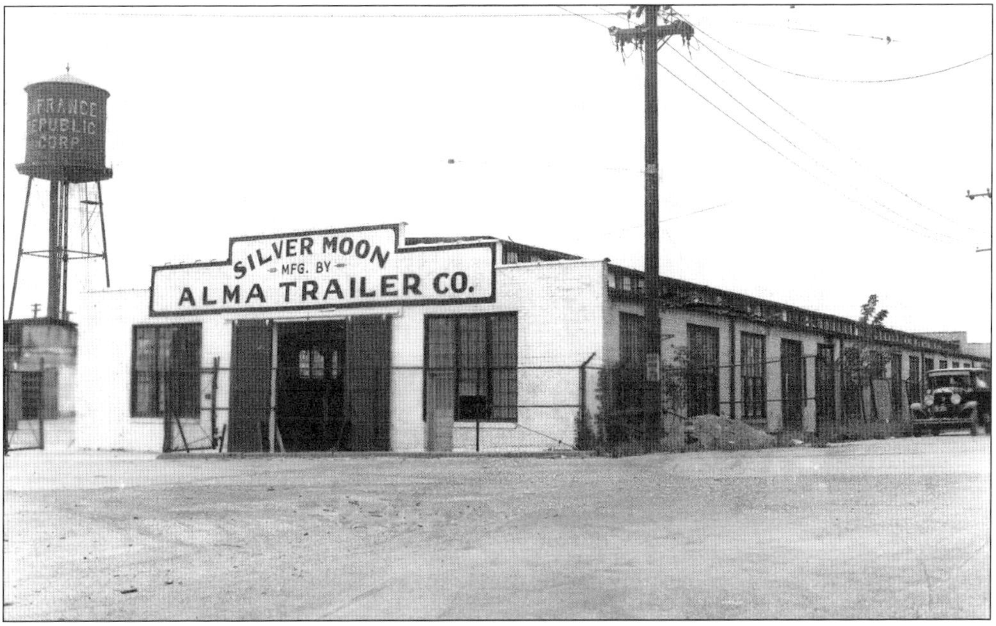


The house-trailer industry in Alma started by chance in 1930 when Harold and William Redman with engineer Allen Hathaway built their first house trailer—a small hunting trailer for the three of them. Other men asked for similar trailers, and the industry was born. The Alma Trailer Company, making the Silvermoon House Trailer, occupied the vacant plant No. 1 of the old Republic Truck Company complex. (Courtesy of Richard Tesman.)

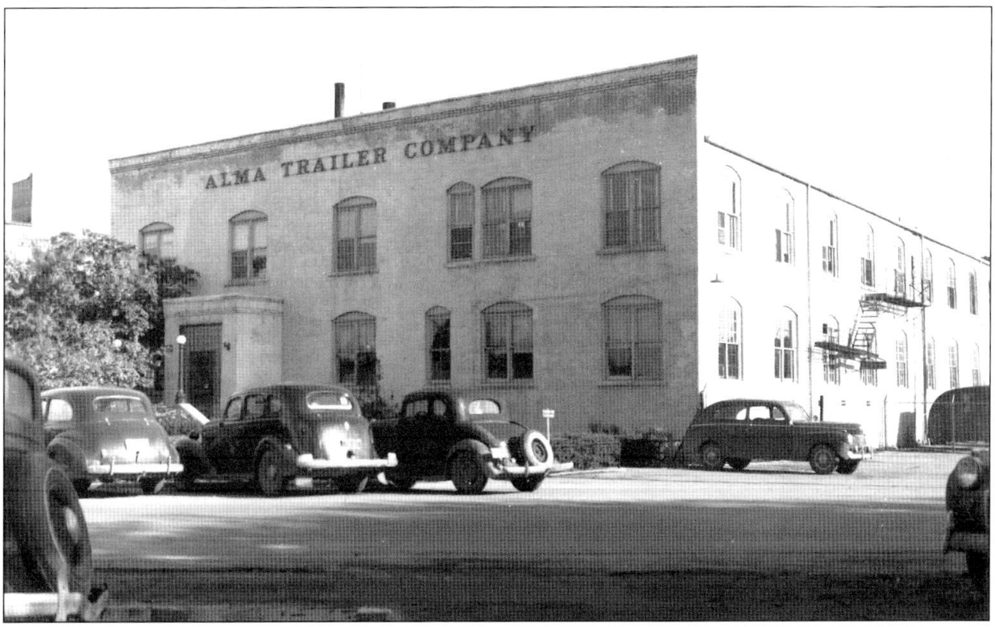


When investor James Ryan bought 51 percent of the stock of the Alma Trailer, a shake-up in the company occurred. The Redmans and Hathaway moved into the vacant Libby, McNeill, and Libby pickle plant across the street and began to manufacture New Moon Trailers and soon were making substantial additions to their factory. A New Moon Trailer was used in the movie *The Long, Long Trailer*, starring Lucille Ball and Desi Arnaz. (Courtesy of Richard Tesman.)

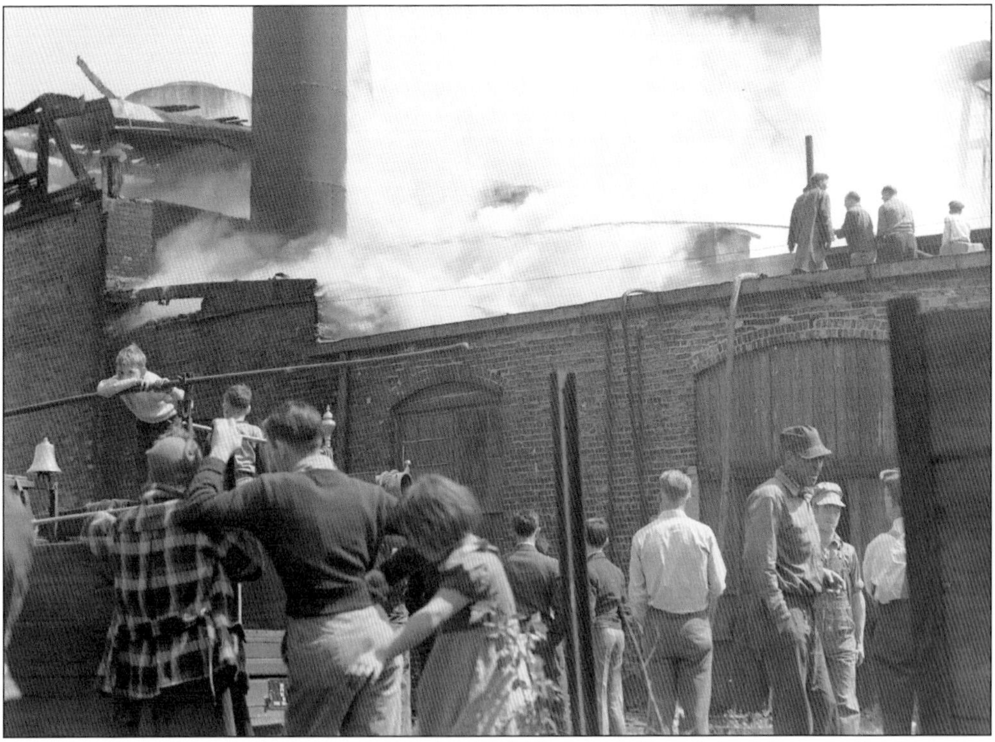

Detroiter Mobile Homes of St. Louis, Michigan, had just purchased the Alma Trailer Company plant in 1962 when a fire broke out in the paint shop and destroyed part of the factory, along with a half dozen new mobile homes. All of Alma's trailer companies were drifting into new factories in the South, and within a few years, the mobile-home industry left Alma completely. (Photograph by Hubert Elias, courtesy of Dale Kemler.)

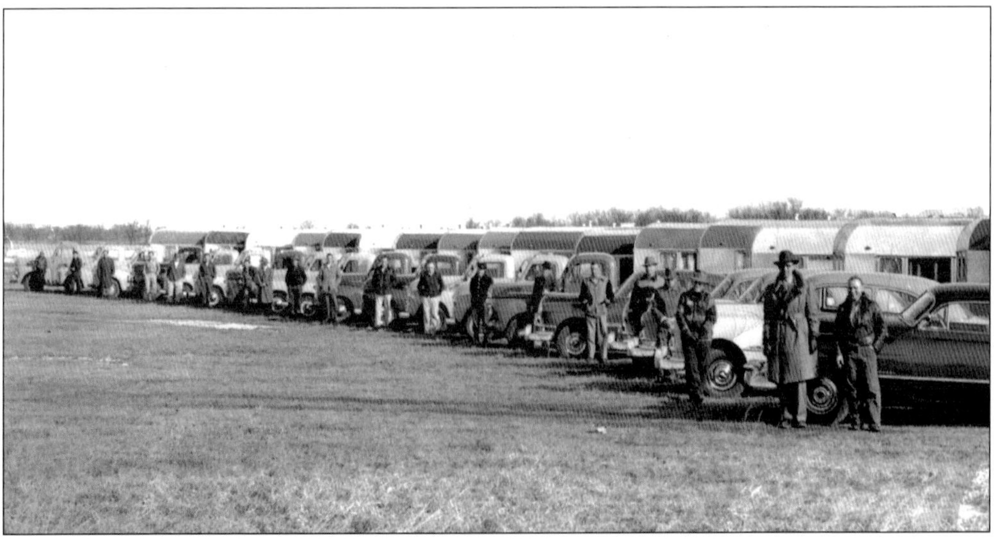

Many drivers were needed to move the hundreds of mobile homes manufactured in Alma to their destinations. Here drivers with trucks and cars prepare to transport them. During World War II, the federal government placed orders for many trailers to be used as dwellings at busy government installations. (Courtesy of the Alma Public Library.)

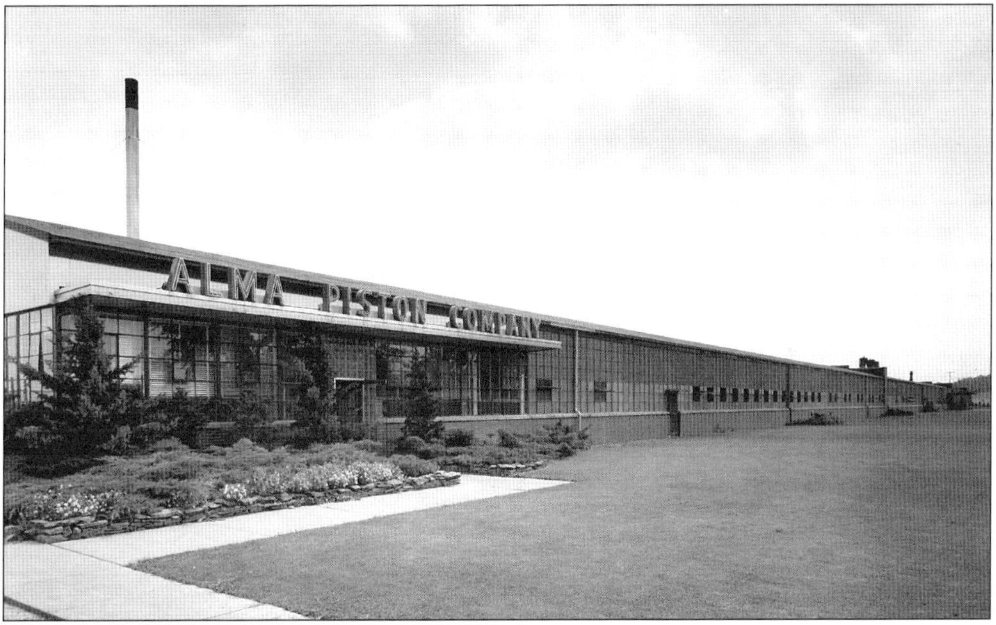


Alma Piston Company was founded in 1943 by Emmet E. Tracy at the Redman trailer plant site to produce service parts for the Ford Motor Company. In 1948, it moved to new quarters at this site on Michigan Avenue. Although its name was changed to Alma Products Company, it has always produced a variety of automobile parts. (Courtesy of Alma Products Company.)

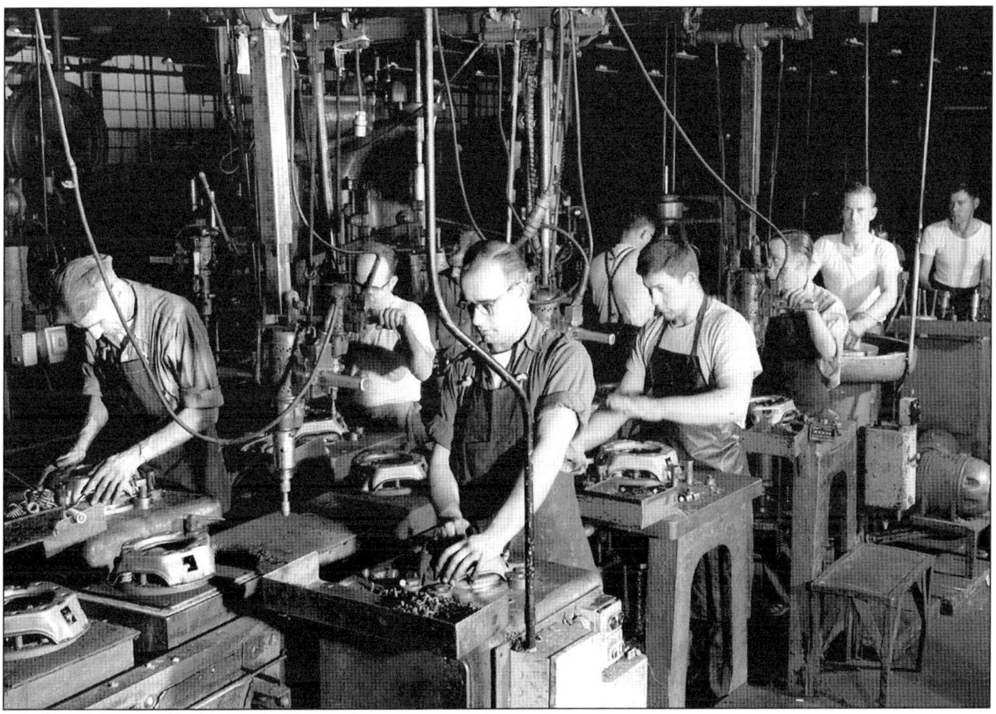

This production line is turning out clutch subassembly units. Boxes of components and stacks of clutch pressure plates provide workmen with pieces for building the units. The company continued to grow as a supplier primarily to Ford Motor Company. (Courtesy of Alma Products Company.)

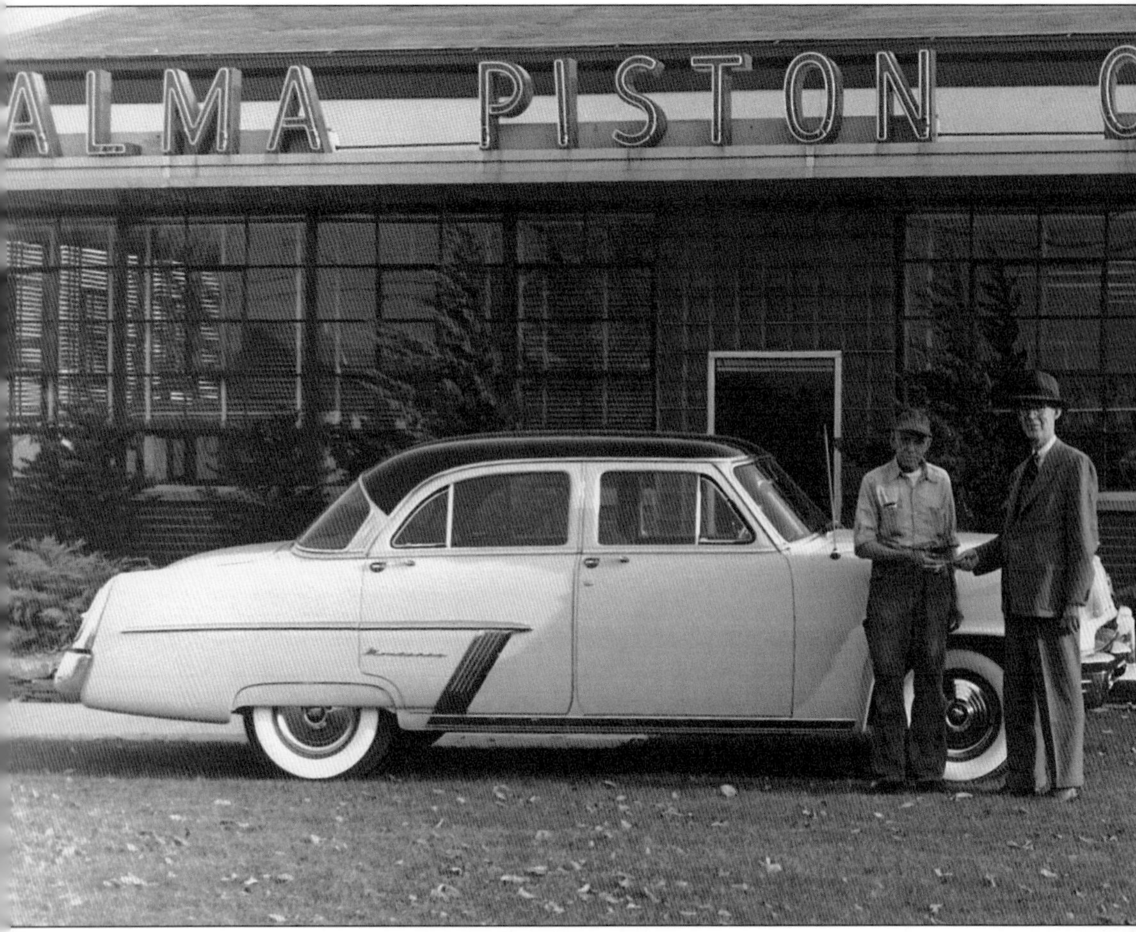


Emmet E. Tracy, chief executive officer of Alma Products Company, presents keys to a 1953 Mercury Monterey to employee Roy Collison. All employees were eligible to win the car, and excitement at the plant was intense. Collison's wife was astounded when he rolled up in front of the house in the new vehicle. "You mean you won that car?" she exclaimed. He assured her it was theirs. (Courtesy of Alma Products Company.)

# *Five*

# IMPROVING LIVES

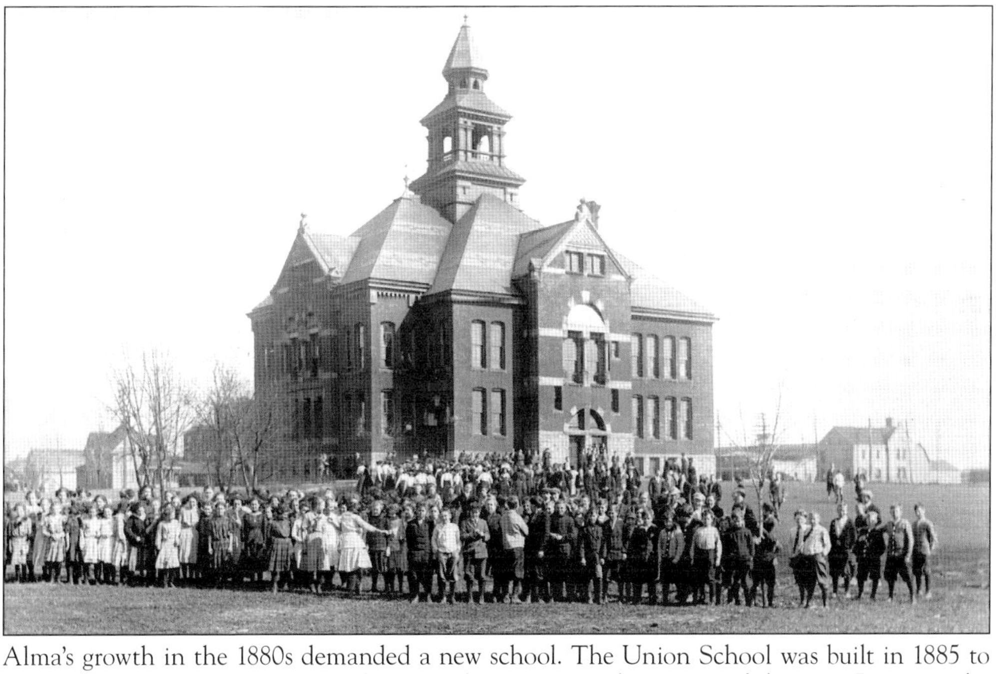

Alma's growth in the 1880s demanded a new school. The Union School was built in 1885 to accommodate the burgeoning student population. Located just east of the Pine River on the south side of Superior Street, it required most students to cross the Superior Street bridge. Some scholars from outlying areas rode horses that were stabled at downtown liveries. (Courtesy of Richard Tesman.)

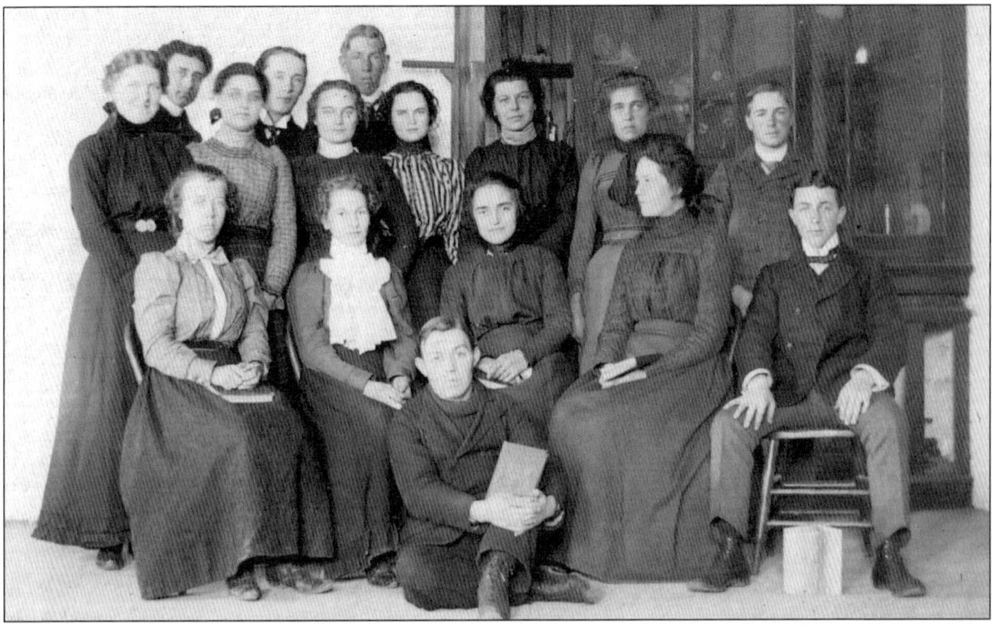

Graduation exercises for the Alma High School class of 1901 were conducted on June 19 at the opera house. Susie Estella Edwards gave a stirring address on behalf of the class. Baccalaureate was held the preceding Sunday at the Baptist church. Class Day exercises on the preceding Tuesday allowed the sophomores and juniors to get back at the departing seniors. (Courtesy of Alma High School.)

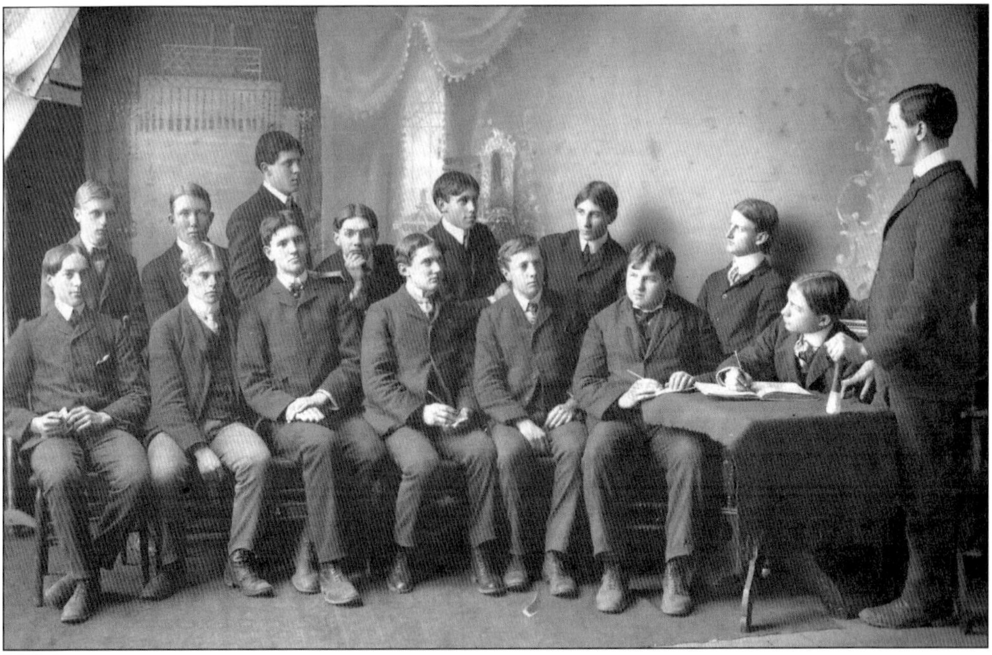

Somber members of the Alma High School Debating Club of 1903 appear to reflect the solemnity of their organization. Membership was limited to 20, and any member who failed to accept the serious nature of the club was blackballed. The favored topic that year was, "Resolved, that literary societies are more beneficial than athletics." (Courtesy of Alma High School.)

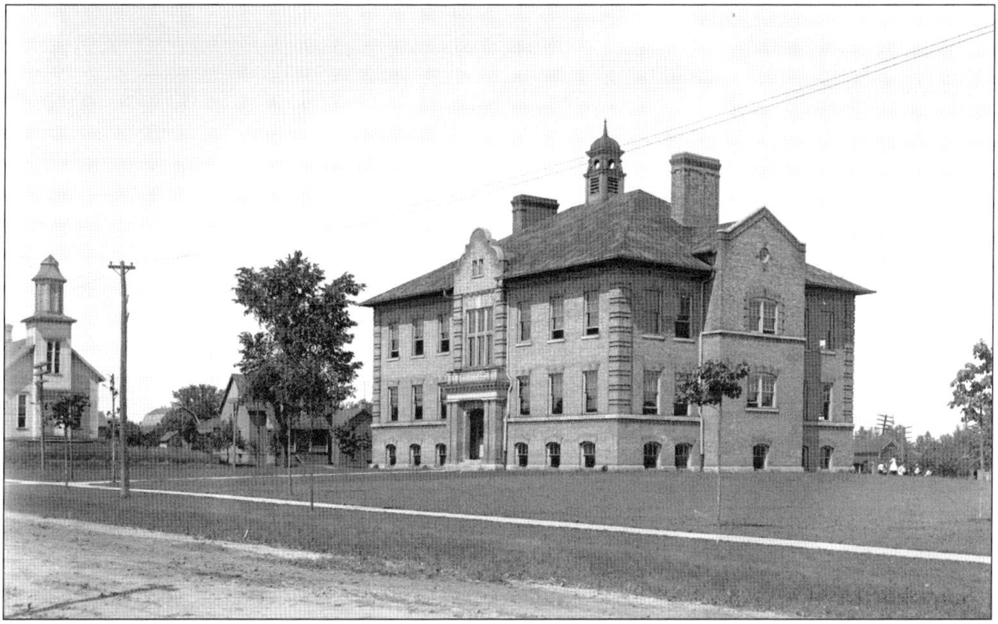

Crowded conditions at the Union School required a new elementary school, and the Ward School was built in 1905 at the corner of Gratiot and Hastings Streets. It cost nearly $20,000 and contained four classrooms on each floor and usable basement space. After serving both elementary and secondary students, it was razed in the 1970s. (Courtesy of Dale Kemler.)

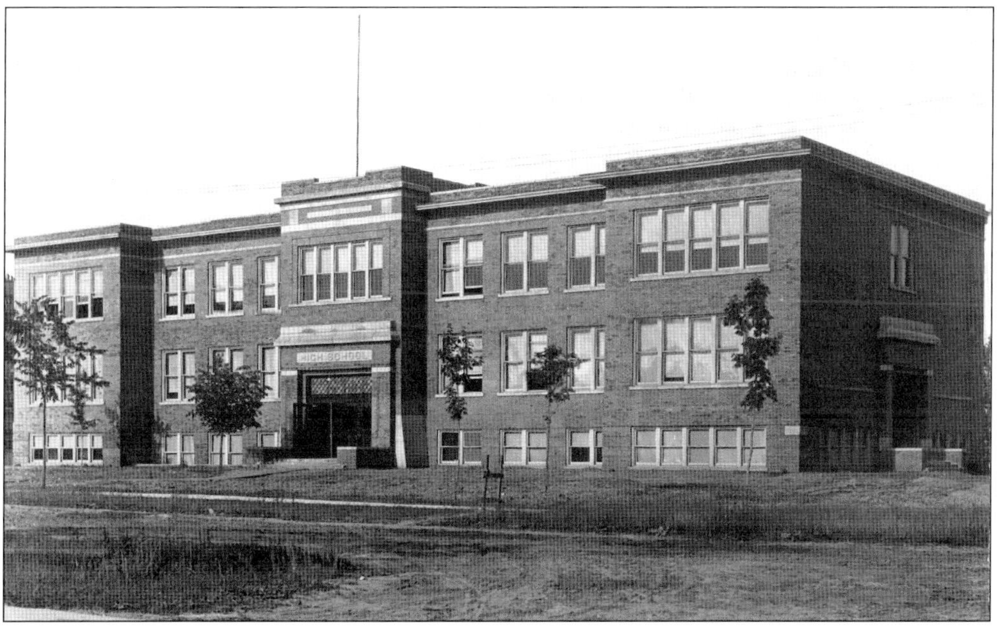


Although the Ward School provided elementary classrooms, a new high school was needed in Alma, and the citizens agreed to bond for $65,000. Located on the same block as the Ward School, the new high school opened in 1913. Building the high school was a wise move, for within three years, the Republic Truck Company drew so many workers and their families to Alma that even with three school buildings, school facilities were severely taxed by the influx of new students. (Courtesy of Richard Tesman.)

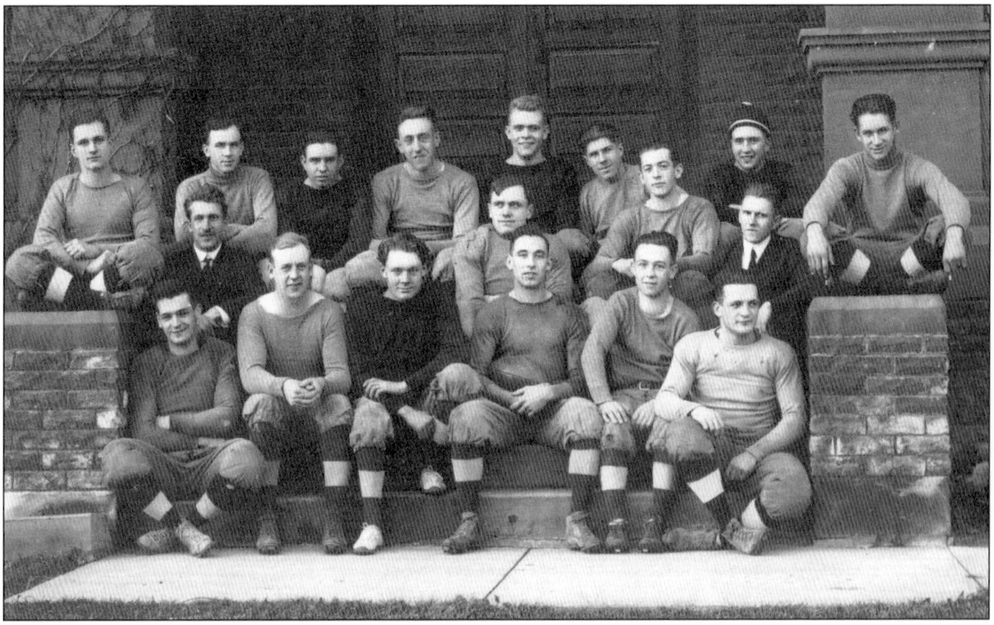

Coaches Collins and Crisp were pleased at the turnout for the Alma High School football team in 1913. They put the boys through grueling practices, resulting in a record of 4-2. Opponents included Bay City Western, Mount Pleasant, Saginaw Arthur Hill, Ithaca, Owosso, and St. Louis. A final season game with Ithaca drew 1,200 spectators and earned Alma High School athletics $157. (Courtesy of Colleen Boyer.)

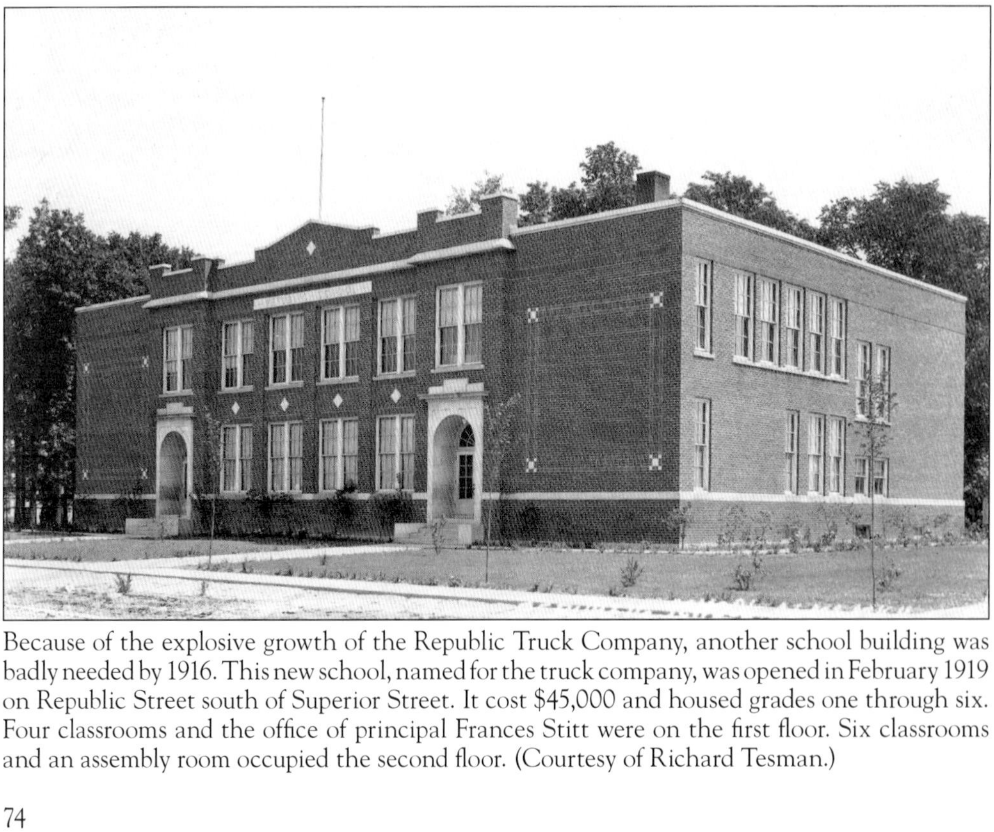

Because of the explosive growth of the Republic Truck Company, another school building was badly needed by 1916. This new school, named for the truck company, was opened in February 1919 on Republic Street south of Superior Street. It cost $45,000 and housed grades one through six. Four classrooms and the office of principal Frances Stitt were on the first floor. Six classrooms and an assembly room occupied the second floor. (Courtesy of Richard Tesman.)

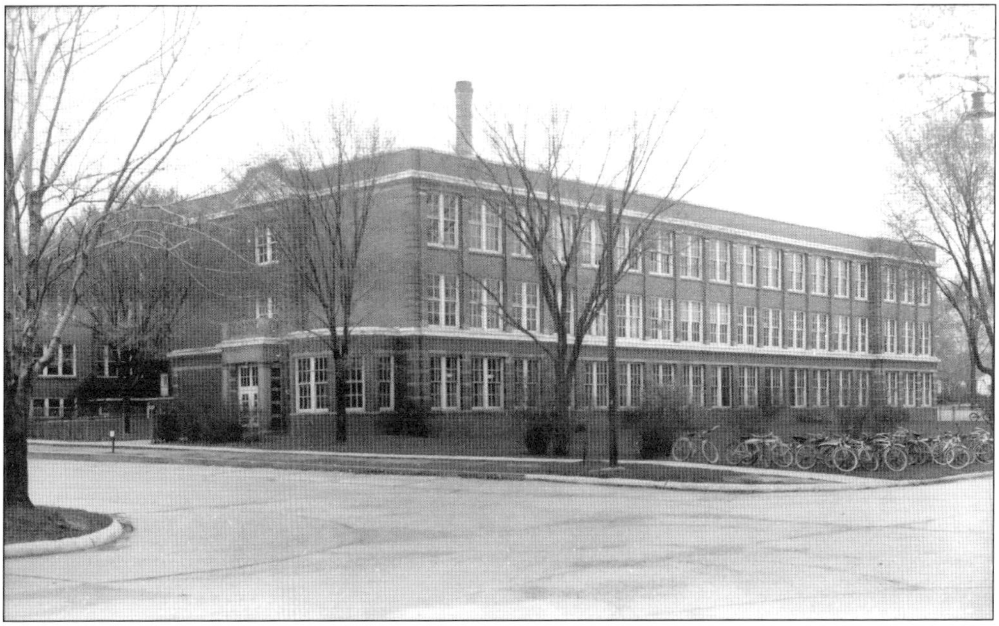

Stilwell Junior High School opened in September 1927 adjacent to the high school. The new building was planned to meet the modern concept of a junior high school. It provided 20 classrooms, a library, a study hall, sewing and cooking rooms for home economics, and corridor lockers rather than cloakrooms. The science room was placed near the school's entrance because of children's fascination with science. (Courtesy of Richard Tesman.)

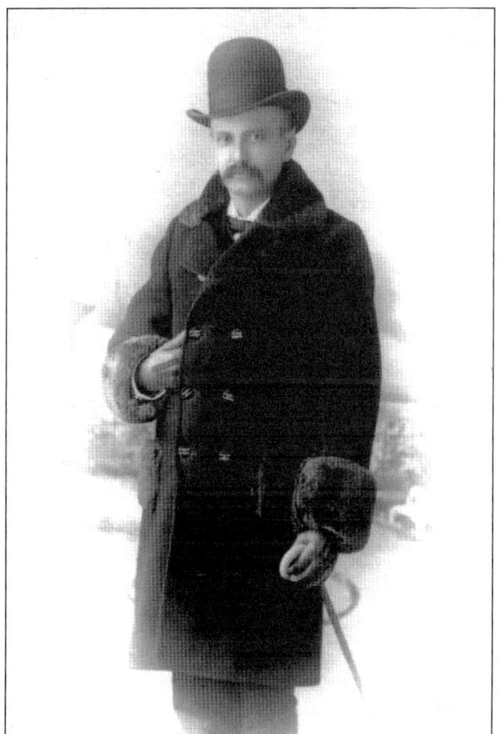

Prof. Oliver J. Stilwell served as superintendent of Alma Public Schools for 10 years. He made a very positive impression on the village before moving to Utah. During his time in Alma, he ran a real estate business on the side, selling 16 houses in 1887. The town honored his memory by naming the new junior high school for him in 1926. (Courtesy of Colleen Boyer.)

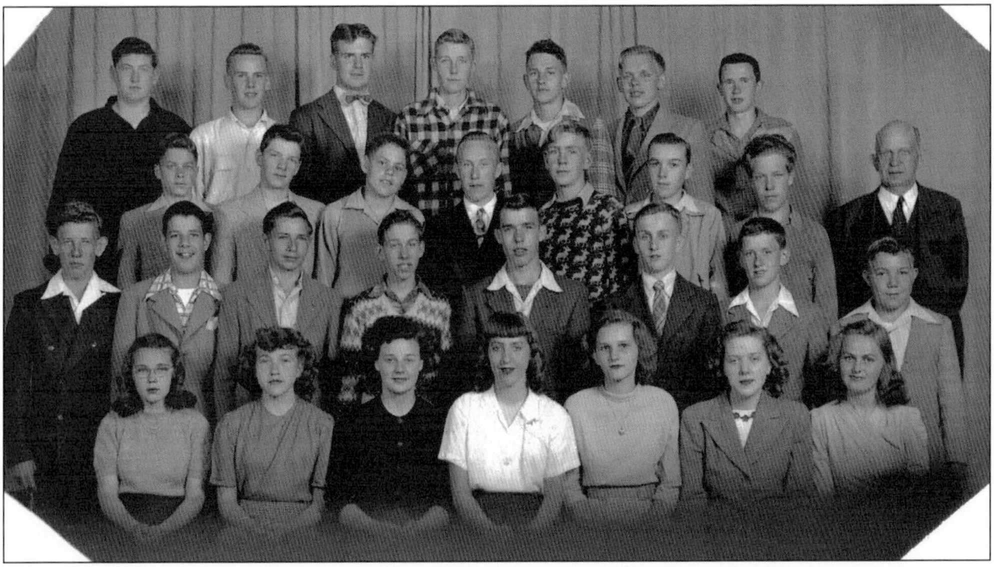

The Stilwell Junior High School ninth graders in 1947 included, from left to right, (first row) Mary Geller, Georgine Stewart, Beverly Hall, Barbara Ramsey, Joyce Maier, Leila Fillhard, and Zelma Miller. The second row includes Cumbo Franks, Tom Bevier, Bernard Chamberlain, Dick VanDemark, Fred Schults, Jim Cox, and Lyle Simmons. In the third row are Eric Beeson, James Bradley, Bill Watson, Robert McGill, ? Orwig, Dale Husted, and Mr. Ericksen (teacher). From left to right in the fourth row are Bill Raycraft, James Watson, ? Tennesee, unidentified, Marvin Sartor, Chuck Hicks, and Lee Woods. (Courtesy of Charles and Diantha Hicks.)

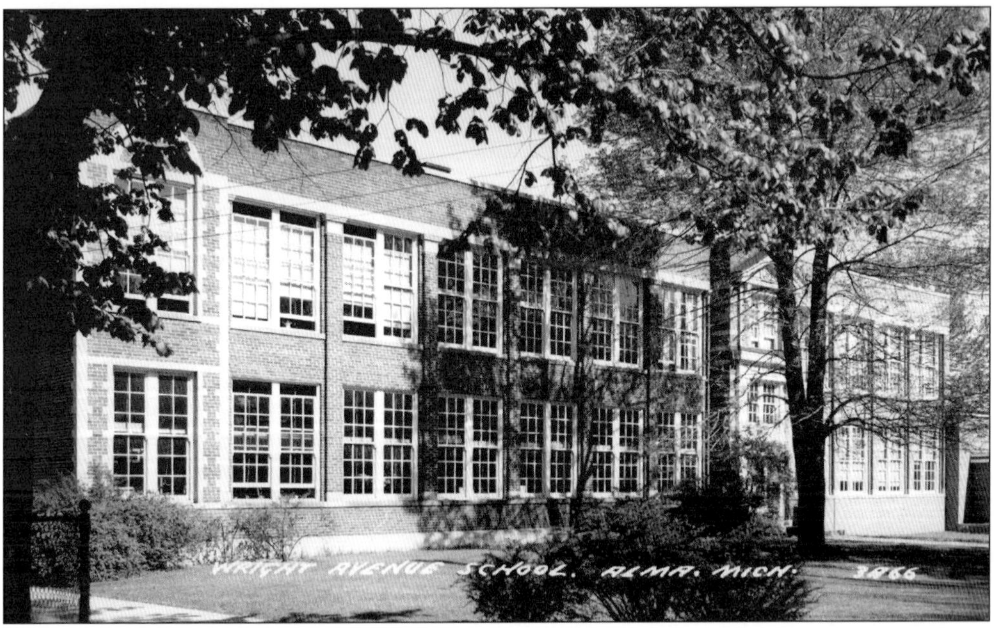


To ease crowding at the Republic School, a new elementary school was built on Wright Avenue next to Wright Park. The Wright Avenue School opened in February 1927. It served students west of State Street and north of the river. School boundaries throughout the city were changed to even out the elementary populations at the city's four elementary schools. (Courtesy of Richard Tesman.)

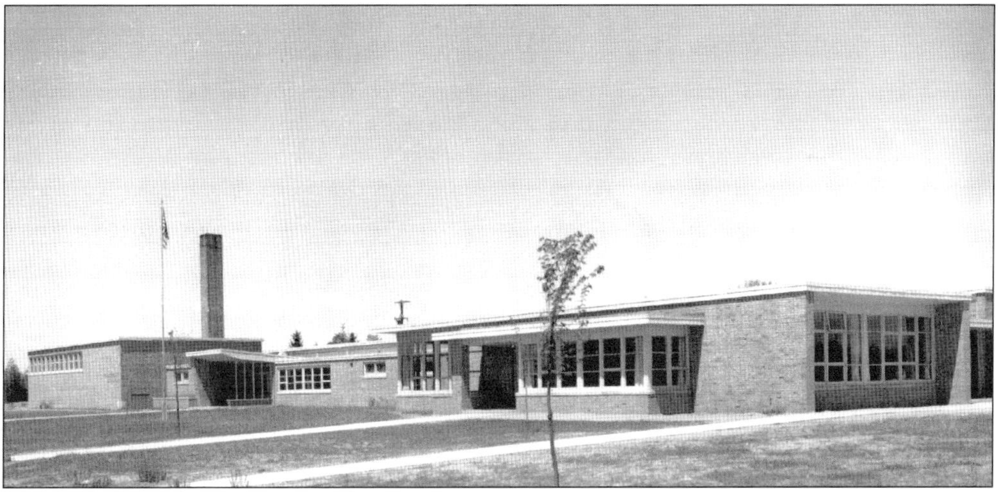

When it became evident that refurbishing the old Union School would be cost prohibitive, a new school was proposed for the south side of Alma where many children lived. Hillcrest Elementary School opened in September 1952. The new school replaced an old three-room frame building that housed three grades. The new school was built at a cost of $284,000. (Courtesy of the Alma Public Library.)

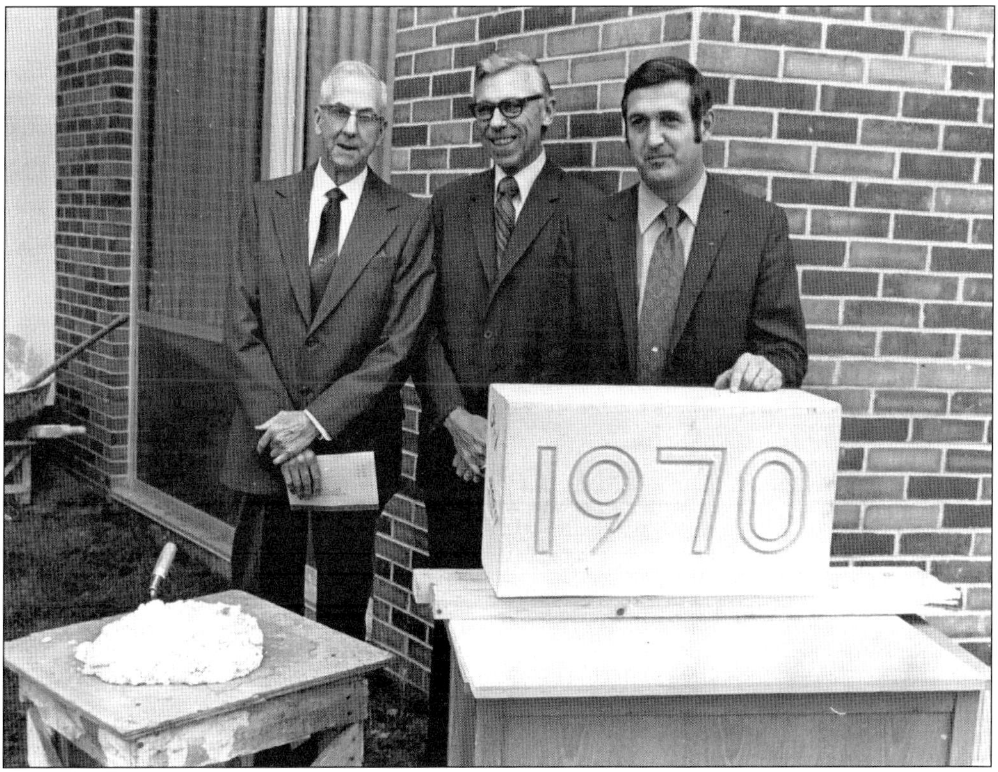


The cornerstone of the new Alma High School was laid on September 26, 1971, as part of the school's dedication ceremonies. Pictured here from left to right are Ward Schults, former principal; Leonard Kaslander, principal; and Don Miller, assistant principal. (Courtesy of Alma High School.)

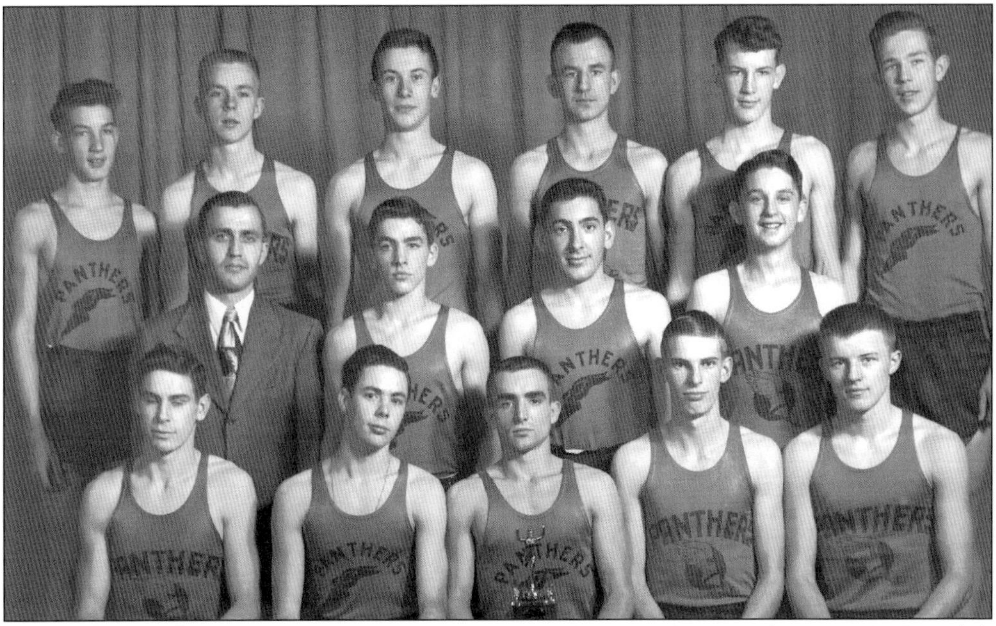


The 1951 Alma High School cross-country team took the state championship in 1951. From left to right, team members include (first row) Junior Mailand, John Goetz, Rocky Wolfgang (captain), Bill Pyle (state champion), and Sam King; (second row) Delmar Brenner (coach), Ron Wolfgang, Eldon Wiltshire, and Jack Schnepp; (third row) Bill McDaid, Bruce Siefker, Larry Houghton, Bruce Gardner, Ed McDaid, and Lawrence Holmes. (Courtesy of Alma High School.)

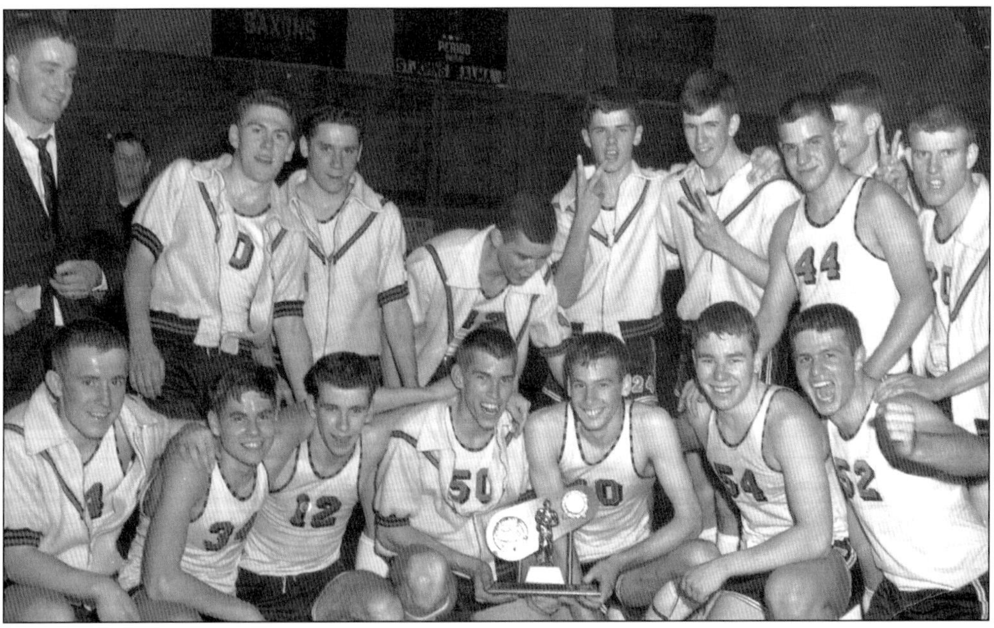

These exuberant Alma High School players beat St. Johns to take the district championship during the 1961–1962 season. From left to right, they include (first row) John Barkman, Doug Yarnell, Jim Gittleman, Jack Young, Harold Robeson, Dave Hoogerland, and Jim Johnston; (second row) Dave Peters (coach), Gordon Peterson, Pat Fleming, Tom Porter, Ron Christensen, Warren Veeder, Rich Skinner, John Morgan, and Dick Anderson. (Courtesy of Alma High School.)

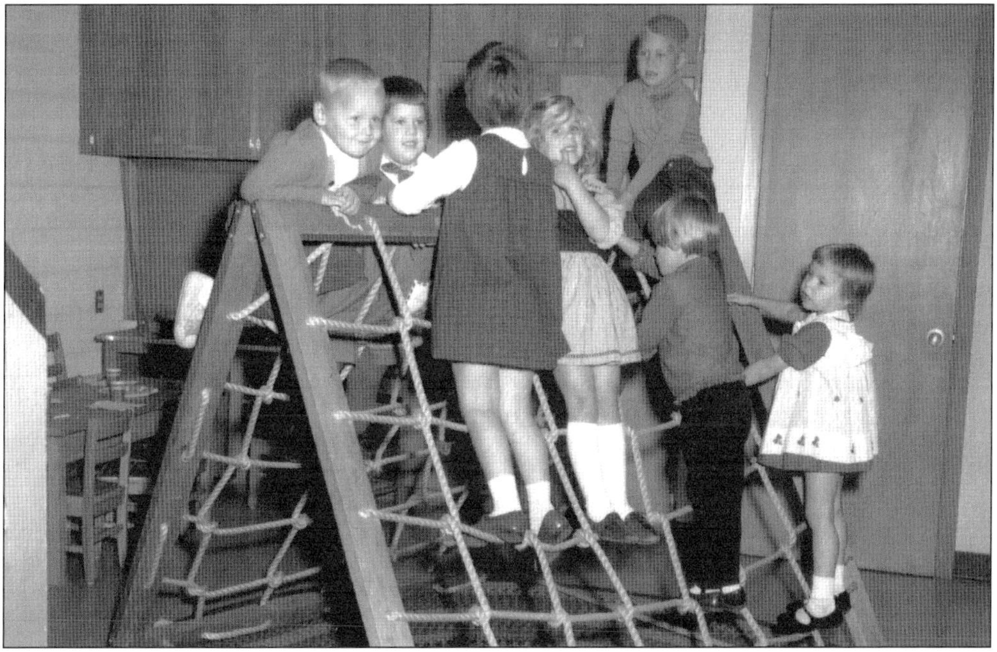

Children enjoy the Land of Oz Nursery School at the Presbyterian church on October 6, 1965. This picture, taken on one of the get-acquainted days, shows one-third of the four-year-old section of the nursery school. On the left is Bill Stolz. On the right is Demoree Hicks. JoAnn Hayward was the teacher. (Courtesy of Charles and Diantha Hicks.)

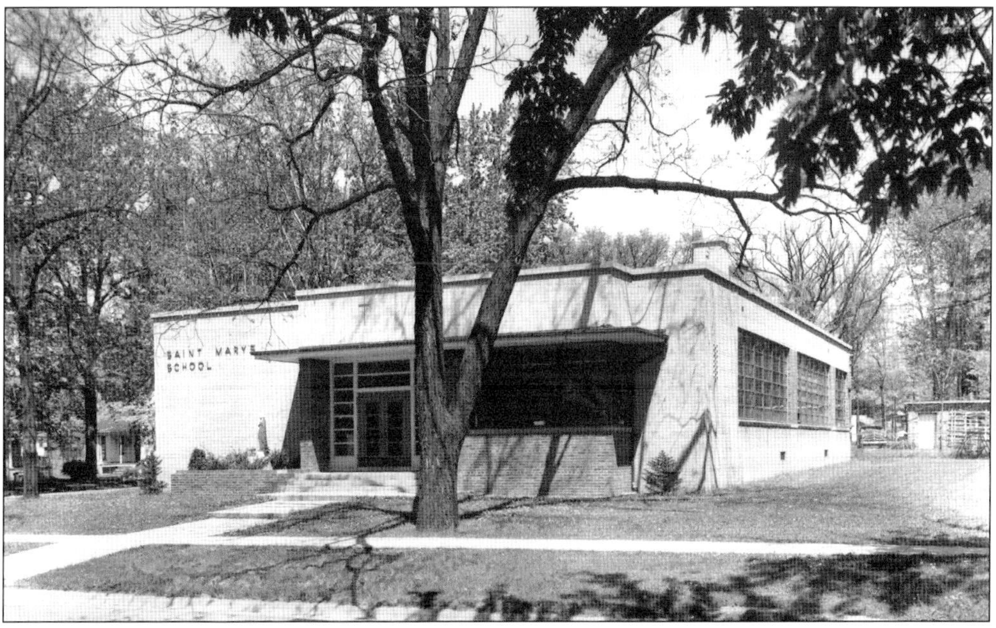


Accommodating grades one through six, St. Mary's Catholic School opened in September 1950. Four nuns from St. Dominic were the teachers. They lived in the Tom Smith house, which was moved to another part of the parish property and remodeled. "We feel we have a school of which we can be justly proud and one which fulfills a need in this community," said Rev. S. A. Van Gessel, the pastor. (Courtesy of Richard Tesman.)

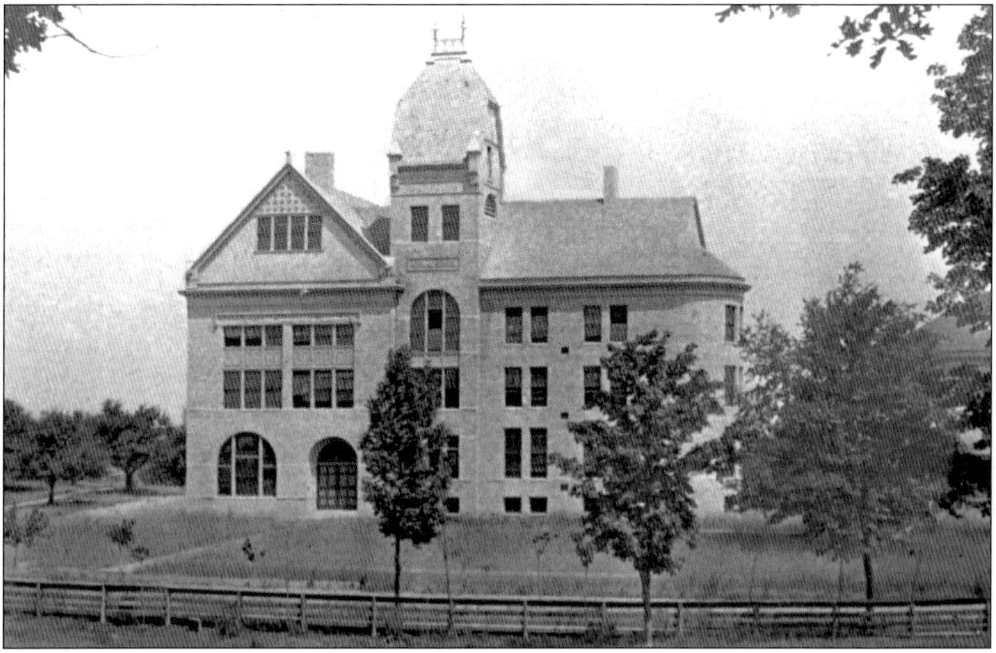

Old Main was the first building of the Central Michigan Normal School, established in 1886. The school was in business only a year before Ammi W. Wright, donor of the building, gave it to the Presbyterians to start Alma College. Old Main and Pioneer Hall, a dormitory, were the first two buildings of the new college. (Courtesy of the Alma College Library.)

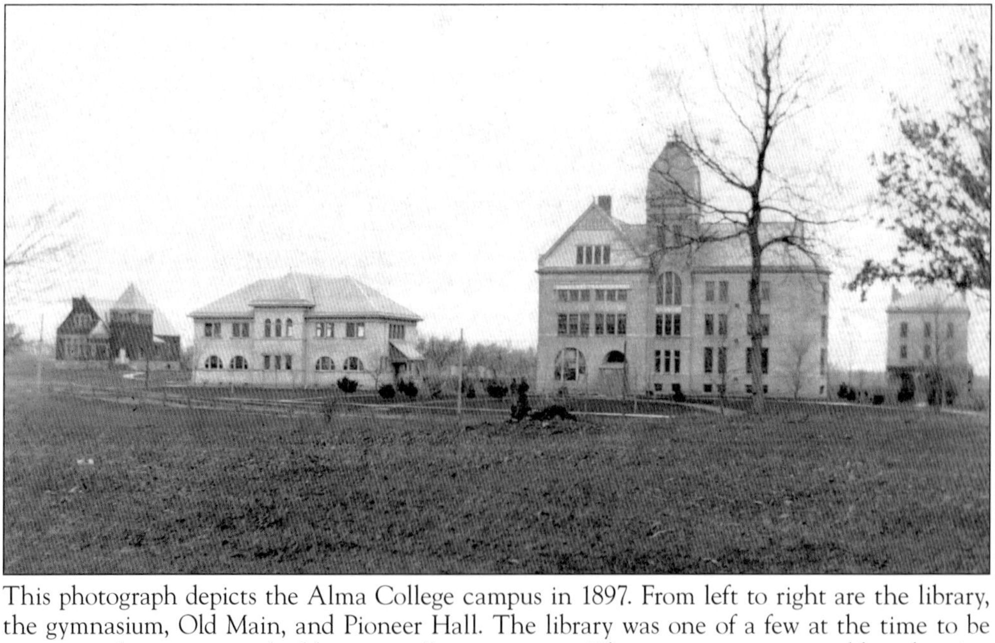

This photograph depicts the Alma College campus in 1897. From left to right are the library, the gymnasium, Old Main, and Pioneer Hall. The library was one of a few at the time to be constructed as a separate building on college campuses. The campus was warmed by a heating plant, reducing the possibility of explosions from housing boilers in individual buildings. (Courtesy of the Alma College Library.)

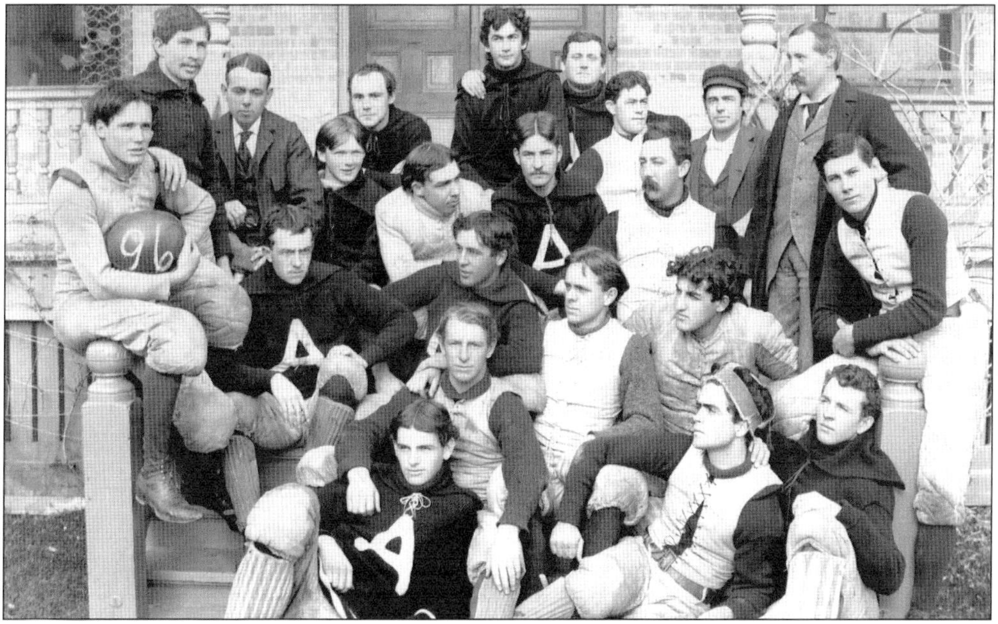


The Alma College football team of 1896 reflects a studied dignity that belies the vigor and excitement these young men showed on the playing field. W. Frank Knox, in the second row, has thrown his arm over Milton Holmes's shoulder. Knox later became a United States vice presidential candidate and secretary of the navy. Holmes, an Alma boy, became a wealthy executive in Alma's Republic Truck Company. (Courtesy of the Alma College Library.)

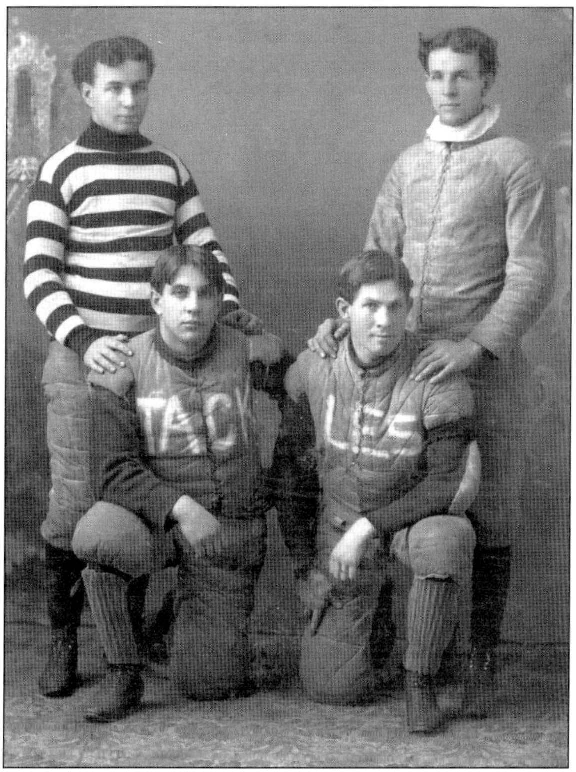


Ends Elton Brock (left) and Amos Eastman and tackles Reuben Brown (left) and Robbie McKee posed for the camera in 1899. In a 1901 game against the Detroit Athletic Club, McKee took a severe blow to the abdomen. Very ill, he came home with the team and was taken to Brainerd's Hospital where three days later he died of the injury. At the time of his death, the Canadian student was 28 and planning to become a missionary. (Courtesy of the Alma College Library.)

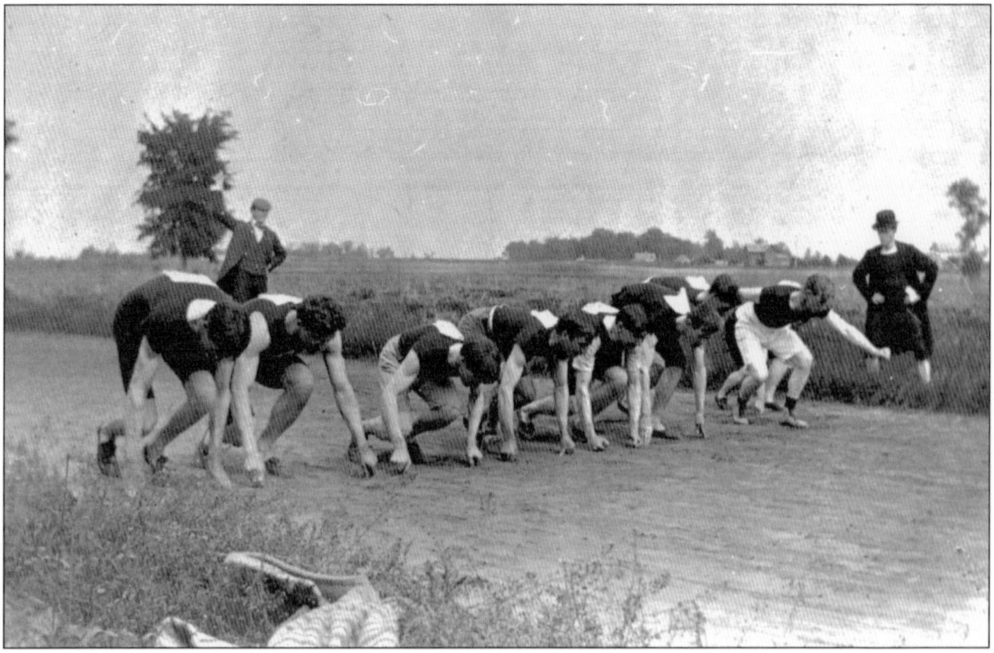

The college track team surprised everyone, including themselves, by winning every event at the Saginaw Valley Field Day sponsored by the Saginaw YMCA on June 6, 1896. The men numbered the least of any college team but brought the college more renown than any other sport. Arriving home, the athletes were greeted by a throng of excited citizens and students at the depot, who lifted them bodily into a carriage for a triumphal trip to the campus. (Courtesy of the Alma College Library.)

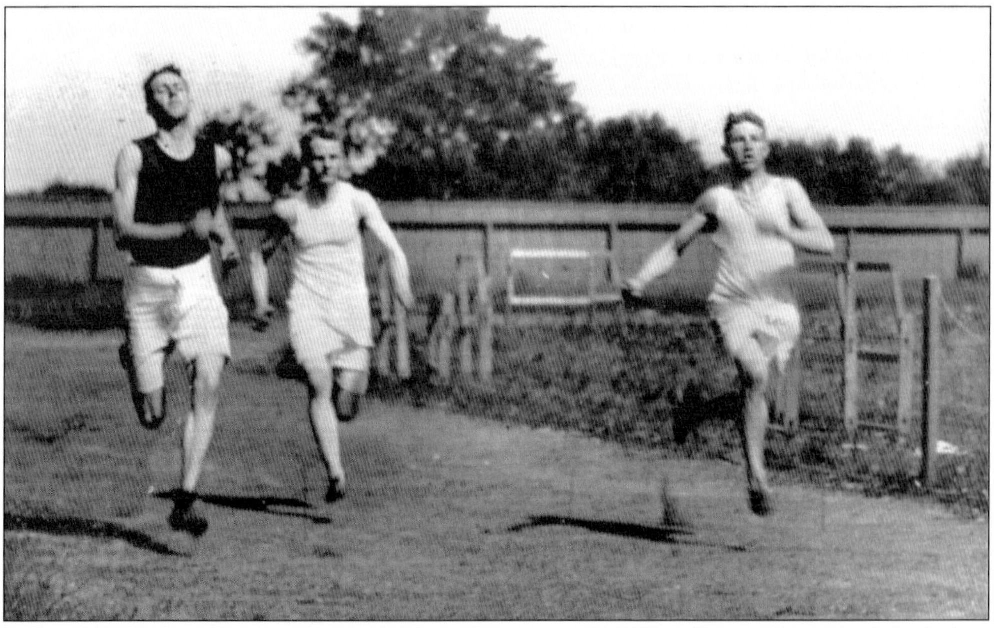

In the 1908 Michigan Intercollegiate Athletic Association Field Day, Byron Chapel (right) of Alma took an early lead in the 100-yard dash, but teammate Frank "Fleety" McComb (center) finished first, and Watkins of Hillsdale College was third. (Courtesy of the Alma College Library.)

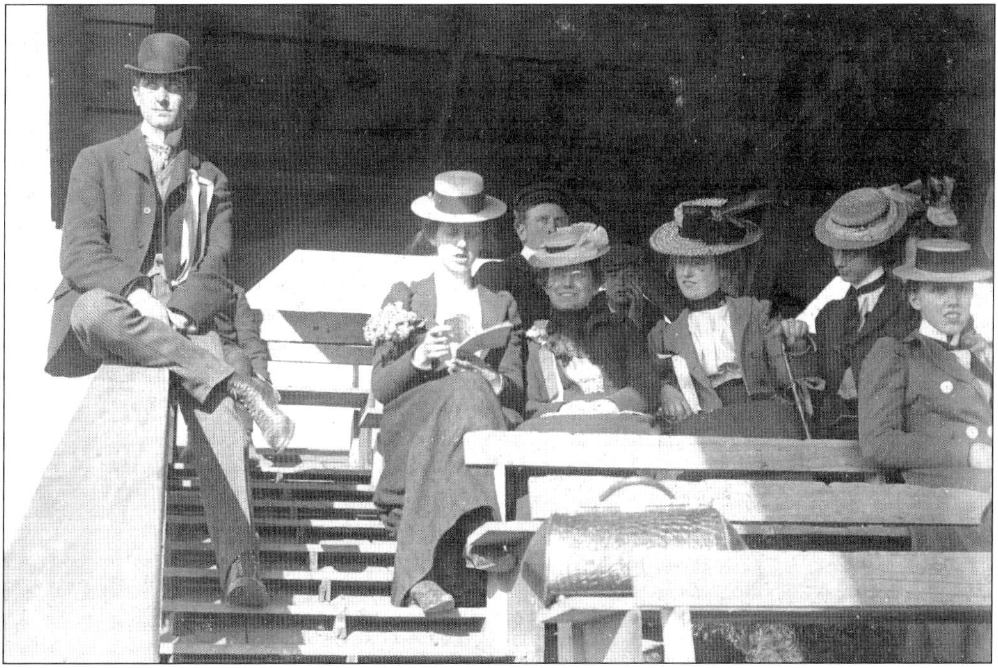

The Davis Field grandstand held crowds for athletic contests and other activities. Here a nattily attired group of students enjoys the view from the grandstand. The field was named for Charles Davis, a generous donor to Alma College in its early days. (Courtesy of the Alma College Library.)

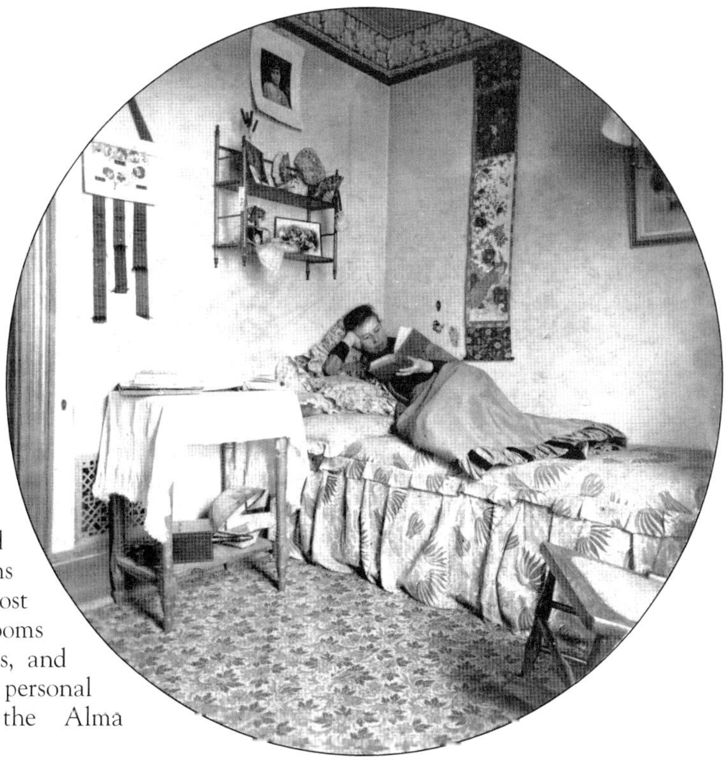

Mary Hill studies in her room in 1897. The rooms sometimes held two students. Bathrooms were down the hall. Most students decorated their rooms with pennants, calendars, and pictures, giving them a personal touch. (Courtesy of the Alma College Library.)

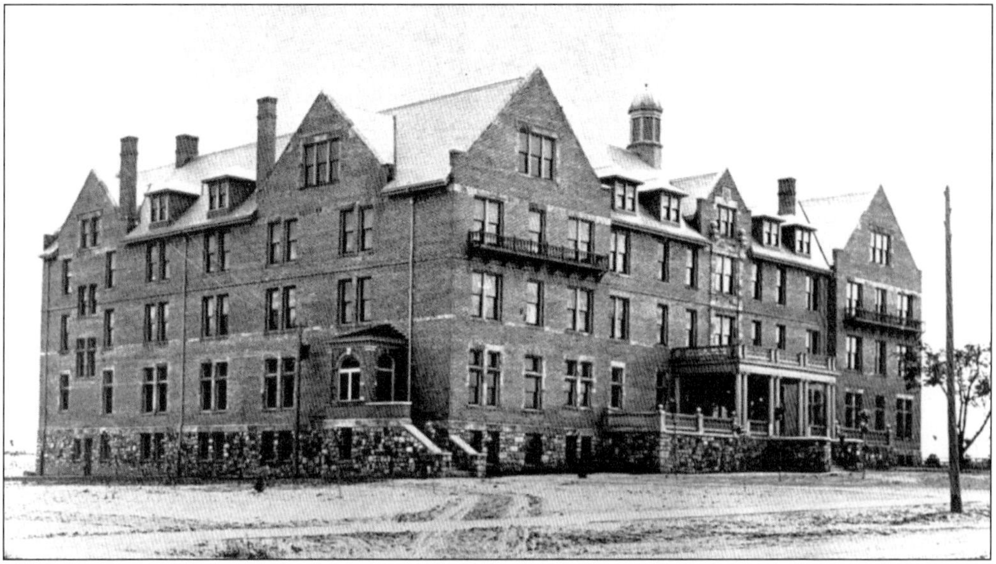

Wright Hall was the gift of the benevolent Ammi W. Wright, who made Alma College possible. One morning in 1901, Wright called on college president August Bruske and said he would fund construction of a girls' dormitory. Upon completion the next year, it proved to be the finest college dormitory in the state. It was built by Alma's master builder George S. Young. (Courtesy of the Alma College Library.)

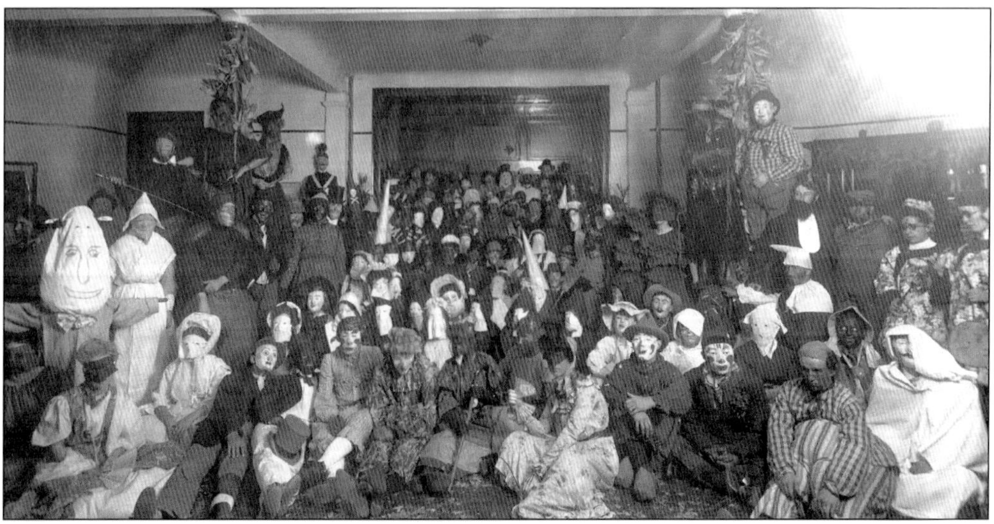

Everyone appeared in costume for the Wright Hall Halloween party in 1906. The maskers included witches, scarecrows, policemen, clowns, cowboys, ghosts, and a number of students in blackface. (Courtesy of the Alma College Library.)

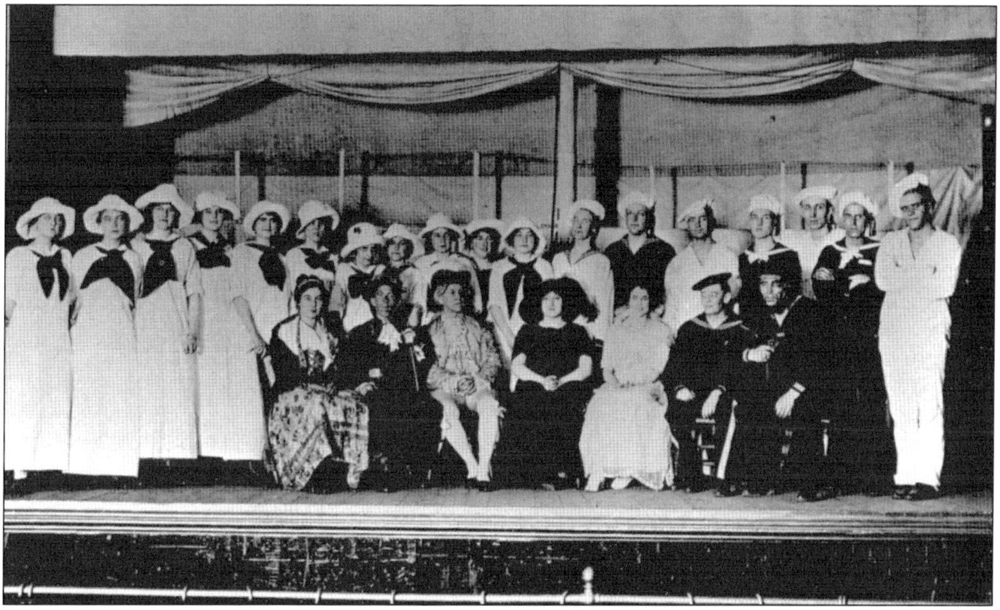

The college drama club performed *HMS Pinafore* on March 14, 1913, in the Realty Opera House downtown. The local paper said, "The production was given with such a degree of finish that the public is anxious for more of the same." John Anderson, assistant vocal instructor, received accolades as producer. (Courtesy of the Alma College Library.)

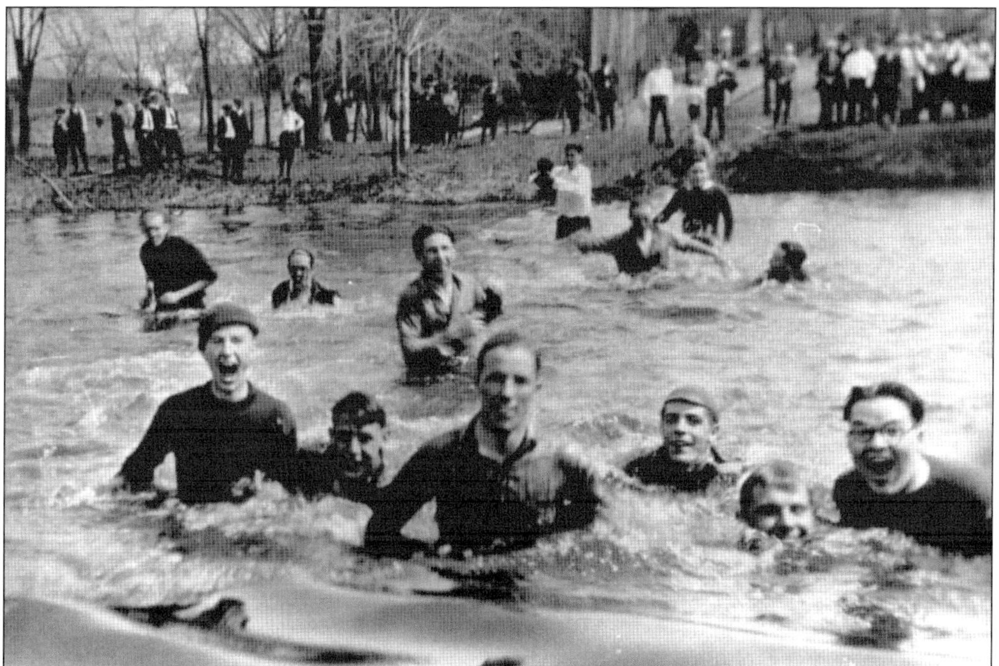

The highlight of the annual College Day was the tug-of-war across the Pine River. The freshman and the sophomores fought it out in 1911, with these cold and exuberant losers clearly trying to make the best of their situation. The tug-of-war in later years became hazardous because of debris in the river, and the event was abandoned. (Courtesy of the Alma College Library.)

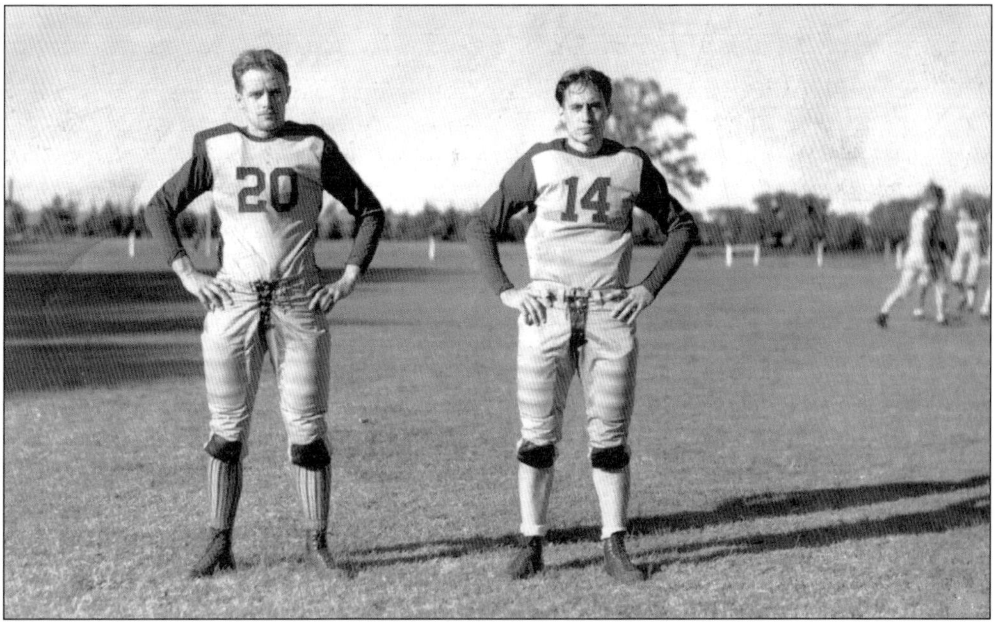

Many college students came from the city of Alma. Pictured here are Harold Dean (left) and Alfred Fortino in their football uniforms. Both remained in the Alma area, Dean as a longtime optometrist and Fortino as an attorney and businessman. (Courtesy of the Fortino family.)

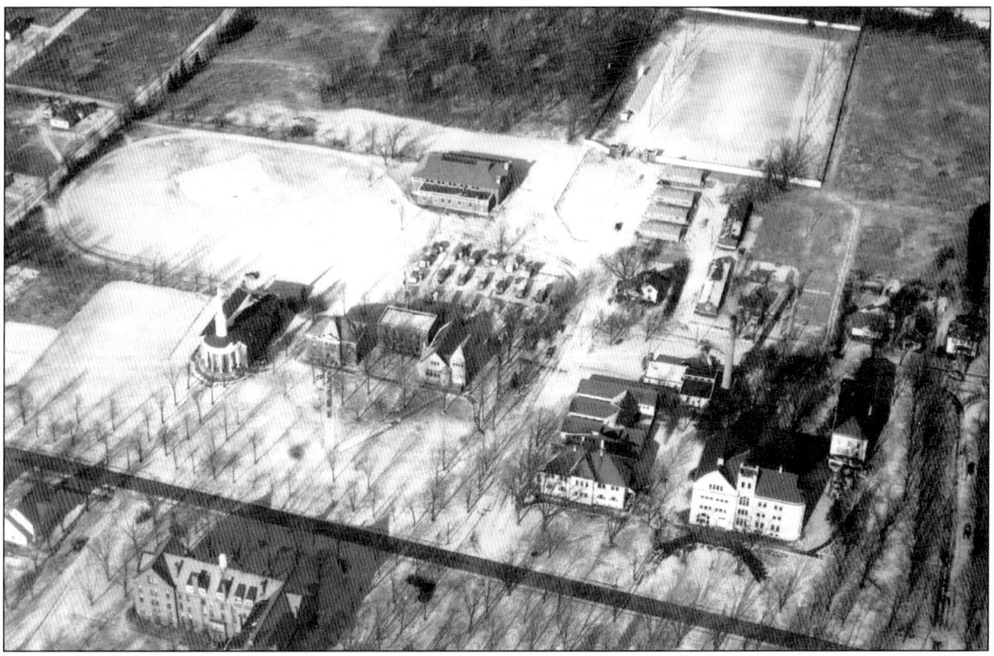

Wars always interrupted normal education at the college. After World War II, an influx of former servicemen taxed the college's facilities. In this aerial view, rows of prefabricated buildings and trailers show attempts to house the overflow. (Courtesy of Richard Tesman.)

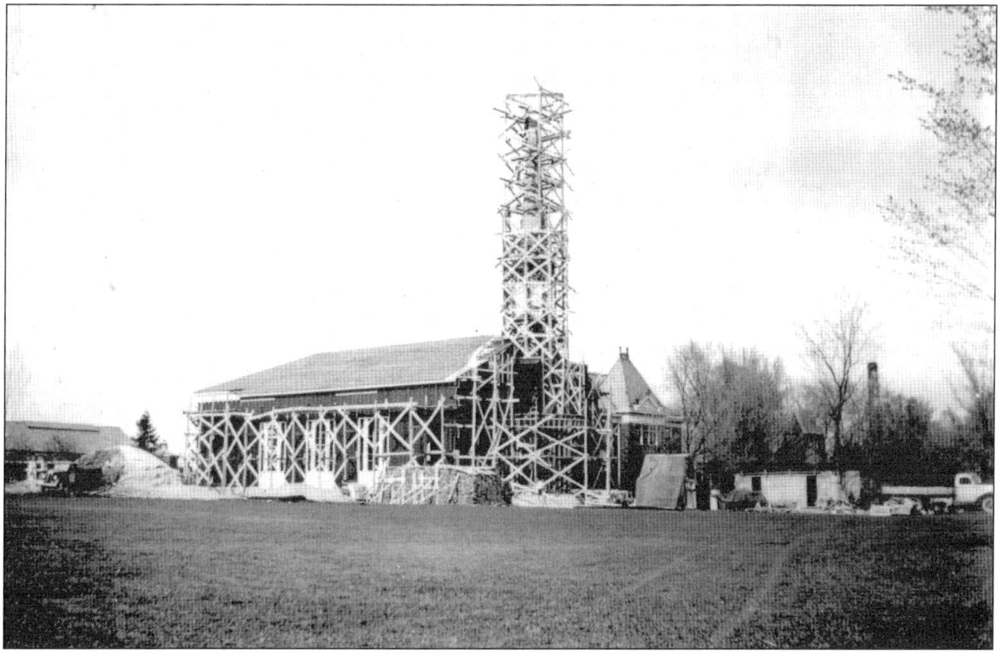

The college chapel, later named for Dr. John Dunning, former college president, was built in 1941. The chapel was funded by generous gifts from several individual donors and the Presbyterian Church. Clad in scaffolding, the steeple is about to receive its 12-foot bronze cross. (Courtesy of the Alma College Library.)

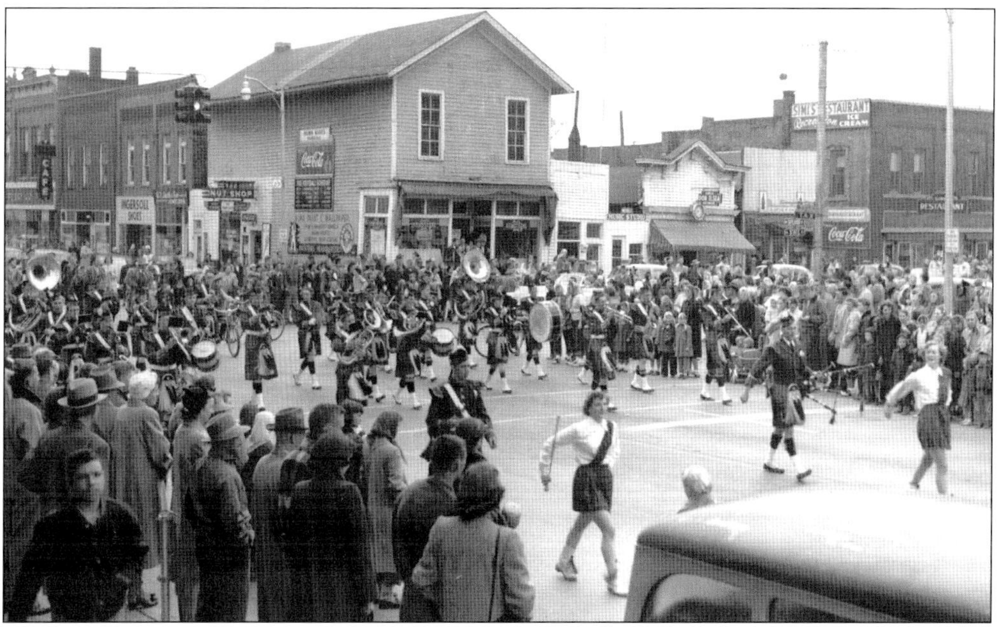


On October 11, 1951, Alma College celebrated its 60th homecoming. The celebration honored Dr. Roy Hamilton, former president of the college. The homecoming parade took a circuitous route through downtown Alma. Here the Kiltie Band moves up Superior Street during the parade. The Scots lost their football game against Hope College 21-13. (Courtesy of the Alma College Library.)

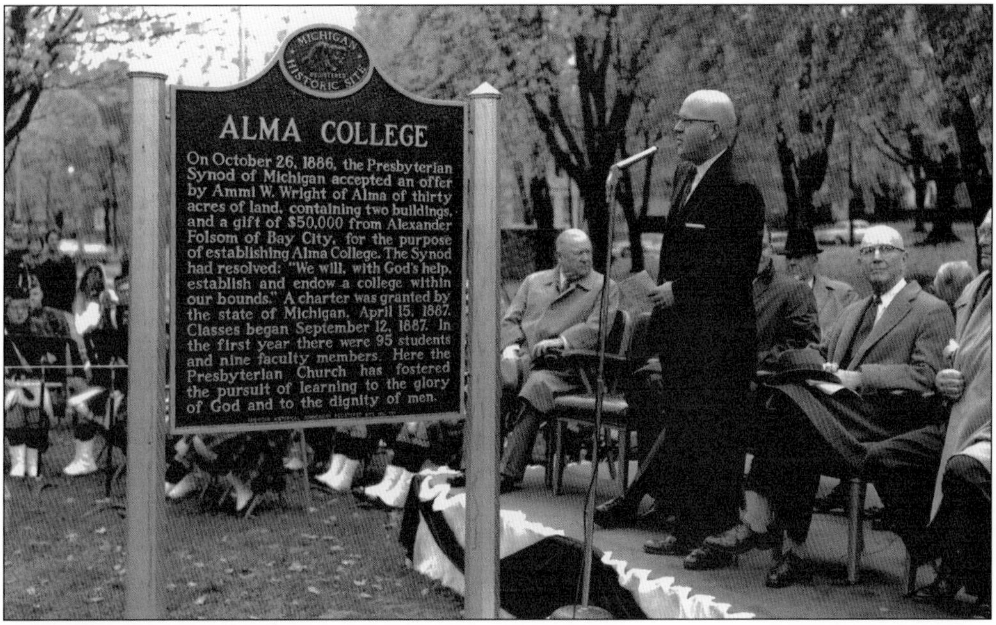


Pres. Robert Swanson speaks at the dedication of a state historical monument on the Alma College campus during Founder's Day in 1961. The plaque memorializes the decision of the state Presbyterian organization to found a college and the response of wealthy lumbermen Ammi W. Wright and Alexander Folsom to finance the new institution. (Courtesy of the Alma College Library.)

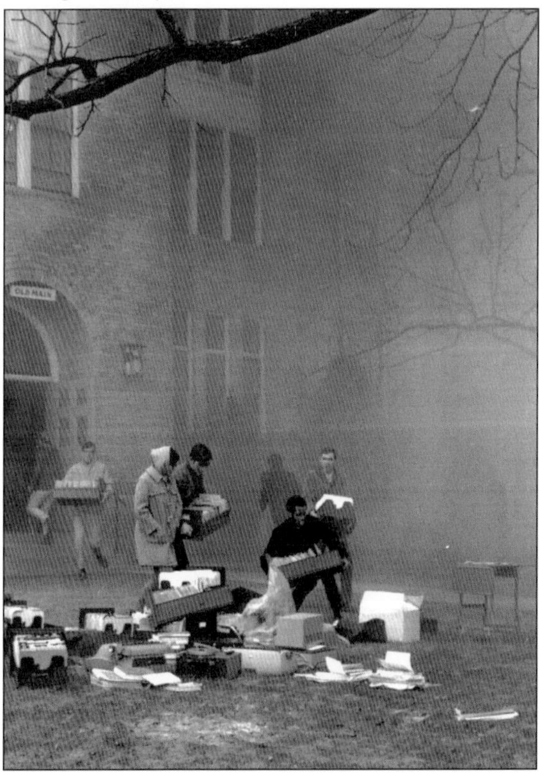


Students on the third floor of Old Main smelled smoke on the morning of March 10, 1969. Flames were already making headway when the building was evacuated. Heedless of the risk, students made repeated trips into the burning building to carry out records and equipment. Within an hour, this symbol of Alma College for more than 80 years was gone. (Courtesy of the Alma College Library.)

The Congregational Church held its first meetings in the village school. Later it built this church. When the congregation united with the Presbyterian congregation, this became the Presbyterian church. In 1899, it was sold to the Baptist congregation because the Presbyterians were planning to build a new church. (Courtesy of the Alma College Library.)

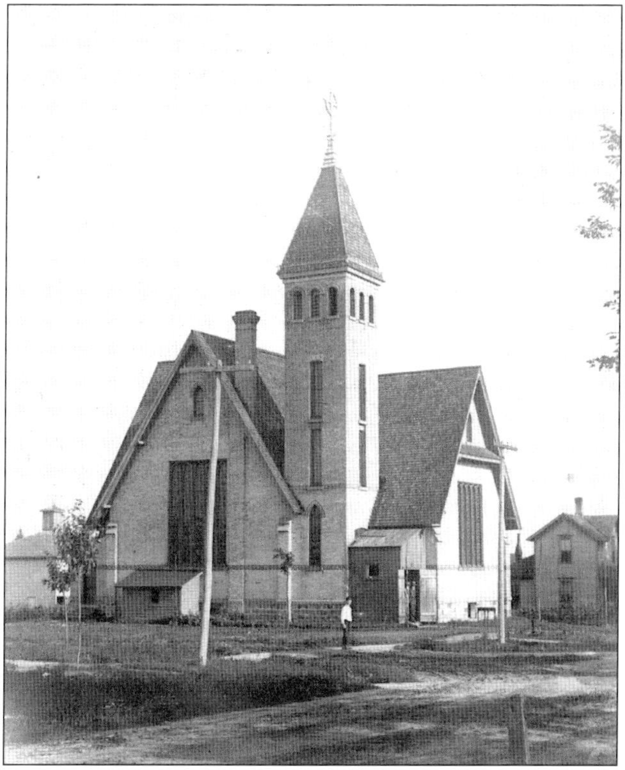

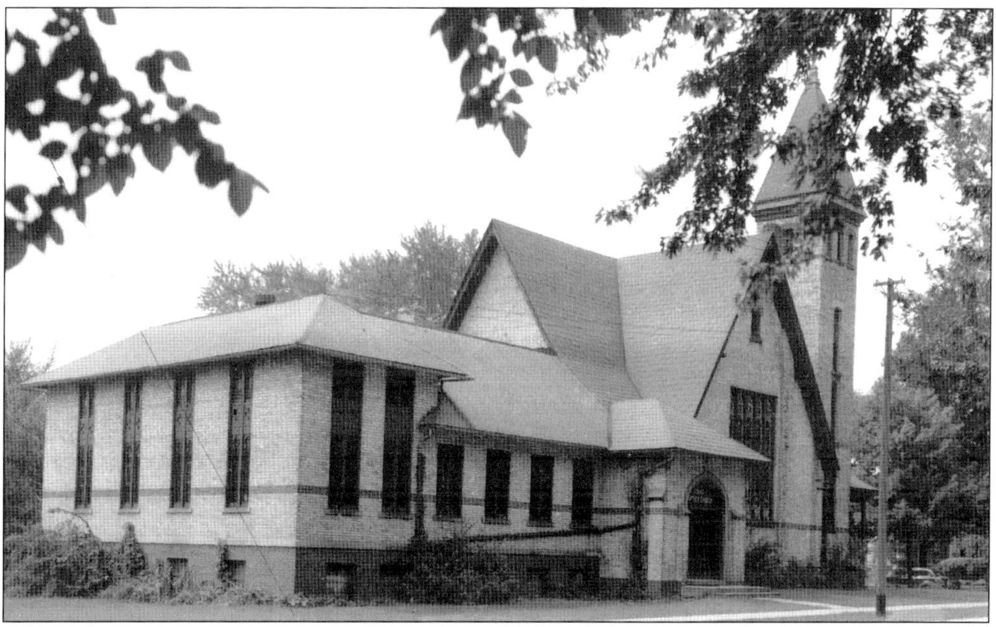

The earliest Baptist churches in Gratiot County were started by farmer and lay pastor Lafayette Church. The Alma congregation first held its meetings in the village school, and then built its first building on Hastings Street in 1873. In 1899, it bought the Presbyterian church building at State and Hastings Streets and in 1917 made a two-story addition for Sunday school rooms. (Courtesy of John Kemler.)

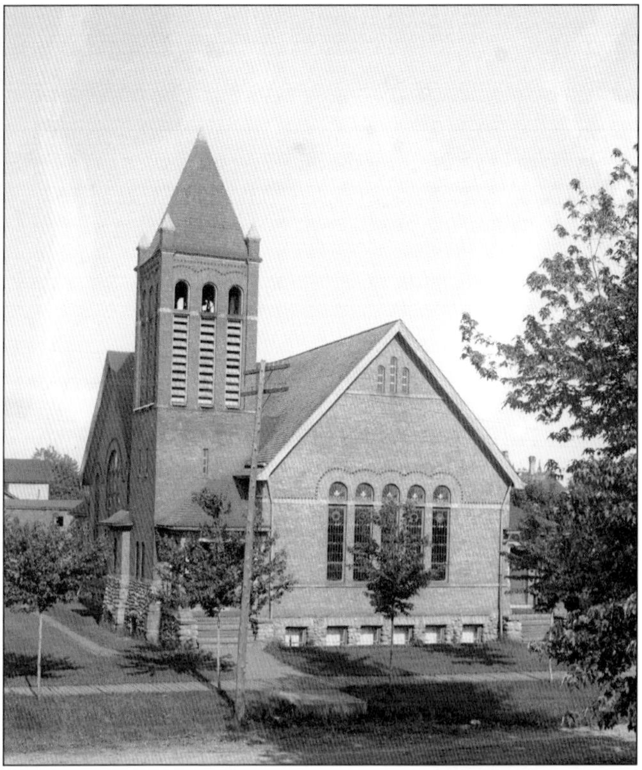

The Methodists began in Alma by holding meetings in the village school at different times from the Baptists. In 1873, they built their church building at the southeast corner of Superior and Prospect Streets. Outgrowing this small church, they built a brick church behind it on Prospect Street. Pictured here is the second church, which burned in 1935. (Courtesy of Dale Kemler.)

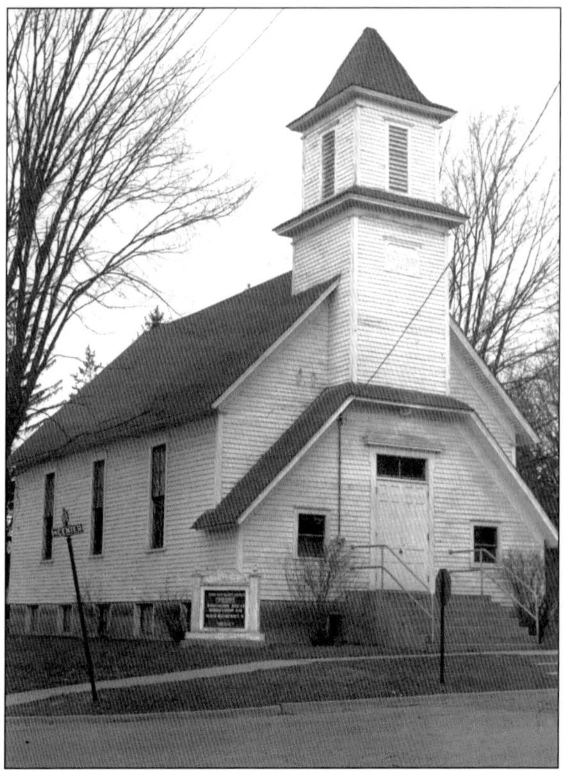

The Free Methodist Church was located at Center and Cedar Streets. It was built in 1896 and served the congregation for many years. Later it was purchased by Alma College and housed the college art department. (Courtesy of the Alma Public Library.)

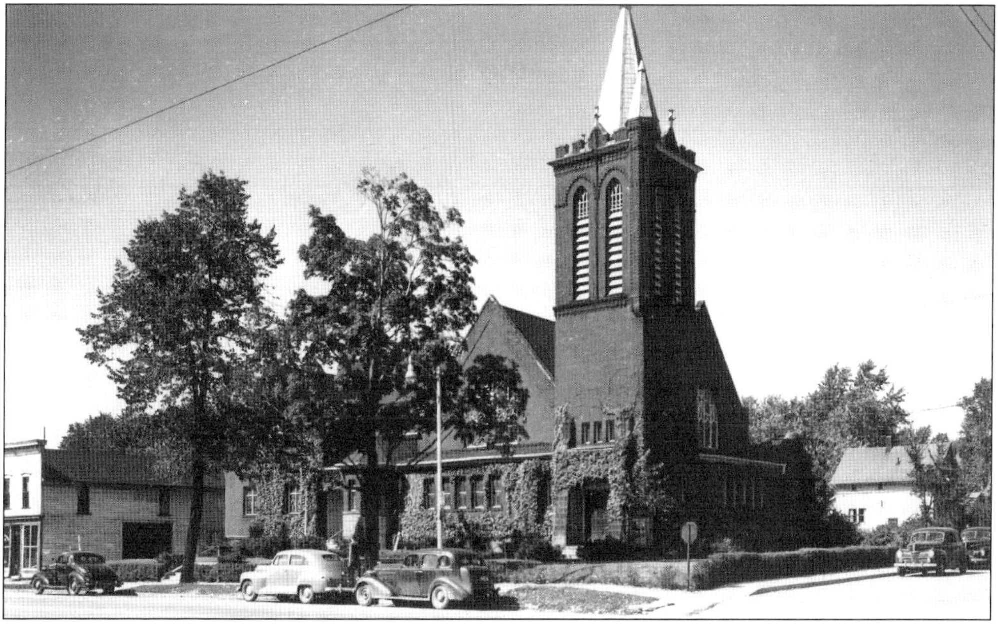

The Presbyterian congregation in Alma developed as a result of the founding of Alma College, a Presbyterian institution. Many teachers at the college were Presbyterians, and a congregation was formed. It united with the Congregationalists and used their church on State Street. In 1900, the Presbyterians built this church on Superior Street. It was called the College Church as many students and staff attended. (Courtesy of Richard Tesman.)

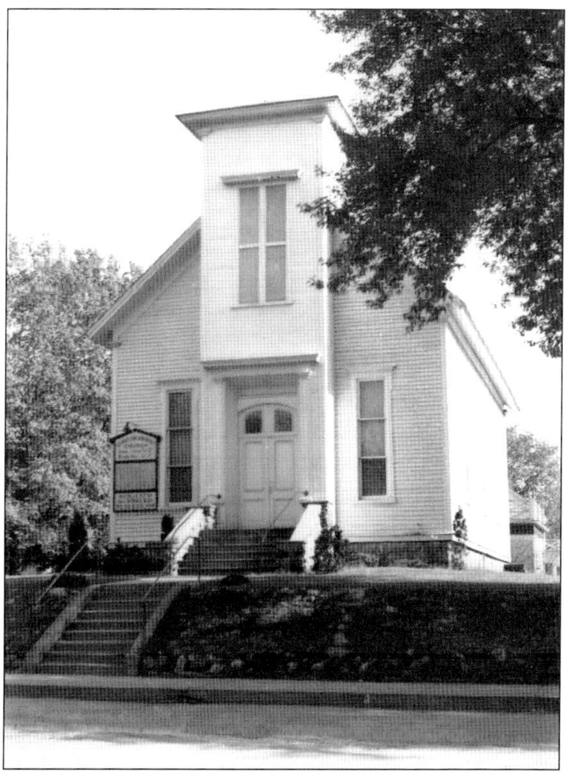

The Seventh-Day Adventists were organized in Alma during pioneer days. James Gargett, who named Alma, was a prime mover in the building of this church at the corner of Hastings and Gratiot Streets in 1880. This building served the congregation until a new facility was built in Pine River Township. Alma Public Schools owned the building for a few years. It has since been razed. (Courtesy of Richard Tesman.)

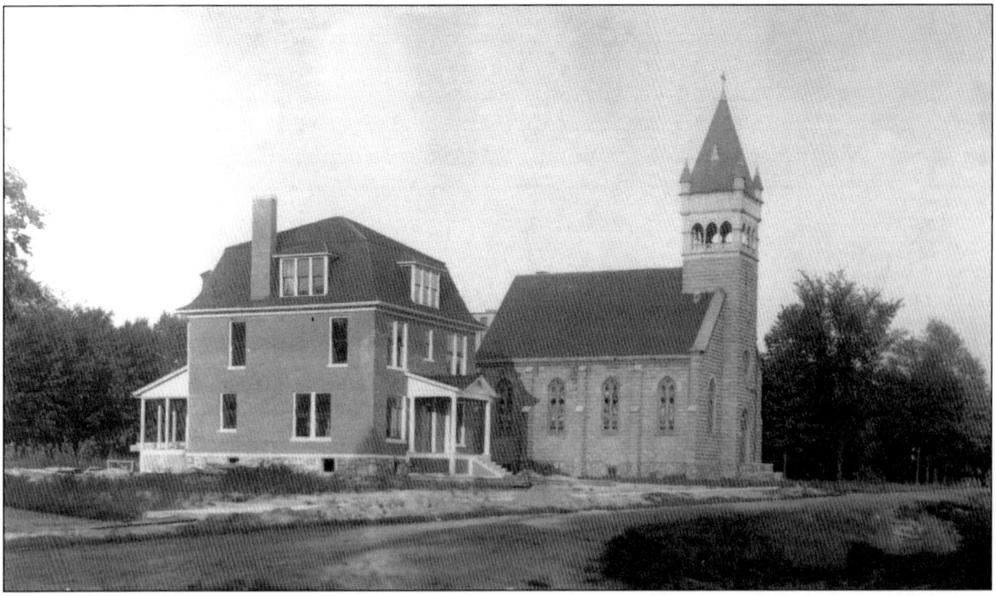

The cornerstone for St. Mary's Catholic Church was laid in impressive ceremonies on June 27, 1905. The Very Reverend Joseph Schrems, representing the diocese, delivered a sermon on the meaning and mission of this new church. Fr. John Troy, the priest of St. Mary's, expressed appreciation for the cordial treatment he received from Alma people. The rectory was built in 1908, the year of this photograph. (Courtesy of Lucille Behler.)

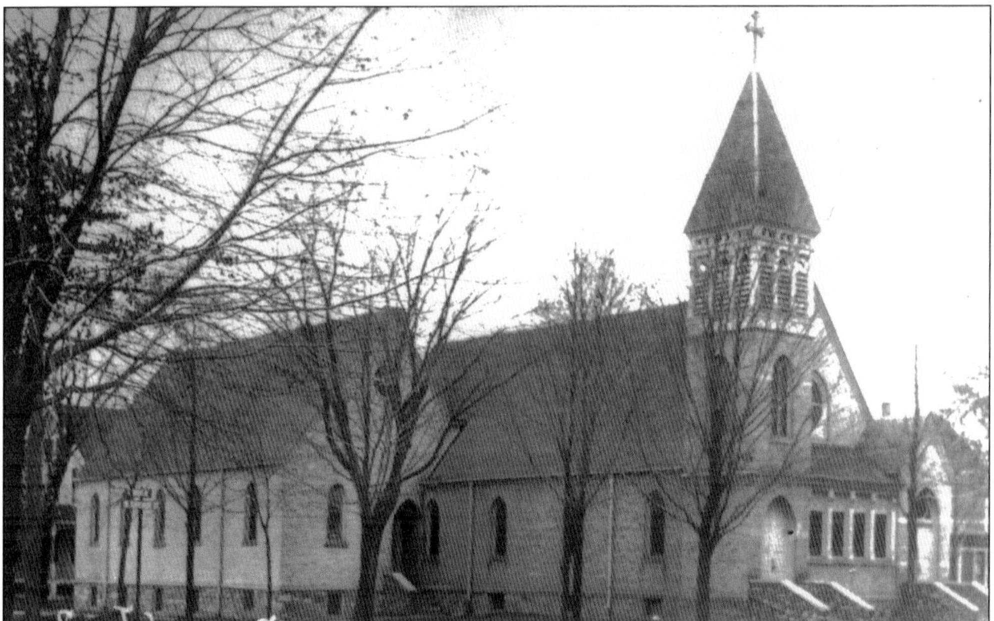


St. John's Episcopal Church was built in 1887 at a cost of $4,000. Located at Wright Avenue and Superior Street, it was brick veneered and seated 350 people. The parish house, built later, was the gift of Ammi W. Wright, whose second wife, Anna Case Wright, was a devout Anglican. The church was demolished in 1966 after construction of its successor on Luce Road. (Courtesy of Lucille Behler.)

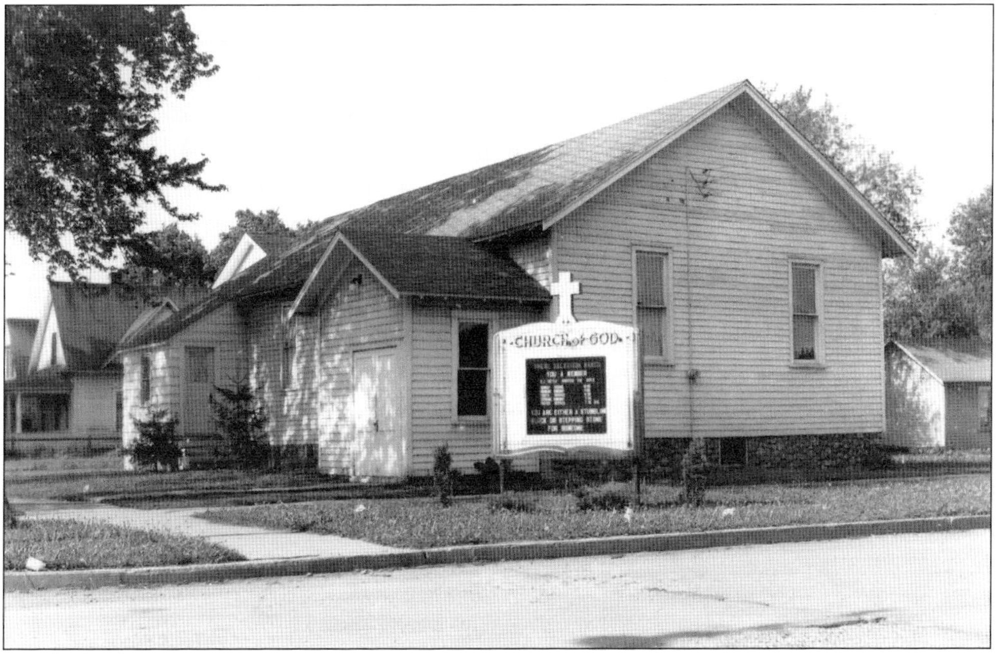


The Church of God congregation first met in a house in the 1930s. Additions to the building resulted in this church at the corner of Center and Prospect Streets. Rapid growth in the 1950s spurred the church to purchase the Presbyterian church on Superior Street, which became available. On October 6, 1957, the congregation marched from their old church to their new one a block north to hold their first service in the new facility. (Courtesy of Richard Tesman.)

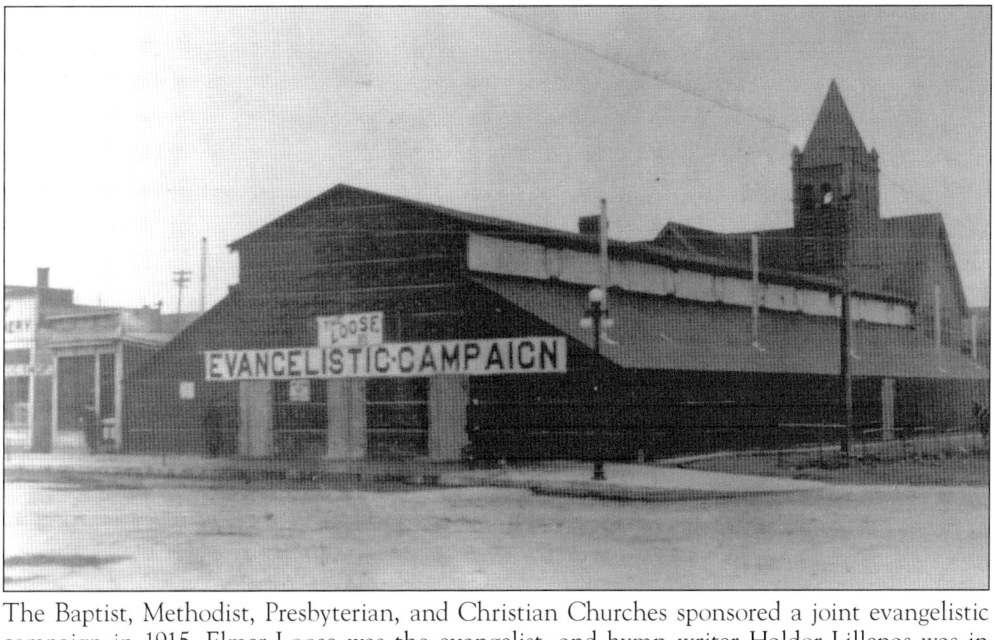


The Baptist, Methodist, Presbyterian, and Christian Churches sponsored a joint evangelistic campaign in 1915. Elmer Loose was the evangelist, and hymn writer Haldor Lillenas was in charge of music. This tabernacle, built in 24 hours at the corner of Superior and Prospect Streets, housed the throngs who attended the meetings. Many new members were added to the churches as a result of the preaching of Loose. (Courtesy of Lucille Behler.)

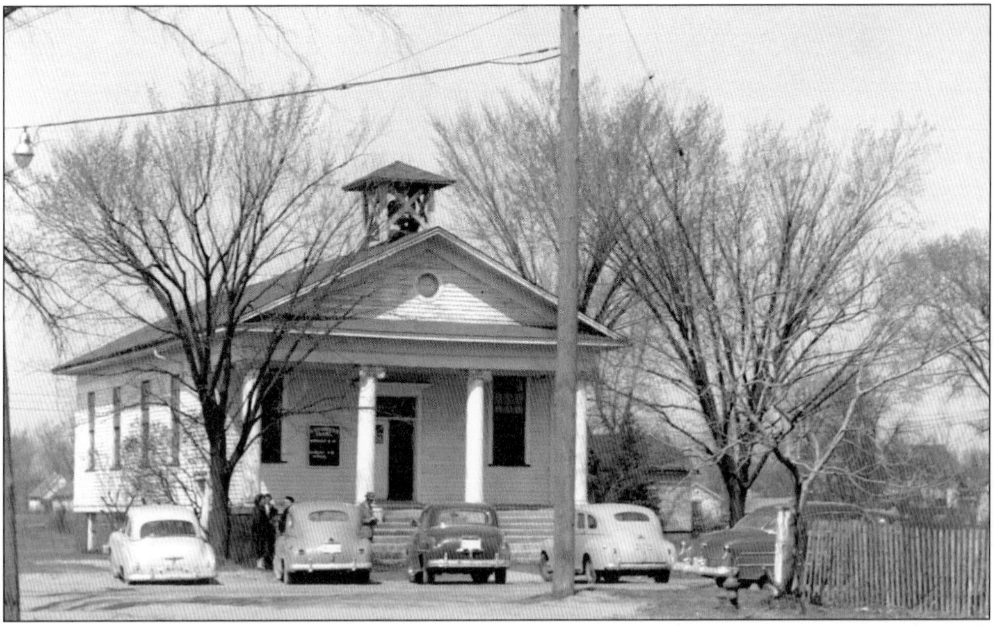

Residents on Alma's east side lacked churches in their community, and the Presbyterian Church organized a Sunday school there in 1914. The school met in a house, the first of six houses it was to occupy before the Eastminster Presbyterian Church was built. Located at the corner of Marquette Street and Republic Avenue, it was dedicated in May 1917. (Photograph by Hubert Elias, courtesy of Dale Kemler.)

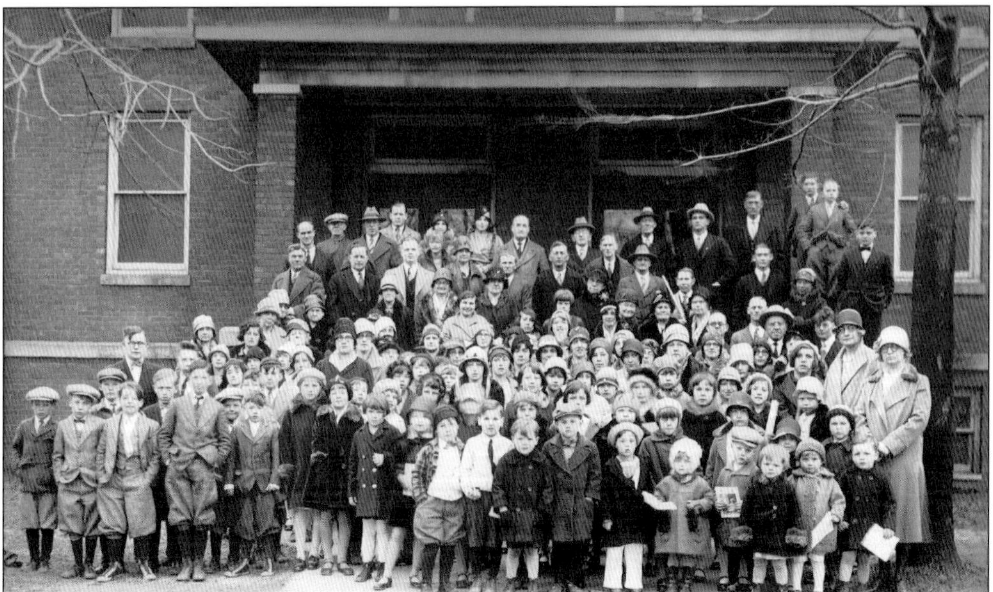

The Christian Church met first in the original Methodist church at Superior and Prospect Streets. In 1912, the congregation bought two vacant lots on Pine Avenue and moved the building to that location. Successful revivals added so many congregants to the church that in 1919 the new Christian church was built on East Superior Street. Here the congregation is pictured in the 1930s. (Courtesy of Charles and Diantha Hicks.)

# *Six*

# The Quest for Health

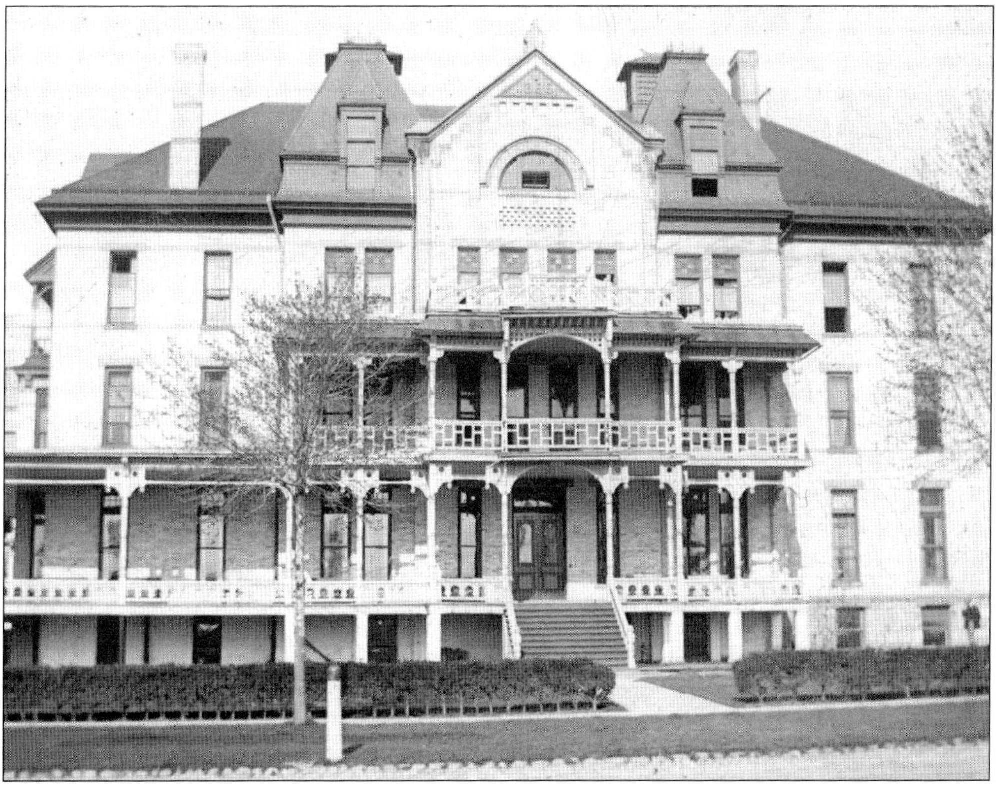

In 1886, entrepreneur Ammi W. Wright opened the Alma Springs Sanitarium on State Street. He had lived in Saratoga Springs, New York, and was familiar with the popularity of spas. A mineral well in the basement of the sanitarium provided water for baths touted to cure a host of diseases. The ill from across the Midwest came to Alma for treatments, including the Studebakers from South Bend, Indiana, and the Dows from Midland, Michigan. (Courtesy of the Alma Public Library.)

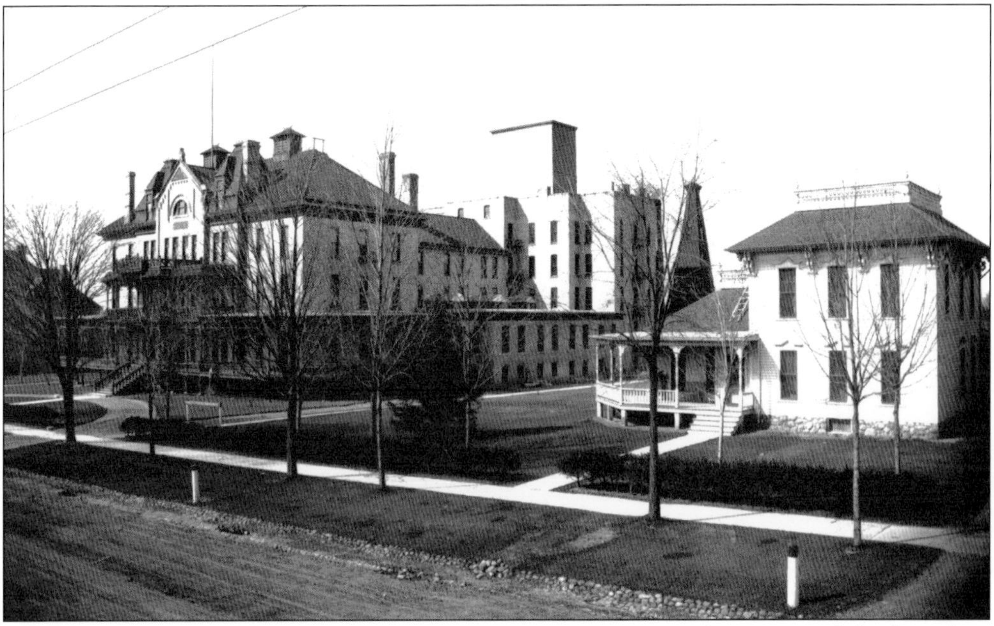

The sanitarium provided medical treatments, pleasant accommodations, good food, and an elegant setting. Its popularity required several additions. The derrick of the second well stands near the rear. This well provided warm water, and the institution became the Alma Hot Springs Sanitarium. The home of the superintendent stands at the right and is presently the Lux Funeral Home. (Author's collection.)

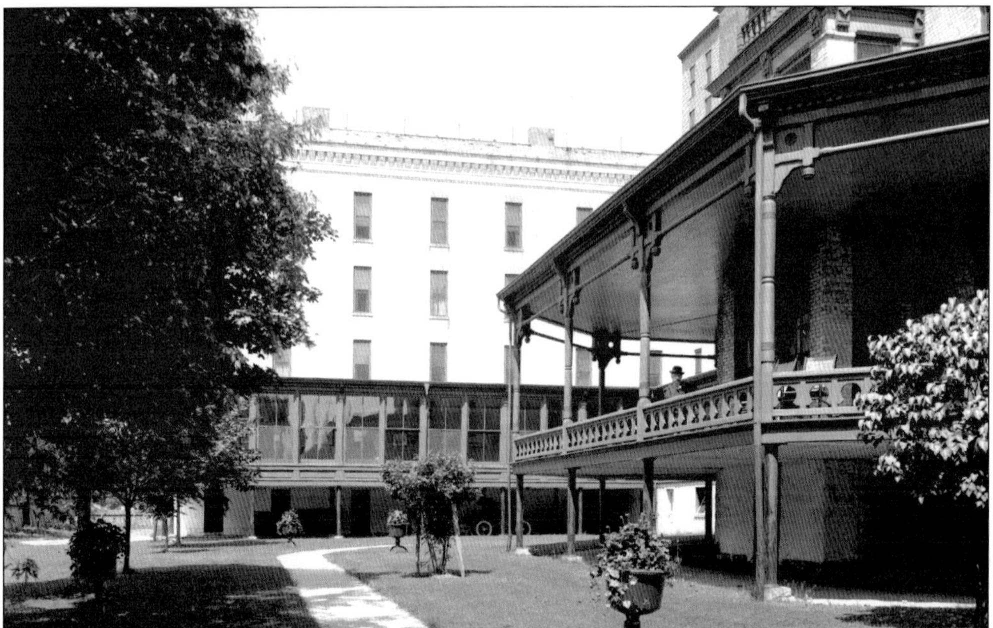

The porches in good weather and the sunroom in bad weather provided popular spots to relax and socialize. Many people of means came to the sanitarium, and they expected and received first-class treatment. By 1900, mineral baths were fading in popularity, and within a few years, this building was closed. (Author's collection.)

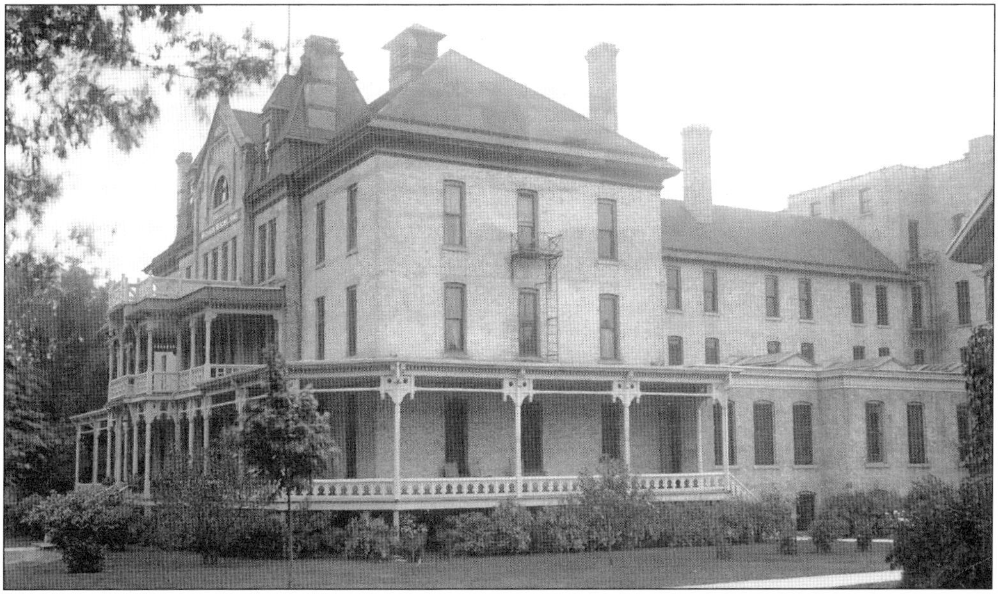

When the Masonic lodge's home for the elderly in Grand Rapids burned in 1910, the lodge began seeking a new facility. The Alma Hot Springs Sanitarium had been closed for several years and was offered to them for sale. They felt Alma was too far from the center of population in the state, and they delayed a decision on the building. Finally, Ammi W. Wright, owner of the building, donated it to the lodge, and it was dedicated as the new Masonic home for the elderly in 1912. (Courtesy of Richard Tesman.)

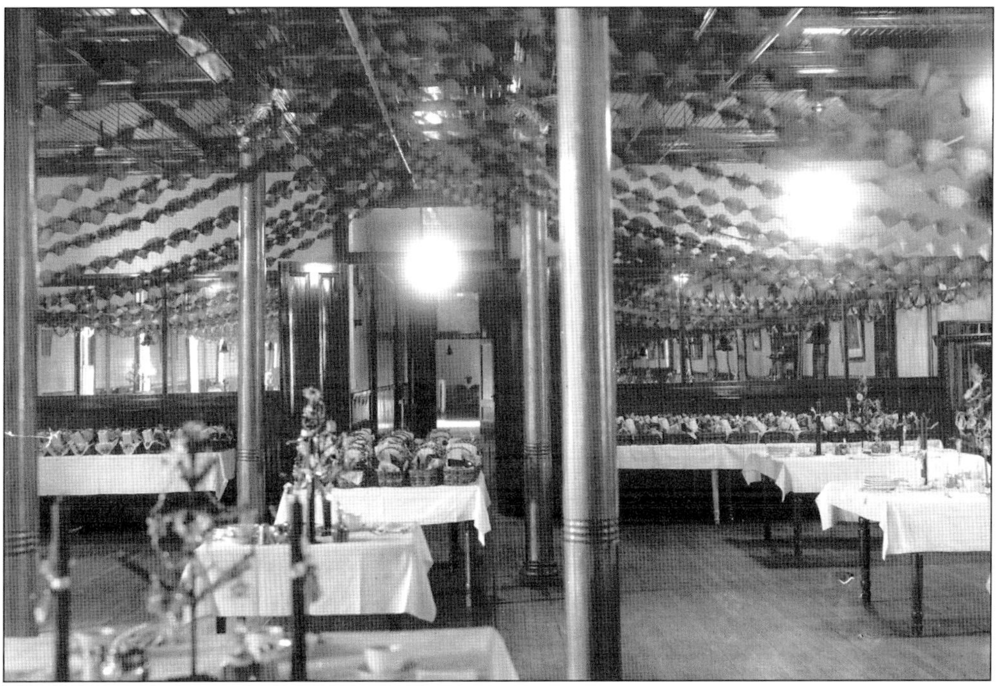

The sanitarium building was elegantly and carefully constructed. The public rooms were spacious and pleasant, including the dining room. Here in the Masonic era, holiday baskets have been prepared for the residents. (Courtesy of Masonic Pathways.)

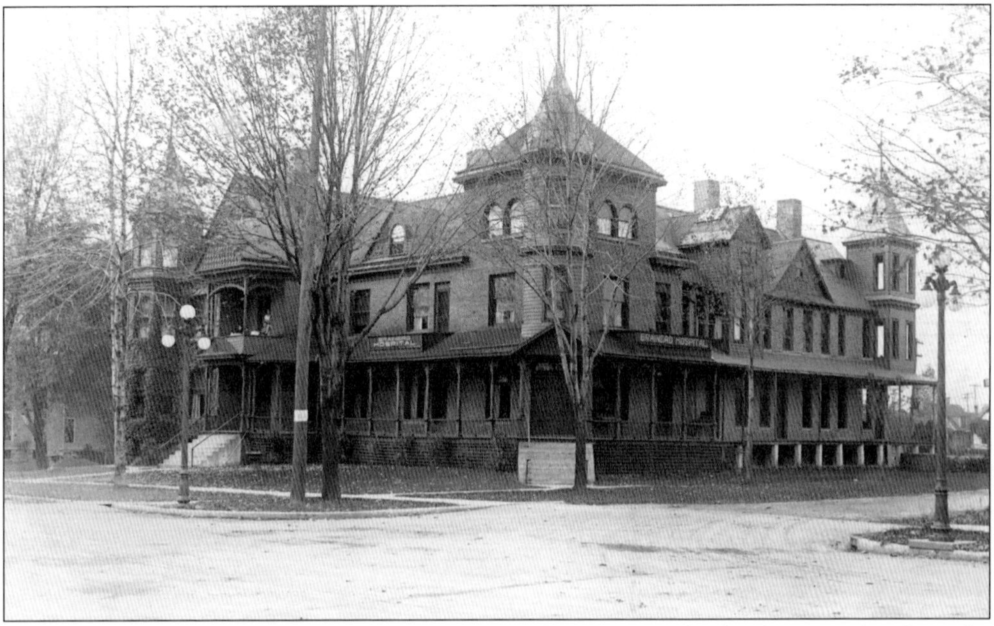

Dr. Ira Brainerd came to Alma with the Central Michigan Normal School as a teacher. Later he established the first hospital in Alma at the corner of State and Center Streets. He constructed the building almost single-handedly, laying bricks and cutting boards when not attending to patients. His scientific approach and his articles in medical journals engendered hard feelings from Alma's less-progressive physicians. (Courtesy of Richard Tesman.)

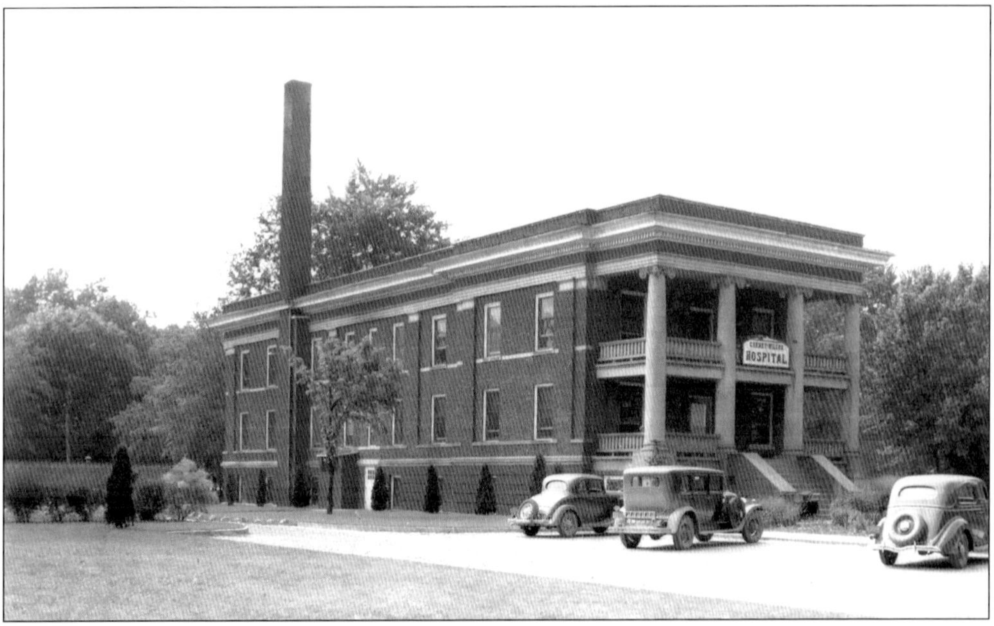


Dr. Thomas Carney came to Alma as a young man and was persuaded to take the position of public health officer. It was a time of outdoor privies and stables in backyards, and Carney took the requisite abuse as he urged city fathers to pass ordinances designed to clean things up. Later he started Carney-Wilcox Hospital in the infirmary addition to the old Masonic building. (Courtesy of Richard Tesman.)

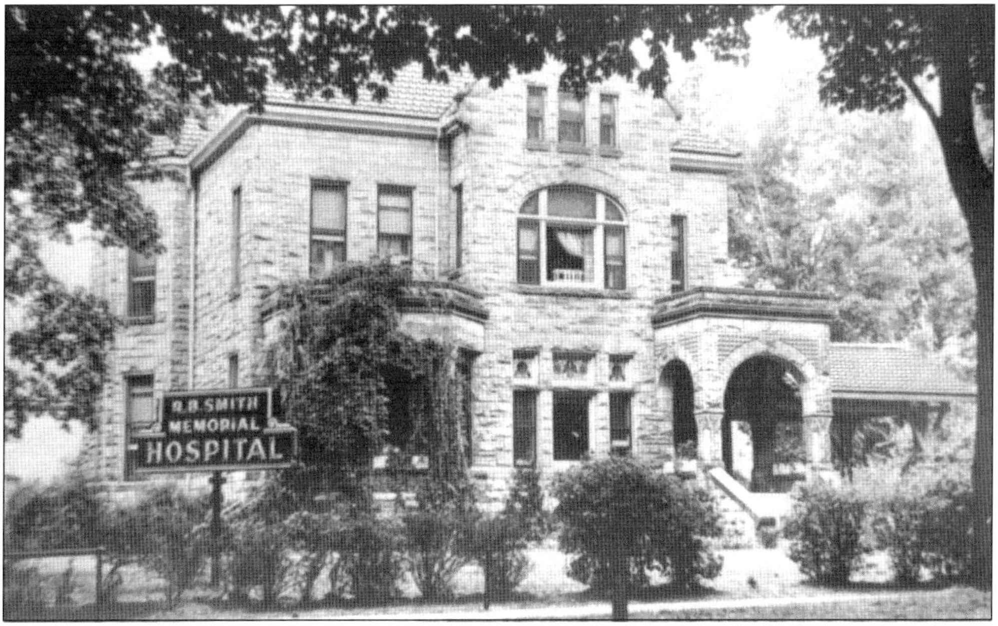


Betsy Smith, widow of a popular Alma physician, was persuaded by a group of Alma physicians to purchase the vacant Ammi W. Wright mansion and make it into R. B. Smith Memorial Hospital in 1934. It was located across a grassy yard from Carney-Wilcox Hospital, and a "feeling" existed between the physicians at the two hospitals. (Author's collection.)

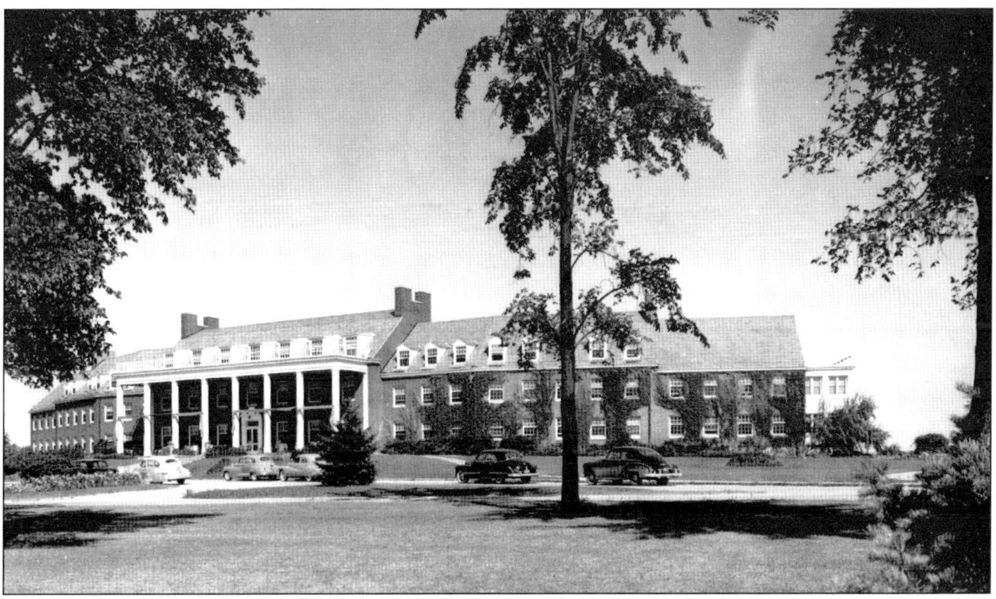

In the early 1930s, the Masonic lodge decided to build a new facility on Alma's north side. The land was purchased from the heirs of Ammi W. Wright. It had been the site of the Links, Alma's first golf course, designed for use by patrons of the Alma Springs Sanitarium. The old sanitarium/Masonic home building was razed. (Courtesy of Masonic Pathways.)

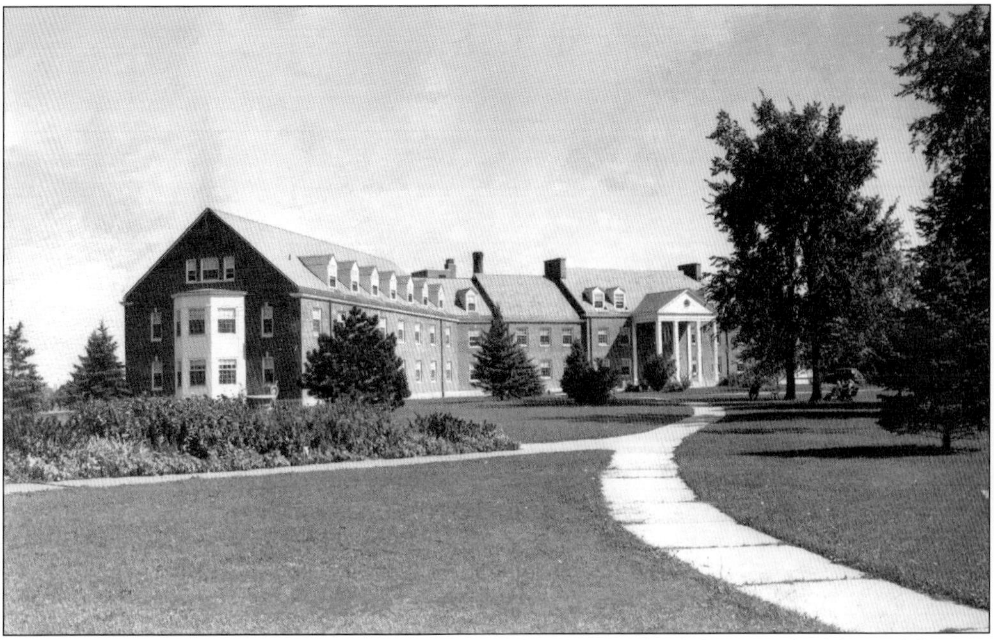

Within a few years, a hospital unit was constructed to the south of the main building of the new Masonic home. The buildings were connected by a 600-foot tunnel. As in the old institution on State Street, residents at the new facility could be cared for at every level of need. (Courtesy of Colleen Boyer.)

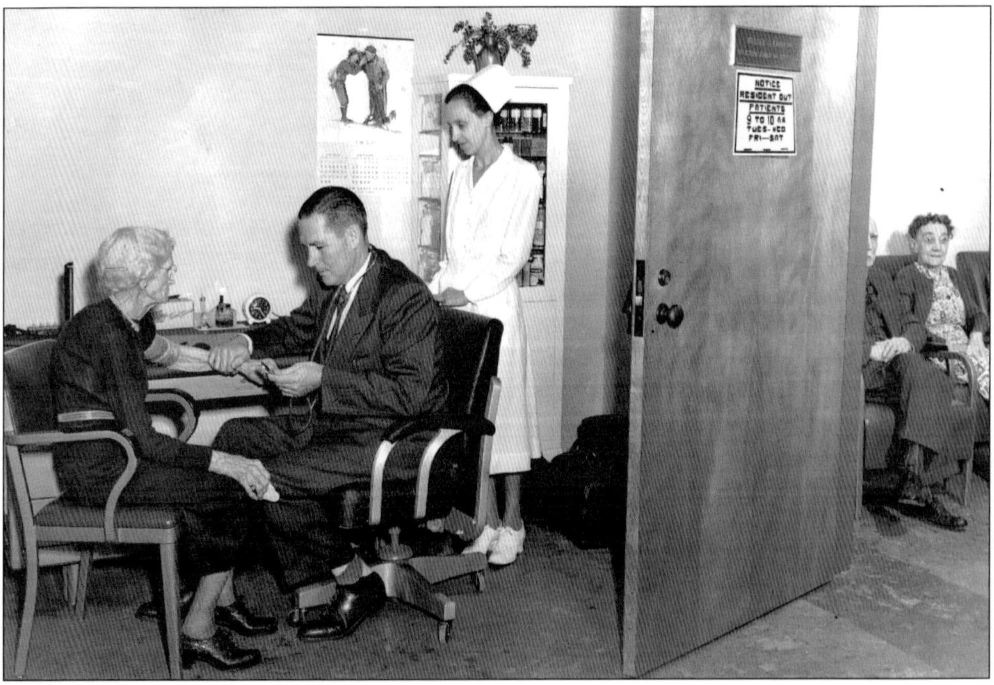


In a scene reminiscent of the 1930s, the home's doctor is examining a patient, attended by a nurse. In the waiting room, other residents wait for the doctor's ministrations. (Courtesy of Masonic Pathways.)

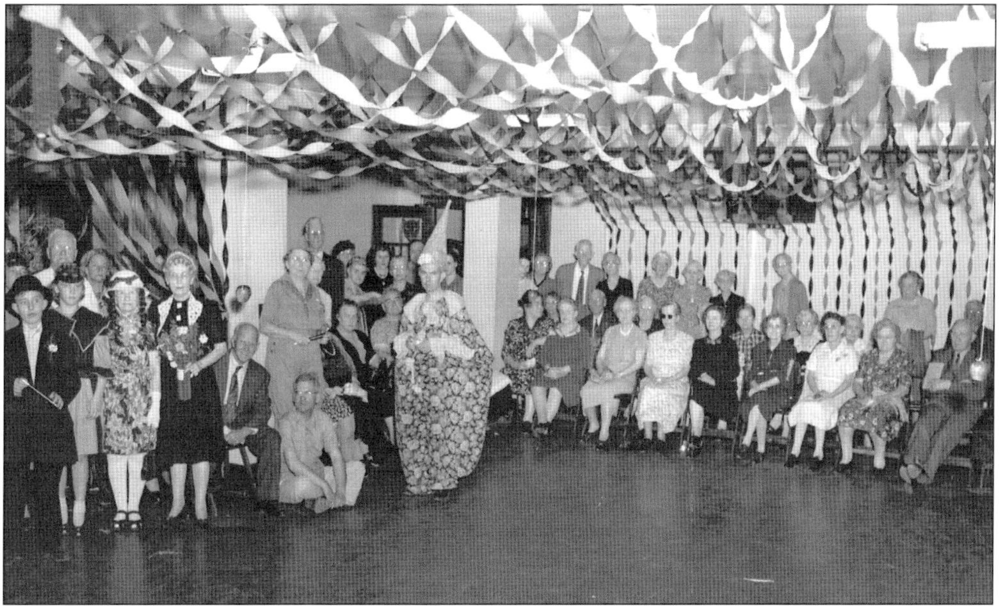

Residents enjoy one of numerous entertainments at the home. Costumed guests have presented a skit. The audience has dressed nicely to attend the party. (Photograph by Maurine Stovall, courtesy of Masonic Pathways.)

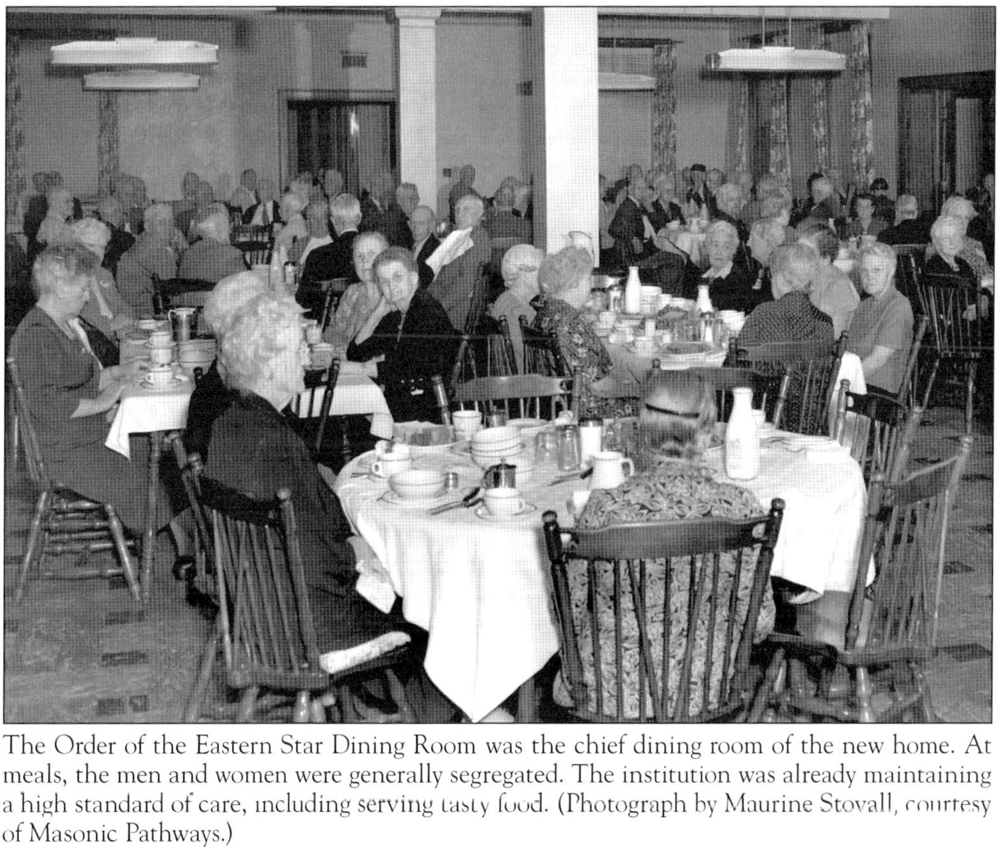

The Order of the Eastern Star Dining Room was the chief dining room of the new home. At meals, the men and women were generally segregated. The institution was already maintaining a high standard of care, including serving tasty food. (Photograph by Maurine Stovall, courtesy of Masonic Pathways.)

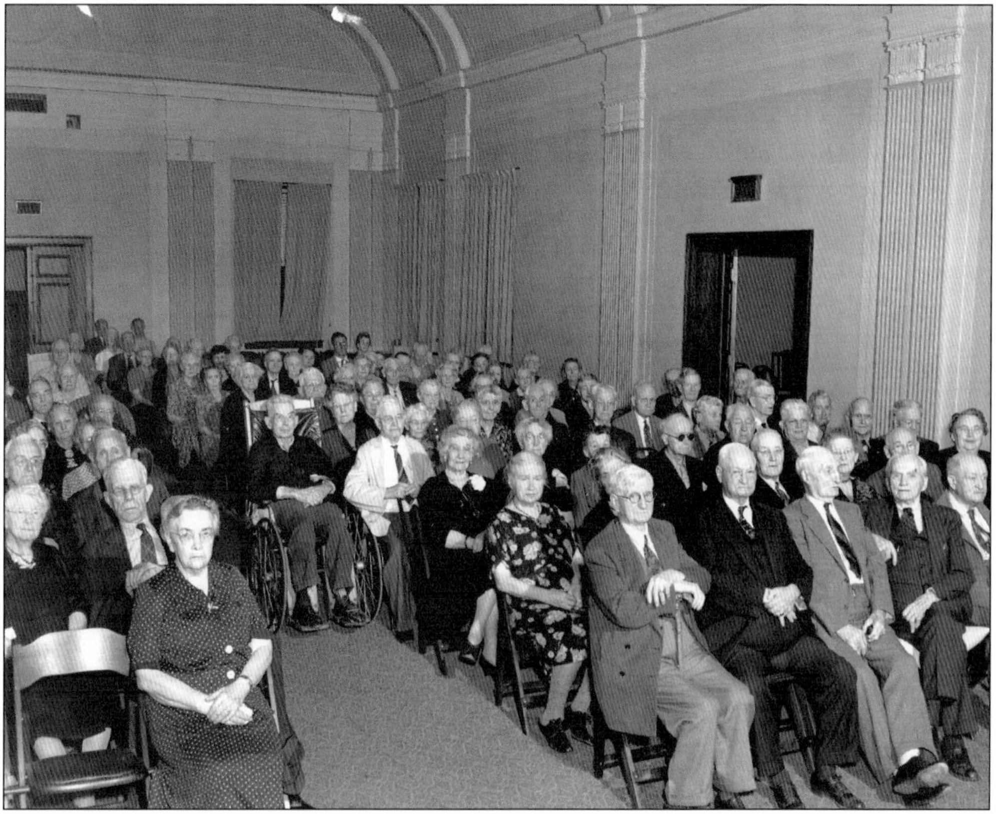

The grand auditorium served the home for many years. Here residents prepare for a performance, and as usual they are dressed very appropriately for a special event. (Photograph by Maurine Stovall, courtesy of Masonic Pathways.)

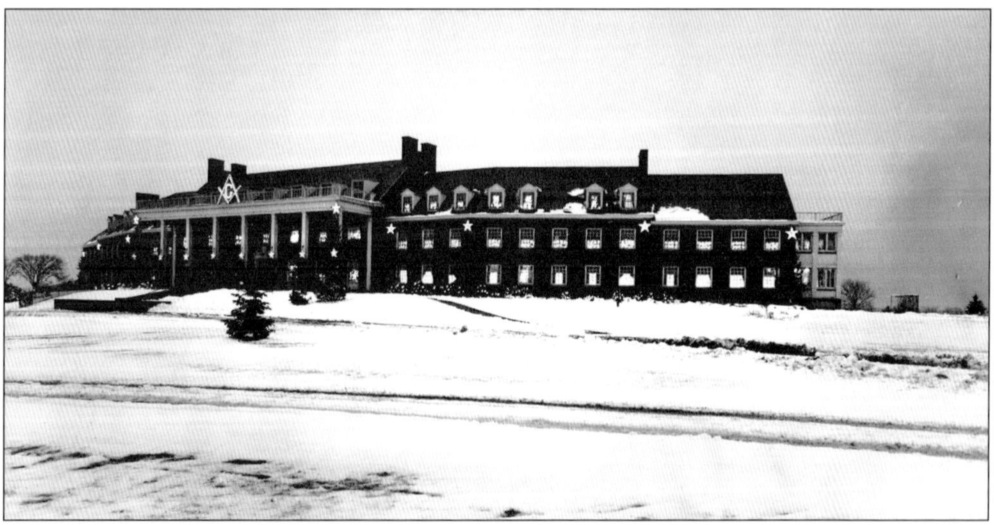

The home was always tastefully decorated for the Christmas season. This night view from the 1940s reflects the simple beauty of the home in winter. (Courtesy of Masonic Pathways.)

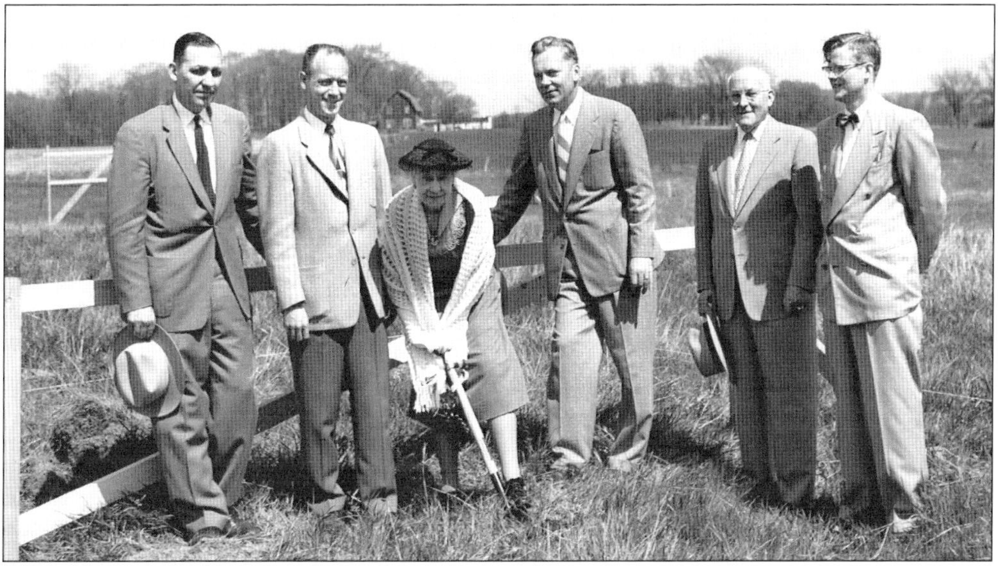

Recognizing the need for a modern hospital to replace the crowded R. B. Smith Memorial Hospital, a new Gratiot Community Hospital was planned for a 10-acre site north of the Masonic home. The million-dollar project began in 1954, and the hospital opened in 1955. Ground is being broken by Lou Nickerson from Smith Memorial Hospital. Also shown from left to right are Everett Thompson, Dr. C. H. Wallman, Earl Brenneman, Lynn Miller, and Robert Anthony. (Courtesy of Gratiot Medical Center.)

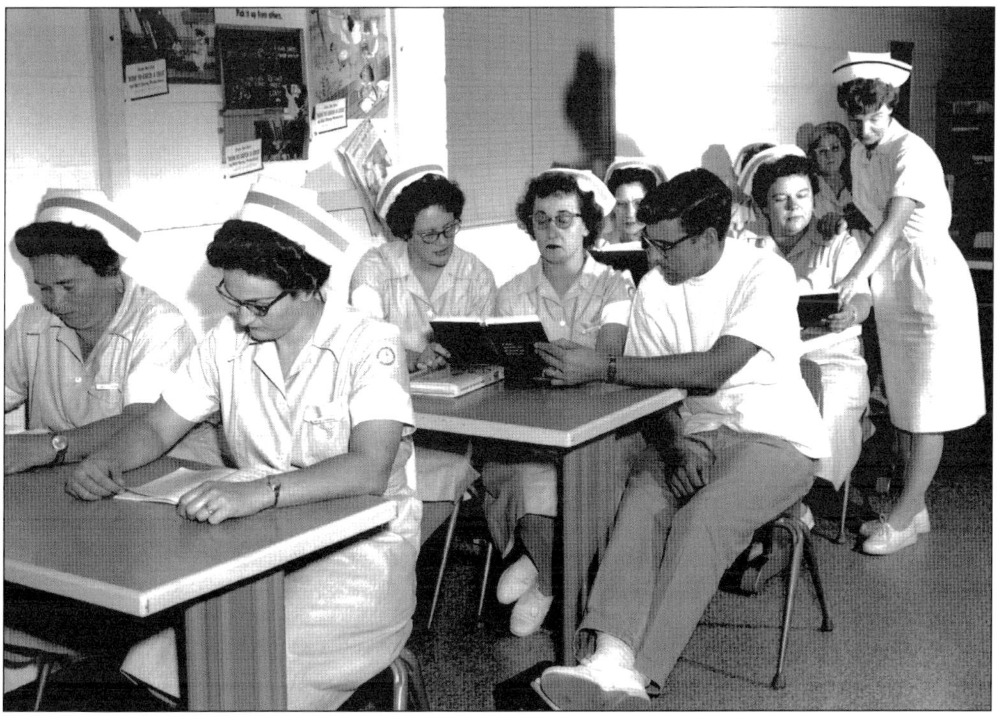

In 1962, a program to train licensed practical nurses was established in cooperation with Alma Public Schools. This program, in various forms, continued to provide training opportunities for these health-care professionals. (Courtesy of Gratiot Medical Center.)

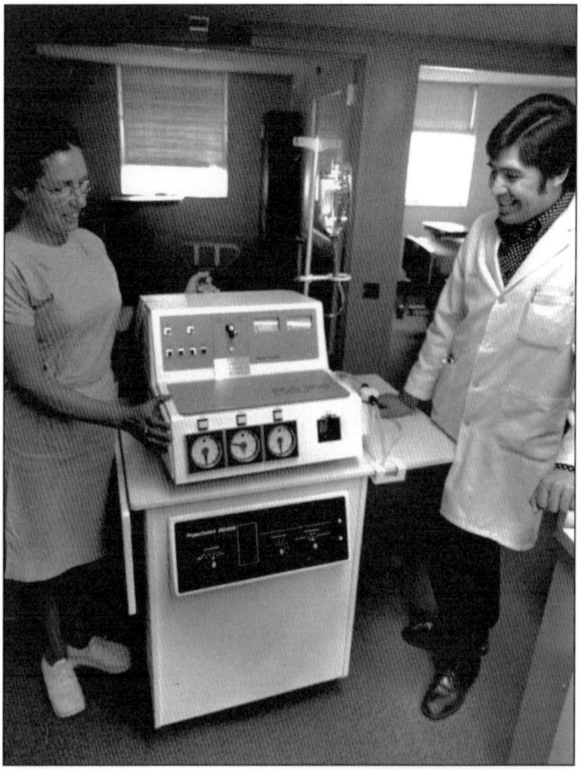

The first hemodialysis unit was purchased in 1968. Here Dr. Victor Rozas examines the new machine. Gratiot Community Hospital was one of the few rural hospitals in the entire country to offer this service. (Courtesy of Gratiot Medical Center.)

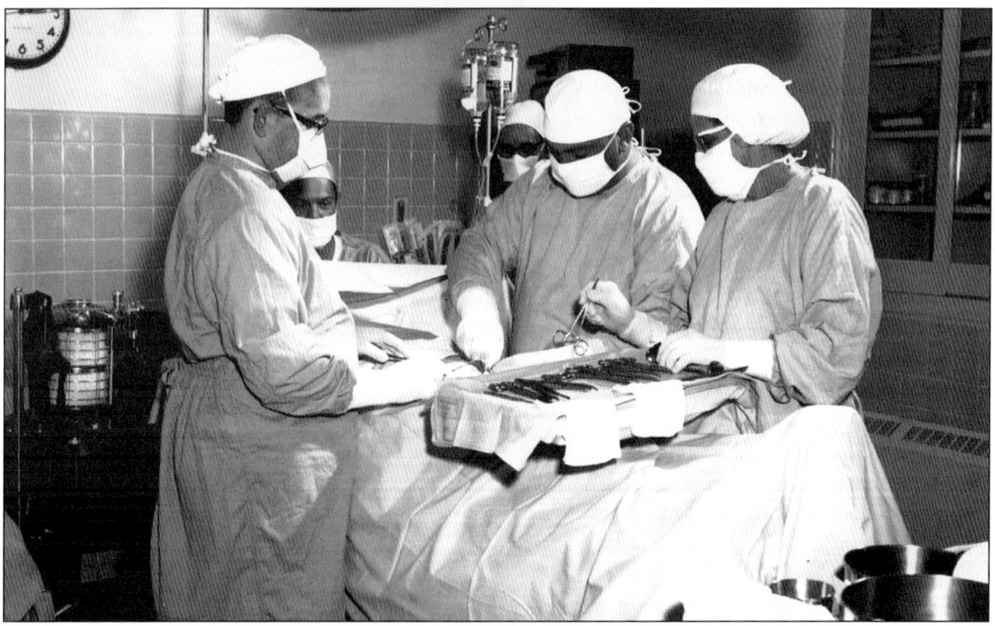

The hospital's operating rooms were only one feature of the hospital, which, from its inception, has consistently attempted to bring the latest in available care and treatments to the people of the Alma area. The new hospital was only the latest facility in a tradition begun by Dr. Ira Brainerd many years before and continued by health-care professionals through the years. (Courtesy of Gratiot Medical Center.)

# Seven

# HAVING SOME FUN

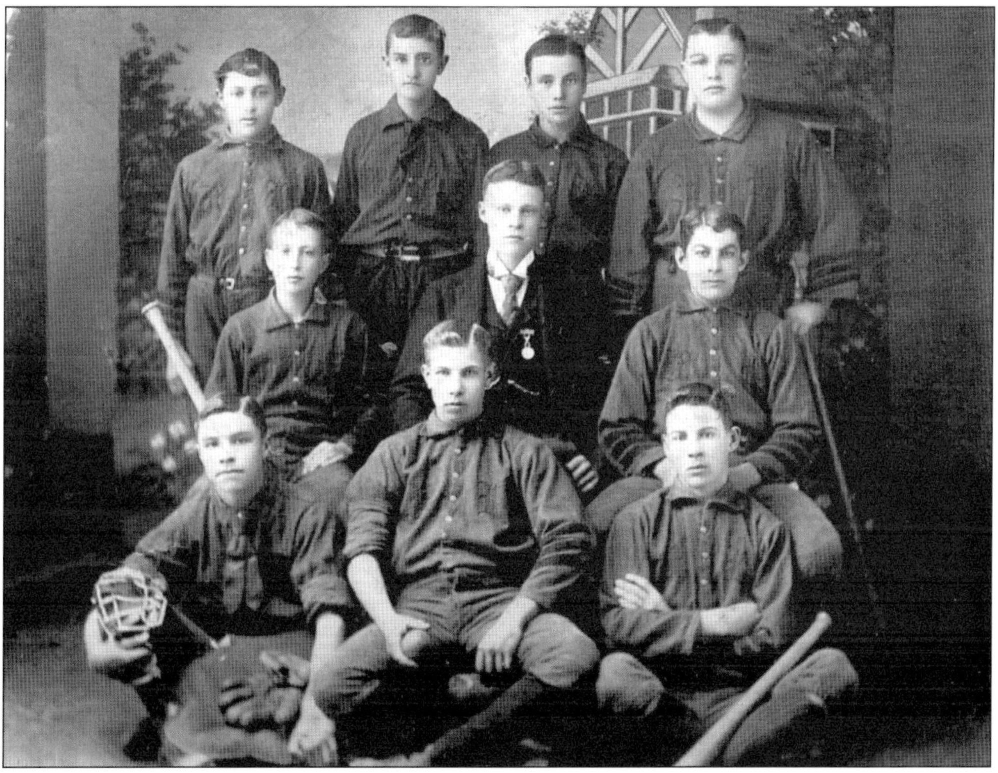

The Alma Maple Leafs were juvenile state baseball champions in 1888. Their regular season included games with local teams from St. Louis and Edmore. The club manager was 20-year-old George N. Wright (center), son of millionaire Ammi W. Wright. After his mother's death, the boy led a troubled adolescence. Four years after this championship year, he died of typhoid fever. (Courtesy of the Alma College Library.)

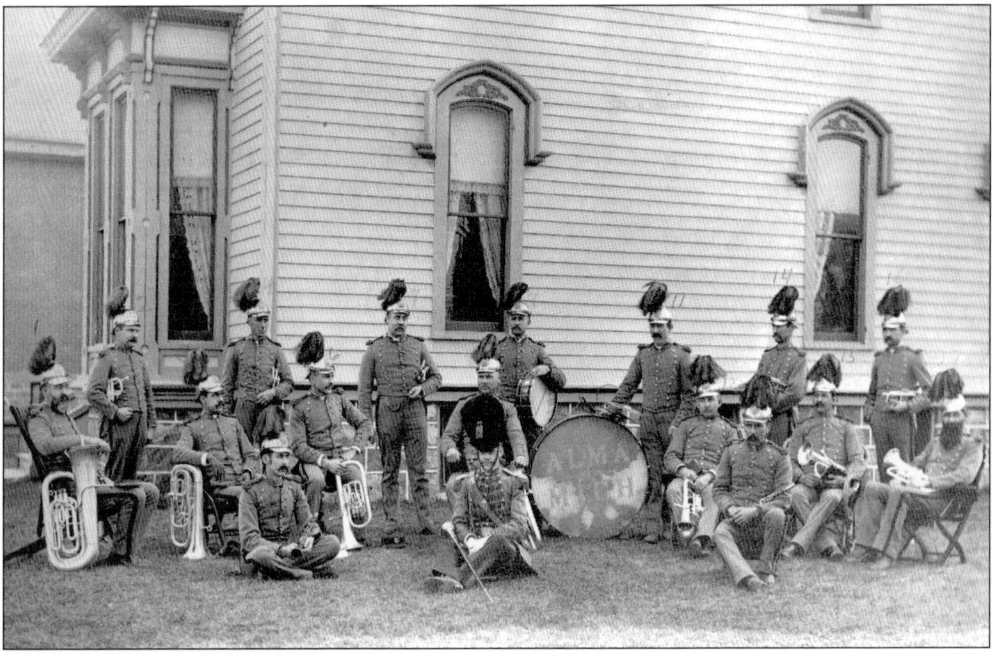


Composed of local musicians, Wright's Opera House Band gave many concerts, marched in every parade, met all dignitaries at the depot, and often played in other towns. This band differed from many town bands because it was composed of trained musicians, most of whom were mature farmers or businessmen committed to producing fine music. (Courtesy of Doris Amsbury.)

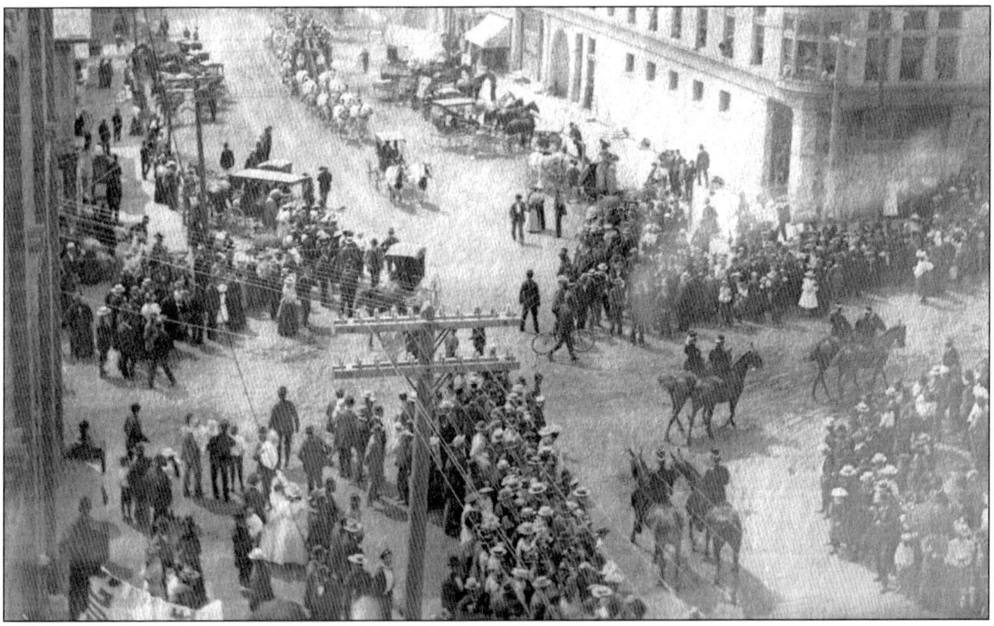

Because it was the crossroads of two rail lines, Alma was for many years a great circus town. Beginning in the 1880s, it was a rare summer when one or more circuses did not visit the village. Big-name shows such as Ringling Brothers and Buffalo Bill's Wild West Show put up their tents in Alma. Often 20,000 people thronged the town on circus day. This circus parade occurred during a visit by the Ringling Brothers in 1898. (Courtesy of the Alma Public Library.)

Not only was the day pleasant, as these two ladies went for a stroll near the Union School, but it was exciting and a bit daring to walk across the railroad trestle over the Pine River. (Courtesy of the Alma College Library.)

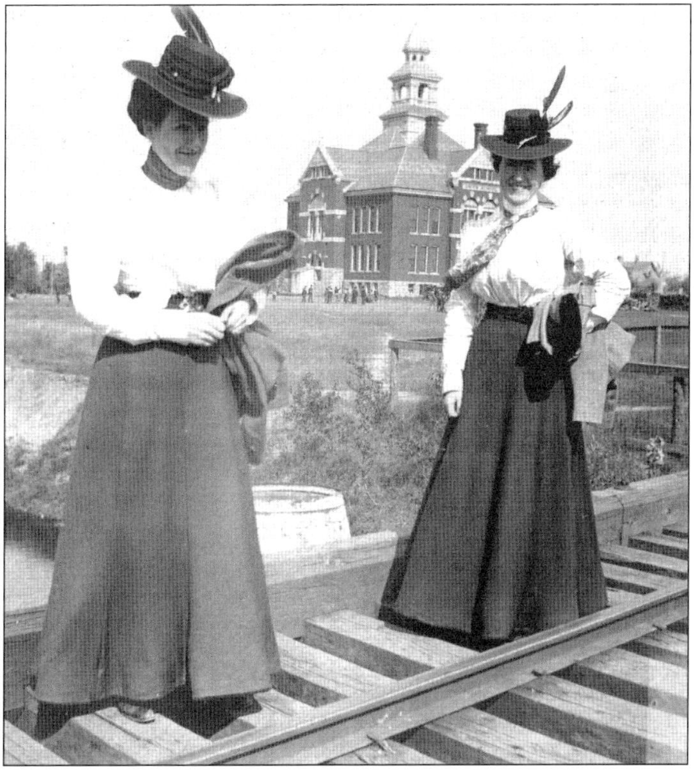

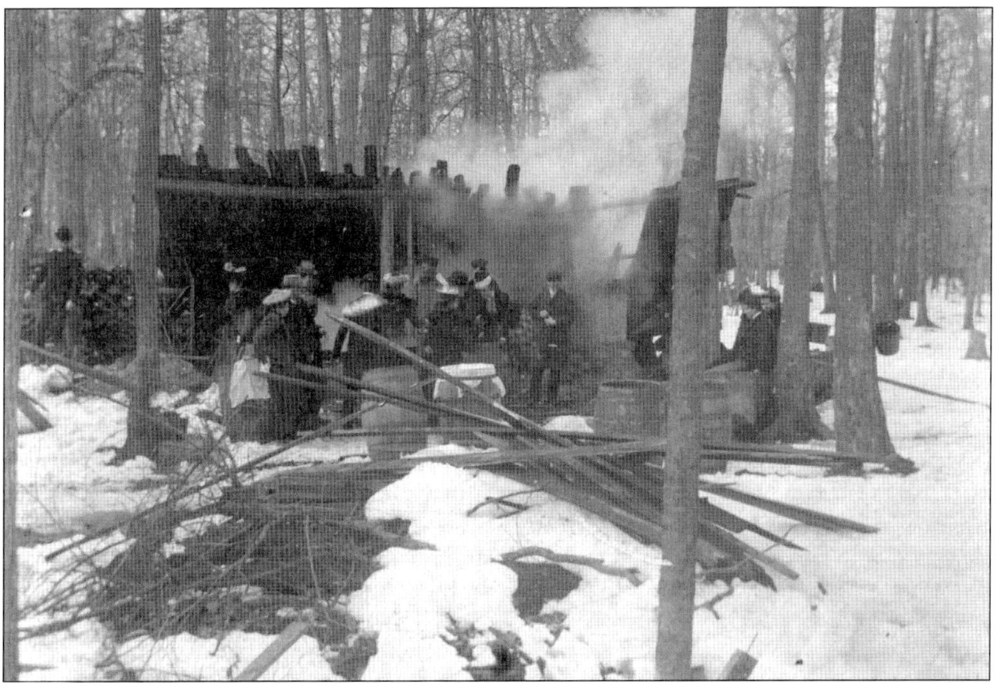

Alma College students are visiting a sugar bush in the woods south of the Pine River. The making of maple syrup and maple sugar had a long history in Gratiot County, as it was the popular sweetener used in pioneering days. (Courtesy of the Alma College Library.)

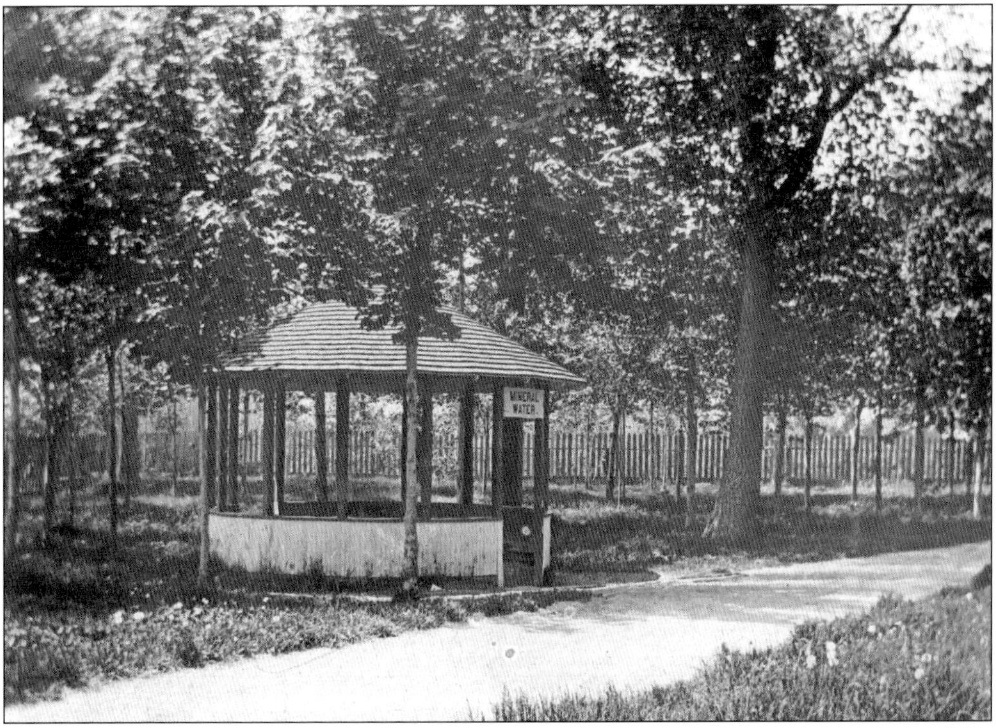


When not enjoying a mineral water bath or socializing with other patients, the guests of the sanitarium could enjoy a drink of fresh water from the mineral well in Sanitarium Park. Another well in the basement of the building furnished water for baths, which were thought to cure a vast number of diseases. (Courtesy of the Alma College Library.)

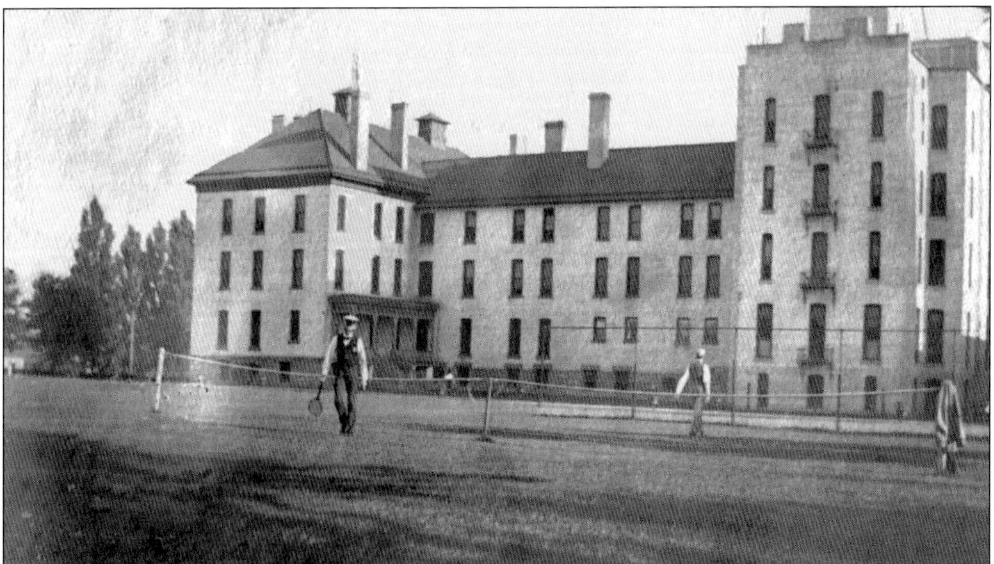

In Sanitarium Park, patrons could stroll, listen to weekly band concerts, ride on horseback, observe the fish in the fishpond, and play croquet. They also could play tennis, as shown by these two gentleman, who are enjoying the courts on the north side of the building. (Courtesy of the Alma College Library.)

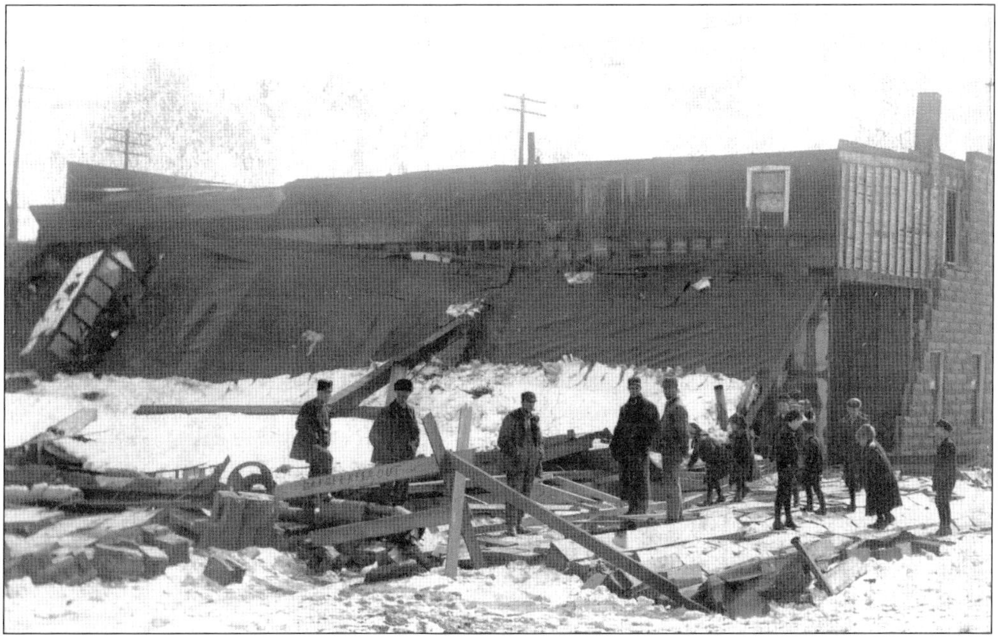

Roller-skating was a popular activity in Alma over the years. Sometimes the local band played at the roller rink. This photograph depicts the fate of a rink newly converted from the Sprague Feed Barn. Two iron trusses supporting the roof of C. M. Grow's rink collapsed under the weight of very wet snow in March 1908. The loss was pegged at $1,000. (Courtesy of the Alma College Library.)

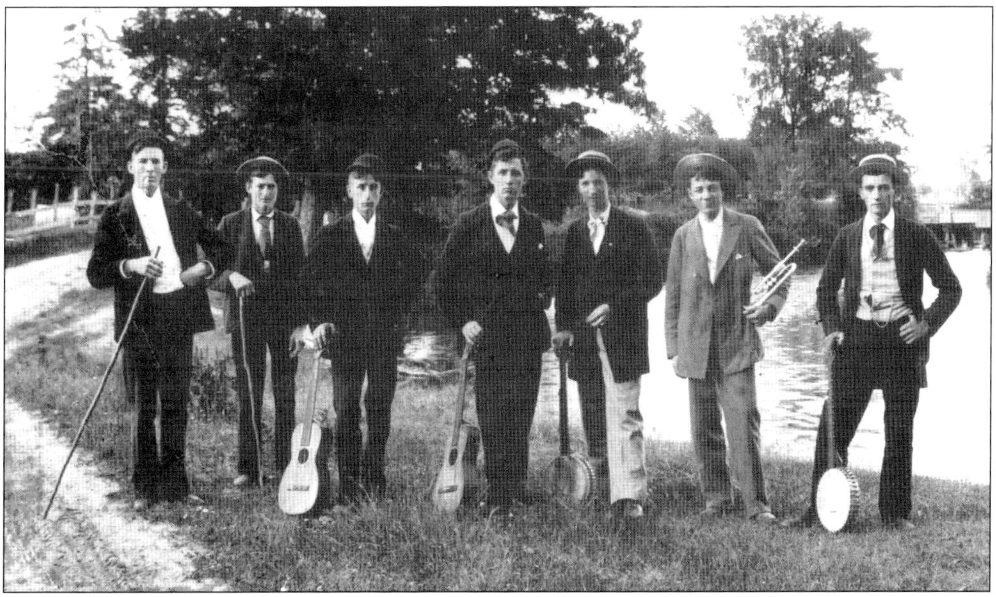

These troubadours, nattily dressed, pose beside the Pine River. The young men, from left to right, are unidentified, unidentified, Floyd Woodward, Tad Davis, Raymond Turck, Charles Ward, and Ed Hutchins. (Courtesy of the Alma Public Library.)

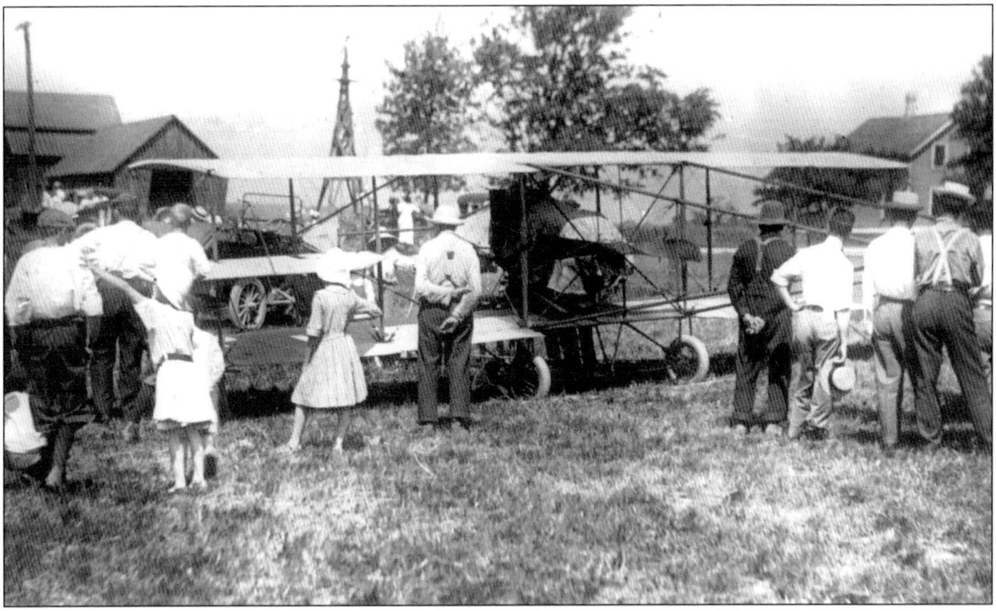

Aviator Floyd Barlow brought his General Curtiss Standard flying machine to Alma for the Fourth of July celebration in 1913. He made several flights out of fields, amazing the old and triggering dreams in the young. (Courtesy of the Alma Public Library.)

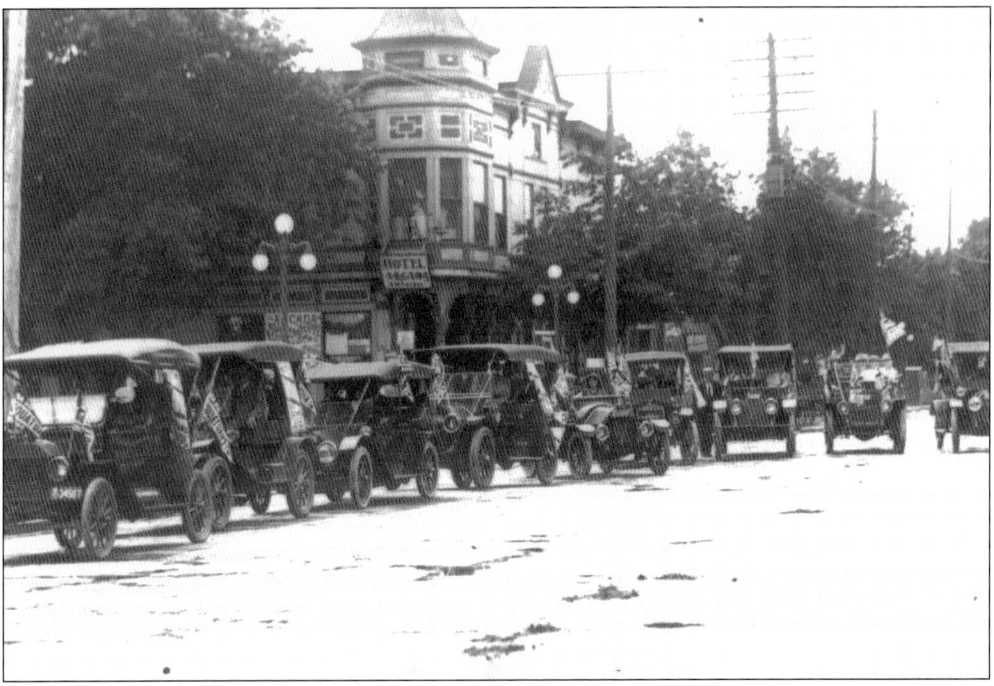


Chautauqua, a weeklong injection of instant culture, set up its tents in or near Wright Park each August from 1913 to 1931. Advertised countywide by this parade of decorated vehicles, the Chautauqua program in 1914 offered well-known vocalists, bands, speakers, and drama companies. It also provided afternoon programs for women and children. A $2 ticket granted admission for the week. (Courtesy of the Alma Public Library.)

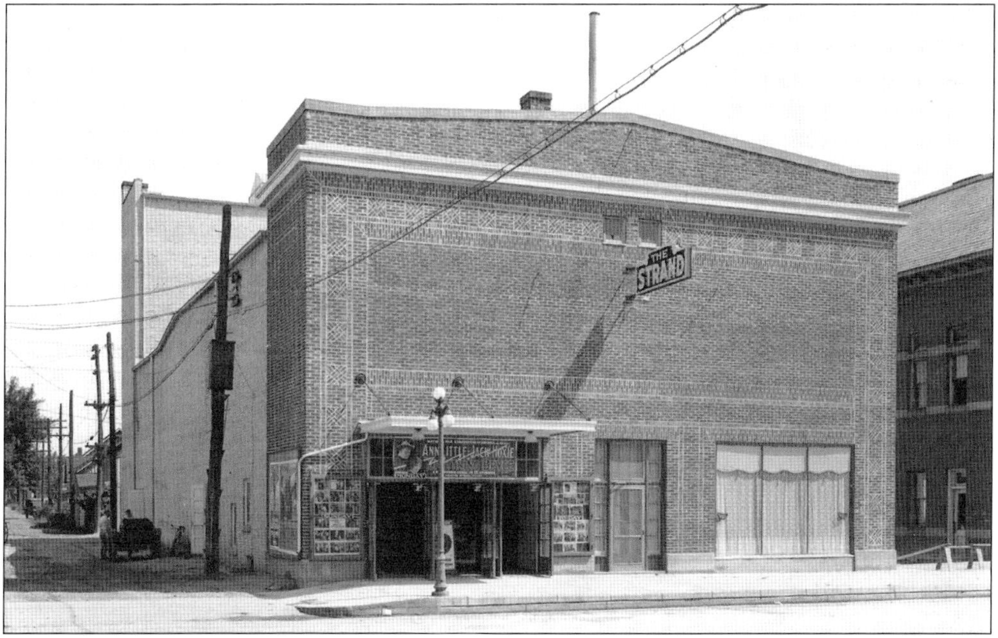


The ultramodern $100,000 Strand theater opened in May 1920. It boasted of more than 900 seats, a fully equipped stage, a $10,000 orchestral pipe organ, the latest in ventilation, and an auxiliary power plant. This building burned in 1960 and was replaced by the Strand Movie Theater. (Courtesy of Richard Tesman.)

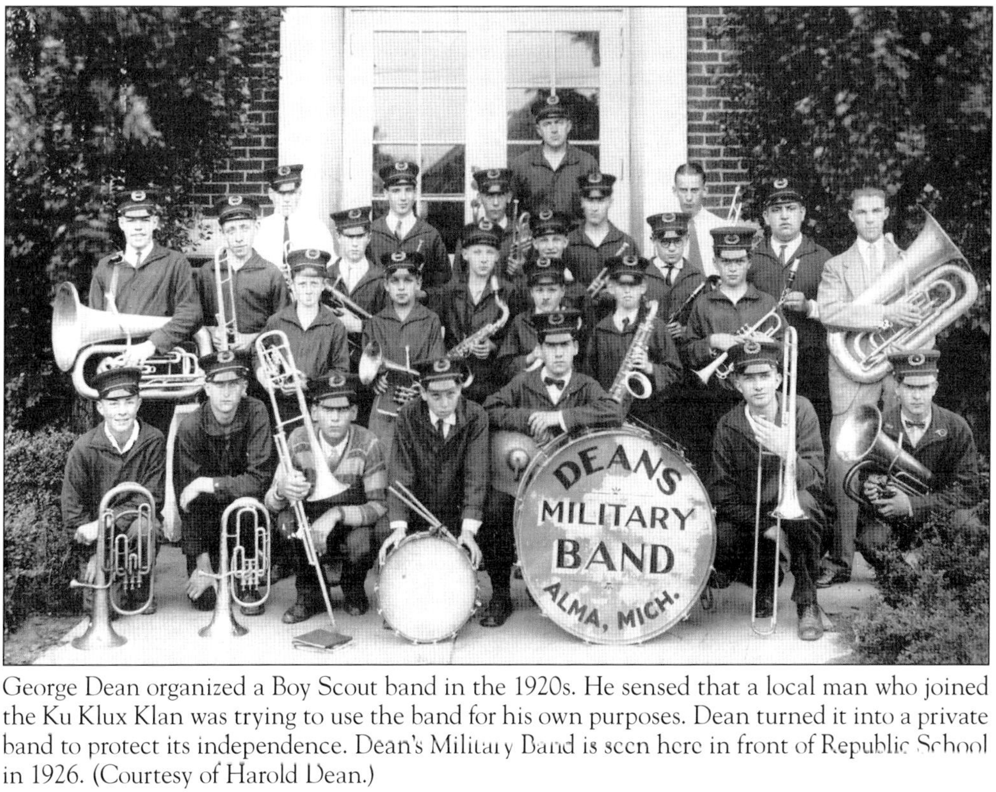


George Dean organized a Boy Scout band in the 1920s. He sensed that a local man who joined the Ku Klux Klan was trying to use the band for his own purposes. Dean turned it into a private band to protect its independence. Dean's Military Band is seen here in front of Republic School in 1926. (Courtesy of Harold Dean.)

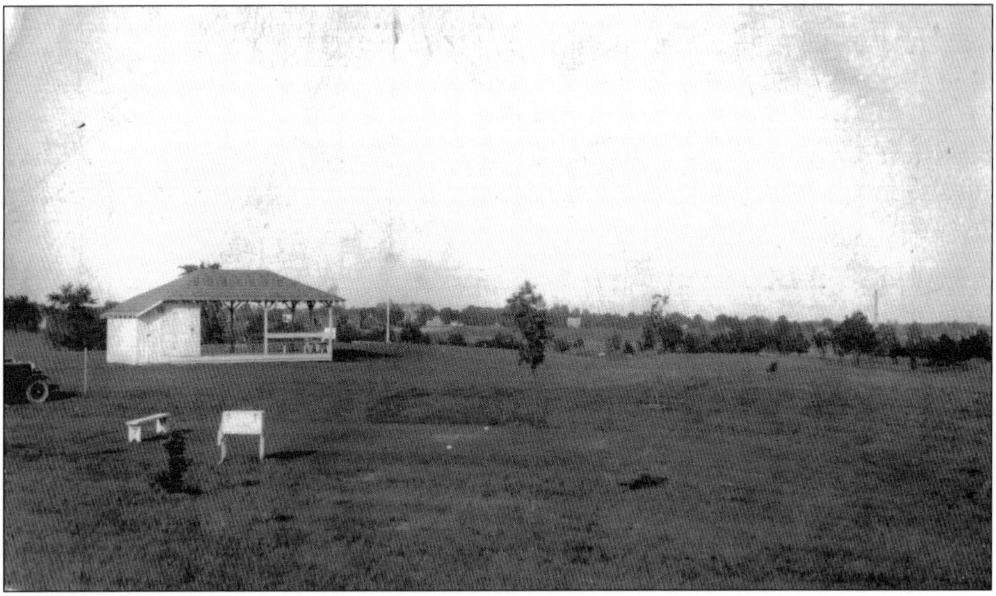

Henry Lancashire, son-in-law of Ammi W. Wright, built Alma's first golf course, the Links, on Alma's north side on the land later to be occupied by the Masonic home. A nine-hole golf course was organized in 1921 by a group of Alma businessmen. They leased 50 acres of the Miller farm west of Alma, and by 1922, membership in the golf club soared to 100. In 1927, the Alma Golf Club became the Pine River Country Club. (Courtesy of Jan Caputo.)

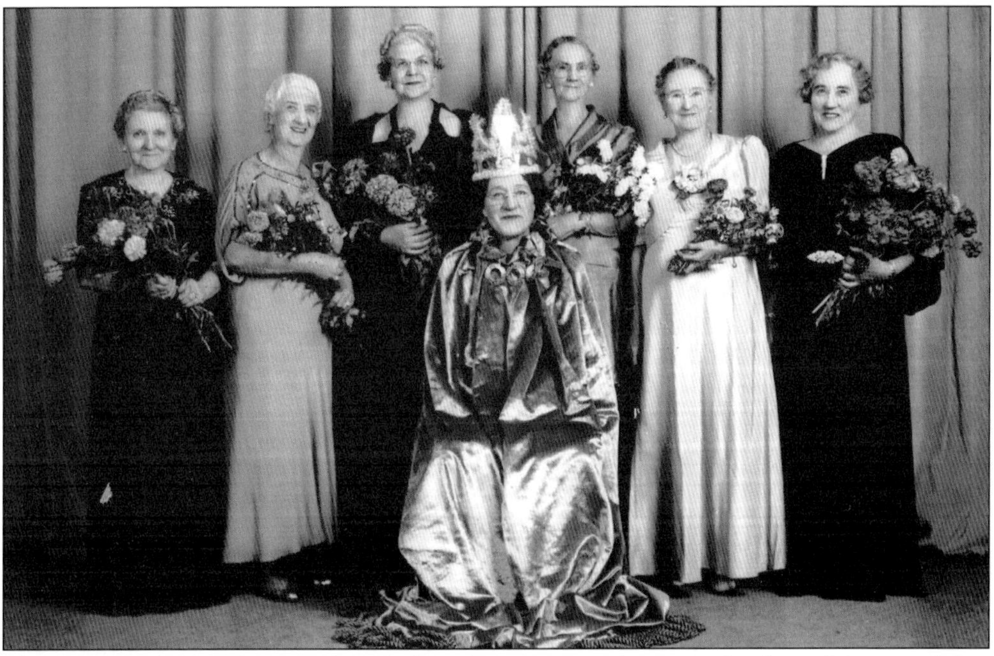

The 1941 Mardi Gras features these ladies who represented pioneer families of the area. They are, from left to right, Genevieve Brewbaker, Eula Gee Hannah, Abbie Wolfe, Nettie Lindsay, Nellie Sullivan, and Della Ward. The queen of the Pioneer Court of Royalty was Charles O. Ward, a man who loved a good joke. He is seen here in his queenly garb. (Courtesy of the Alma Public Library.)

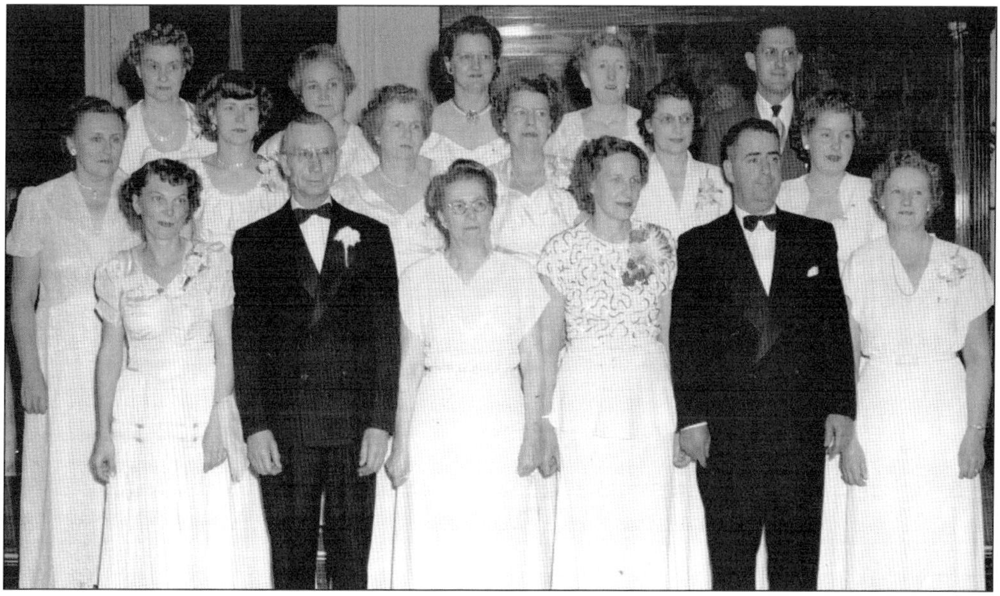

The Masonic lodge has a long history in Alma. Shown here are officers of Alma Chapter 43 Order of the Eastern Star of Michigan in October 1949. From left to right are (first row) Doris Peterson, Herbert Gardner, Laura Argent, Genevieve Wolfe, Gerald Wolfe, and Ann Pollard; (second row) Frances Hicks, Phyllis Scott, Sadie Hinkle, Jean Gardner, Ida Matthews, and Mabel Nelson; (third row) Marjorie Hinderleider, Maretta Wolfe, Adelaide Weeks, Minnie Yahn, and Charles Peterson. (Courtesy of Charles and Diantha Hicks.)

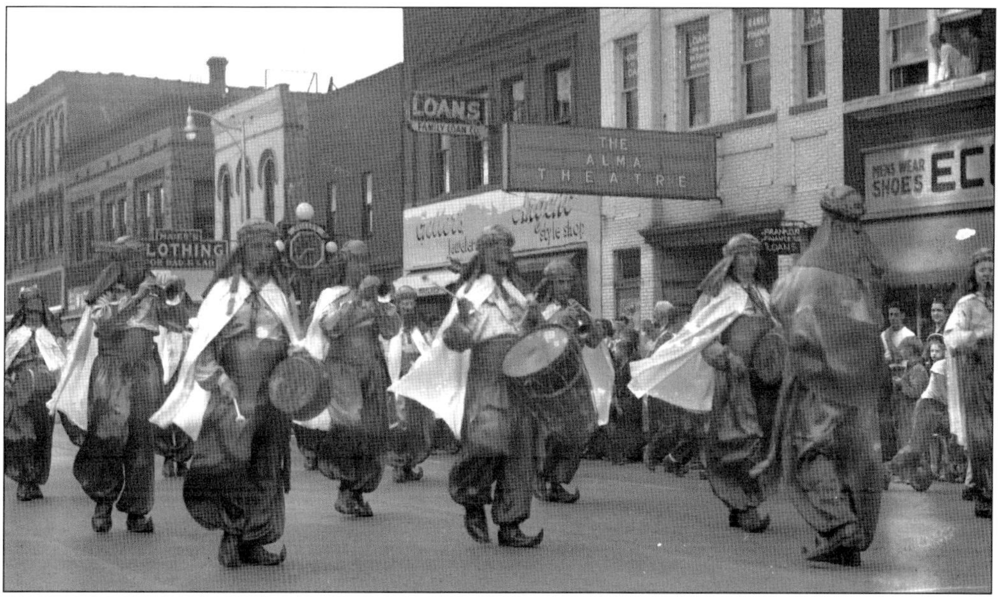


Colorfully robed, the Oriental Band of the Moslem Temple Shrine of Detroit plays its tom-toms and musettes. It was the final unit in a Masonic parade held on Saturday, September 16, 1950, on Superior Street. Also marching in the parade was the 16-platoon Moslem Arab patrol, regarded as one of the most-famous precision marching units in North America at the time. Following the parade, the Shriners entertained guests at the Masonic home. (Photograph by Hubert Elias, courtesy of Dale Kemler.)

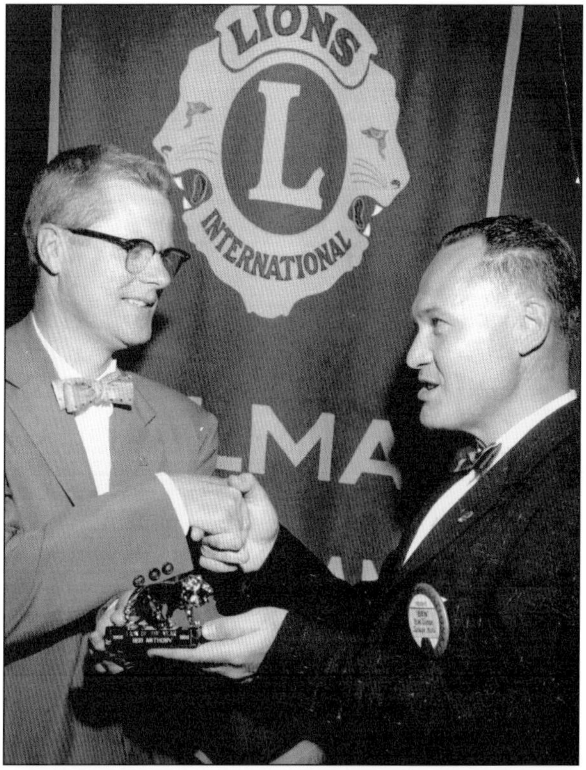


A longtime civic servant, Robert Anthony (left) served for many years as Alma's mayor. Here he receives the Lion of the Year award in 1959. It is being presented by Alma businessman Ben Simon. (Courtesy of Robert Smith.)

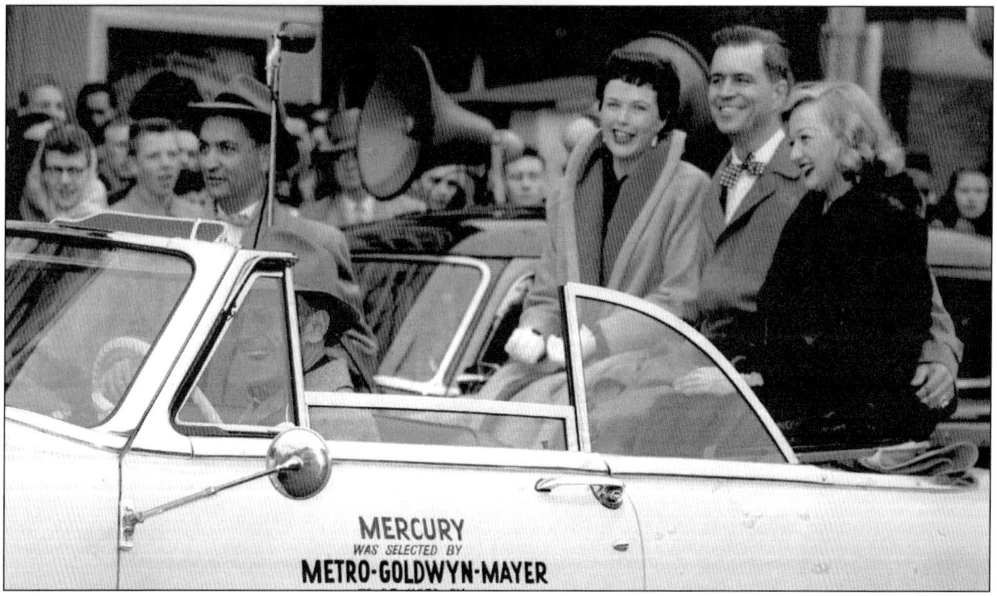


Lucille Ball and Desi Arnaz starred in *The Long, Long Trailer*, a slapdash comedy that took them on a motor journey through the mountains towing a long house trailer. The featured trailer was a New Moon model made in Alma. To promote the 1954 film, two starlets from the film company came to Alma, and a parade ensued. Gov. G. Mennen Williams was in town on other business but was a willing guest of the two ladies in their Mercury convertible in front of the Strand theater. (Courtesy of Jim Sommerville.)

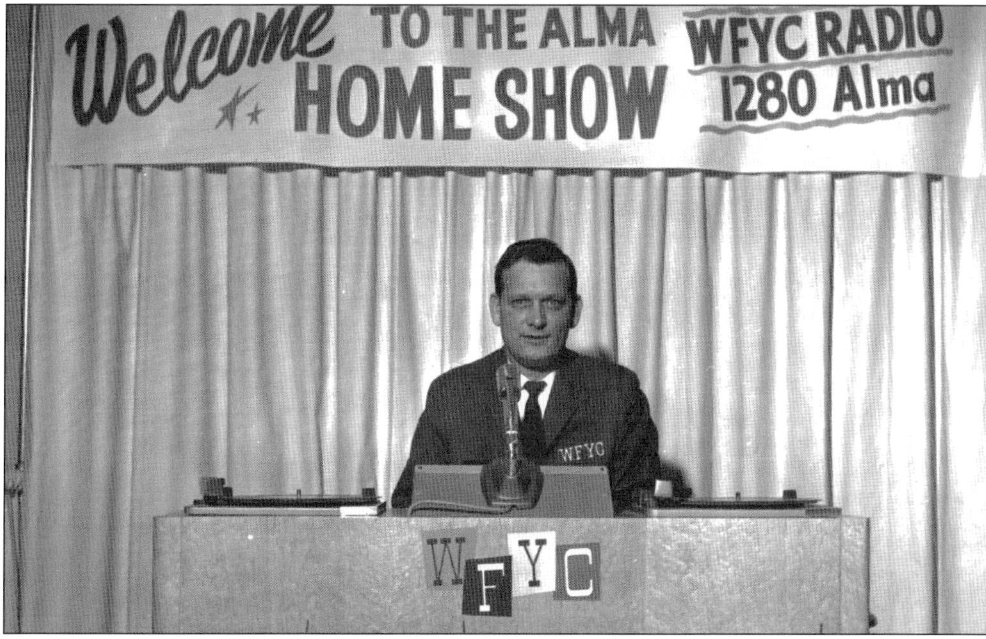

Dave Sommerville, the voice of WFYC AM radio, reports from a home show at the Alma Armory in the early 1960s. Leaving the navy after World War II, Sommerville went to broadcasting school in Pasadena, California. He joined WFYC in August 1948, and its studios were located in the Medler Building in downtown Alma. He made $1 an hour. The station moved to its present State Road location in 1951. (Courtesy of Jim Sommerville.)

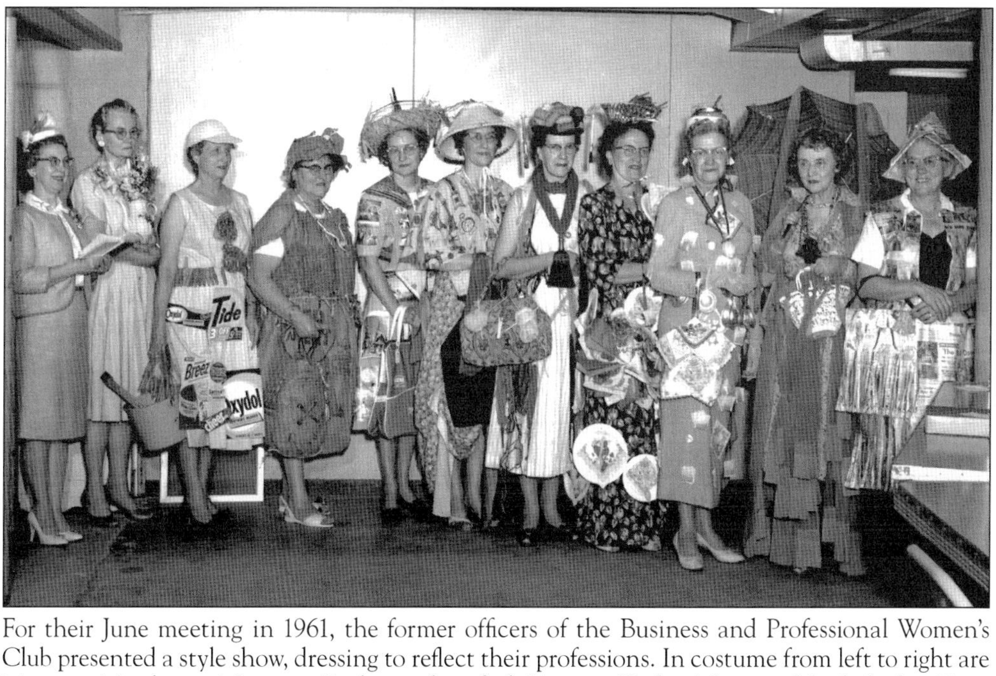
For their June meeting in 1961, the former officers of the Business and Professional Women's Club presented a style show, dressing to reflect their professions. In costume from left to right are Marjorie Matthews, Margaret Bush, unidentified, Frances Hicks, Marjorie Hinderleider, Nina Anderson, Lois McGill, Ruth Remsberg, Thelma Dewey, Ruth Palmer, and Jessie Rockwell. (Courtesy of the Alma Public Library.)

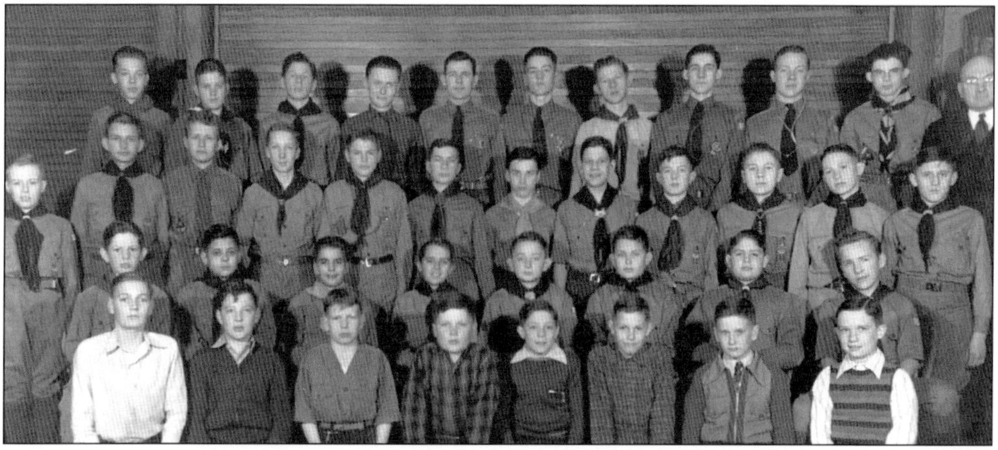

Scouting has had a long tradition in Alma. Here is Troop 101 in 1940. From left to right, the scouts are (first row) Neil Fenner, Don Rice, Lemoyne Wilkenson, Jim Wilson, John Manzullo, Bob Daily, Ralph Hinderleider, and Bob Ellis; (second row) Larry Porter, George Stamas, ? Anderson, Don Redman, Jerry Hungerford, Don Howell, Dick Roberts, and Bob Sharp; (third row) Jim Wolfe, Larry Fisher, Don Berg, Sonny Stewart, Dale McClure, Larry Ferris, Chuck O'Mera, Bill Bevier, Bob Sexton, Ron Mantey, Dave Stein, and John Wilkens; (fourth row) Vance Fulton, David Anthony, Bruce Devero, Bob McDonald, David Gainey, Paul Kaufman, Bill Fishbeck, Bob Thompson, Tom Stein, Richard Small, and Rev. Albert Anthony (acting scoutmaster). (Courtesy of Charles and Diantha Hicks.)

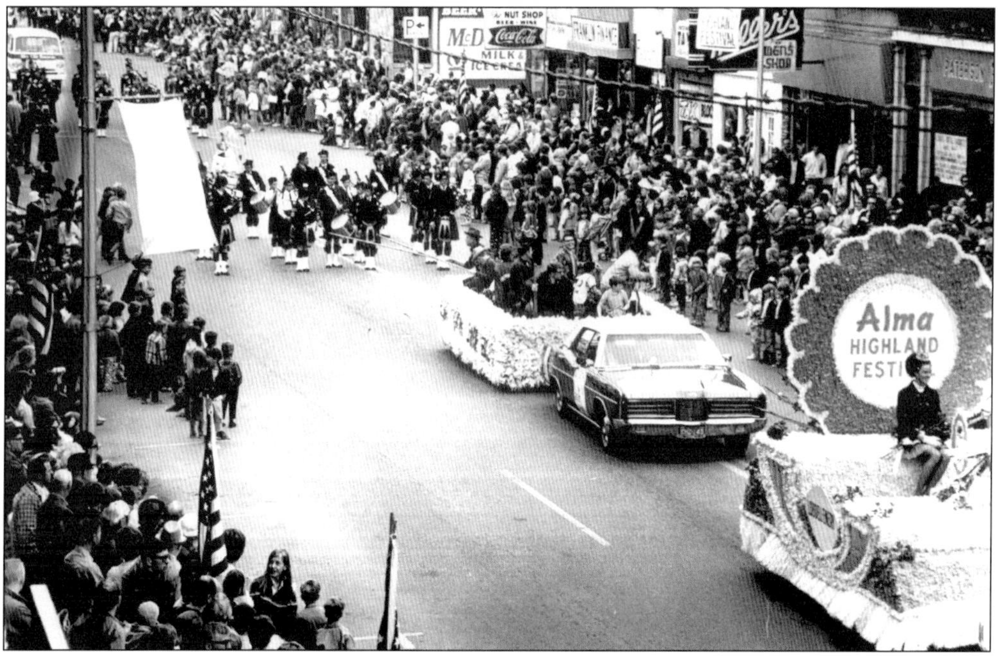


Perceiving a Scottish heritage through Alma College, a Presbyterian school, the Alma Highland Festival was begun in 1968. It attracted pipe bands from across the country and grew into one of the major Scottish festivals in North America. Here the lengthy festival parade, which attracted thousands of spectators, wends its way down Superior Street heading toward the Alma College campus, headquarters of the celebration. (Photograph by Gordon Beld, courtesy of the Alma College Library.)

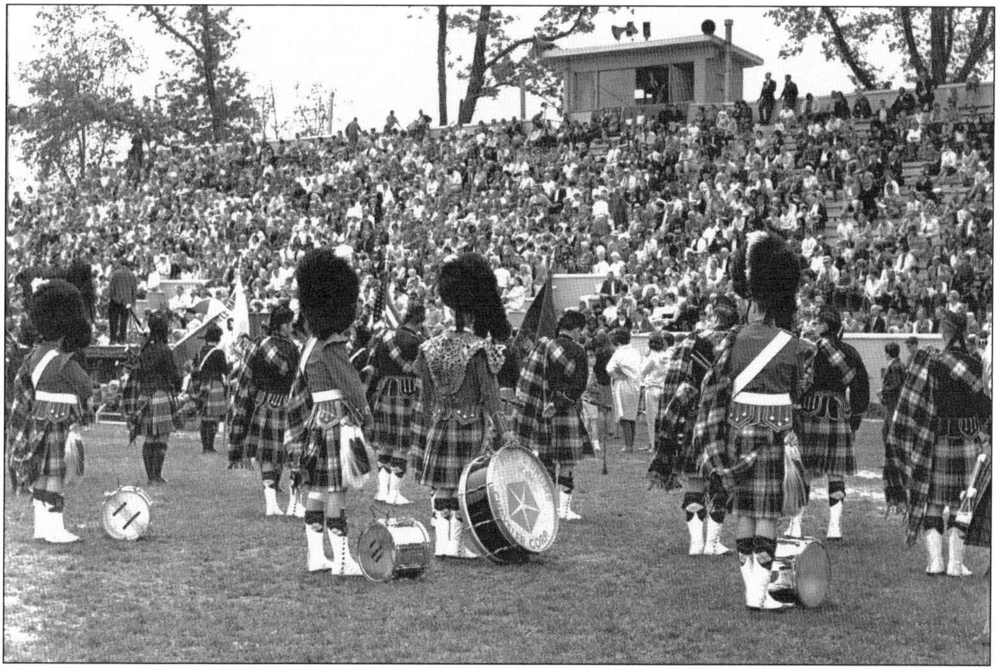

The skirling of massed pipe bands playing at the opening ceremonies of the Alma Highland Festival creates strong emotions in spectators in the stands, whether Scottish or otherwise. These bands take the field during the first festival in 1968. (Courtesy of the Alma College Library.)

Politicians, including Michigan's governors, often attend the festival. Here Gov. William Milliken, resplendent in his kilt, laughs with festival queen Deidre Corbett during opening ceremonies of the 1979 festival. (Courtesy of the Alma College Library.)

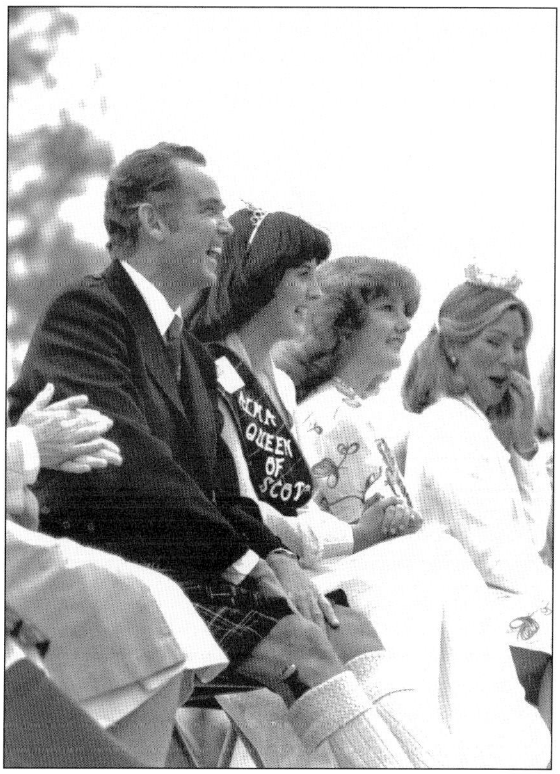

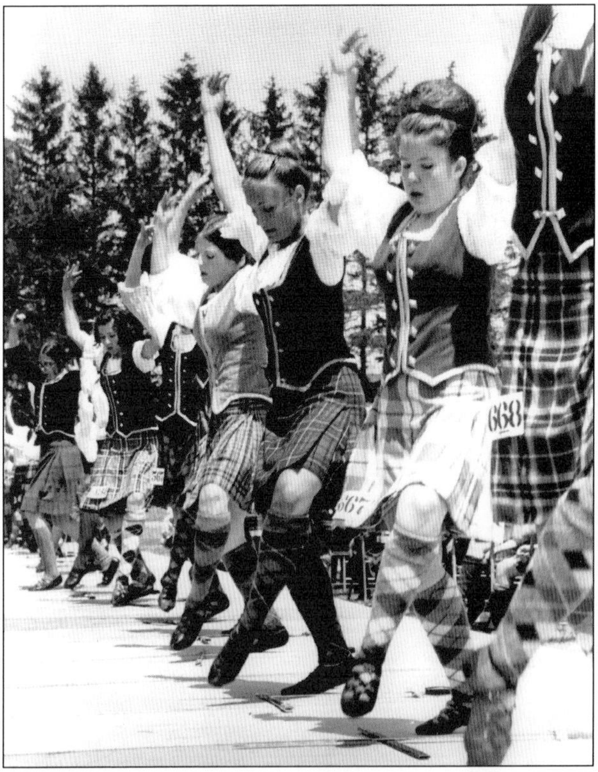

Highland dancing competition, as with many traditional Scottish games, is a major feature of the festival. Numerous talented dancers have been associated with the games, including world champions. (Courtesy of the Alma College Library.)

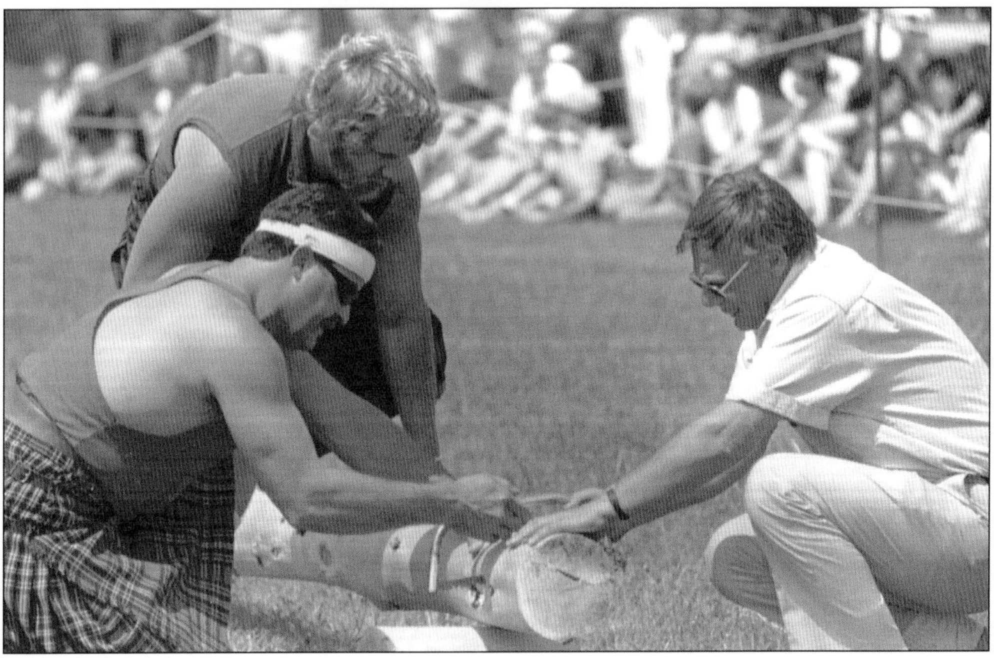

The caber, a long pole carried by running contestants, is thrown and flipped, and must land on its other end. Here the caber is being sawed to achieve the correct length. Tossing the sheaf with a fork and carrying heavy weights in the farmer's walk are other Highland games designed for professionals and amateurs alike. (Courtesy of the Alma College Library.)

*Eight*

# On the River

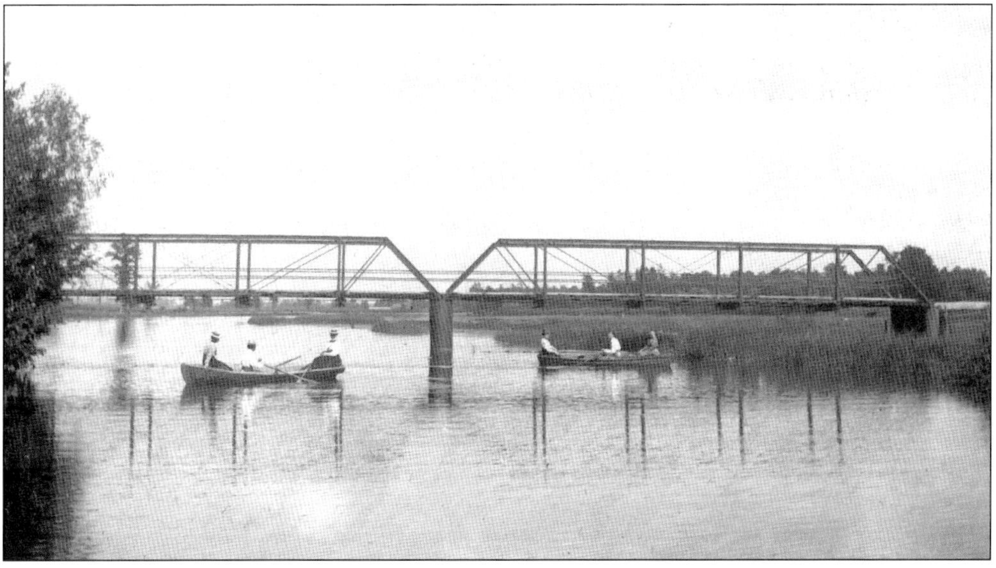

Located near the farmhouse of pioneer Isaac Wolfe, this bridge carried traffic between Alma and the area southwest of town. Wolfe's Bridge was located on what later became Luce Road and spanned the backwater of the dam. As part of the millpond, the waters near the bridge attracted many boaters, canoeists, and anglers. (Courtesy of the Alma College Library.)

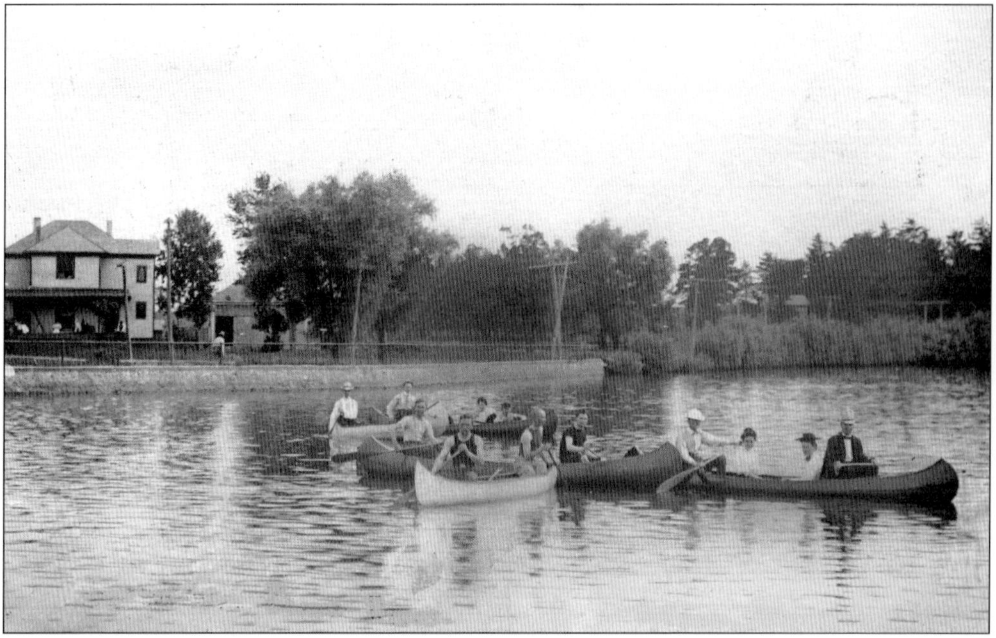

What better way to show canoeing skills or court a favorite girl than to take to the waters of the millpond just above the dam. Some of these young folks are dressed in their Sunday best. Others are dressed in athletic attire, ready for a spirited race. (Courtesy of Richard Tesman.)

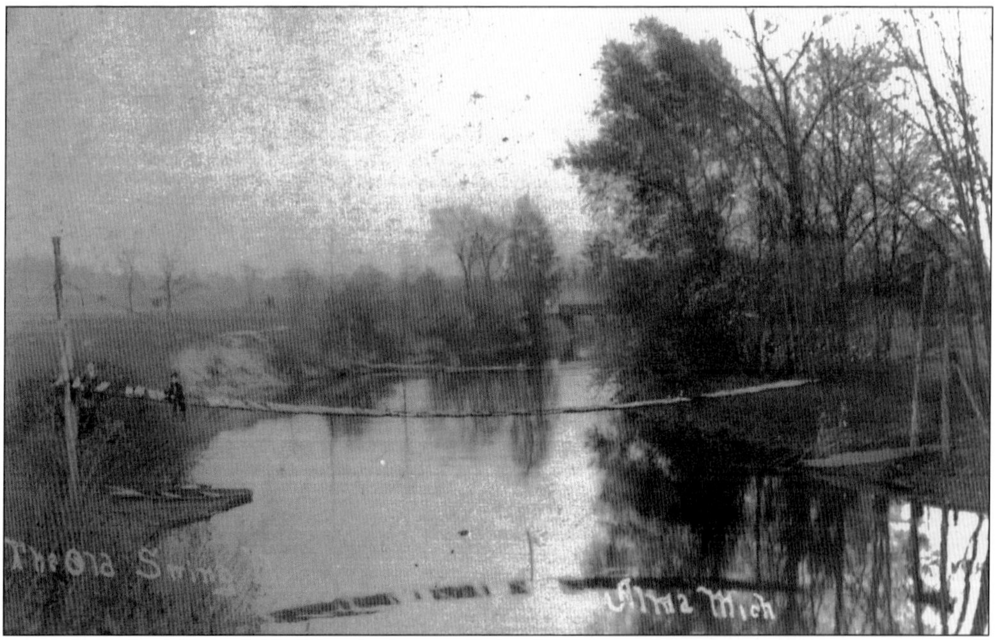


The old swinging bridge attracted many strollers, especially children who escaped adult supervision. By the time this photograph was taken, the bridge had become ragged and unsafe. This did not deter boys from climbing on it and managing to get across. (Courtesy of the Alma Public Library.)

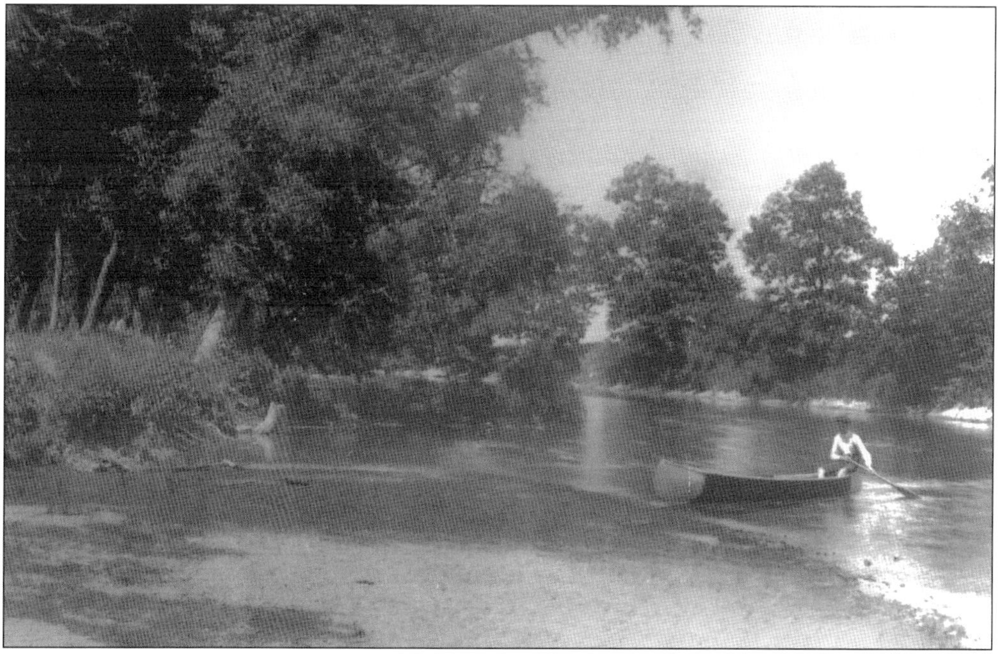

This lad, out for a gentle trip on the river, has found one of the many idyllic spots that attracted water lovers to the Pine River through the years. Parts of the river were stocked with trout during the early days of settlement, and fishing the clear and gently flowing waters became a common activity for Alma folks. (Courtesy of Lucille Behler.)

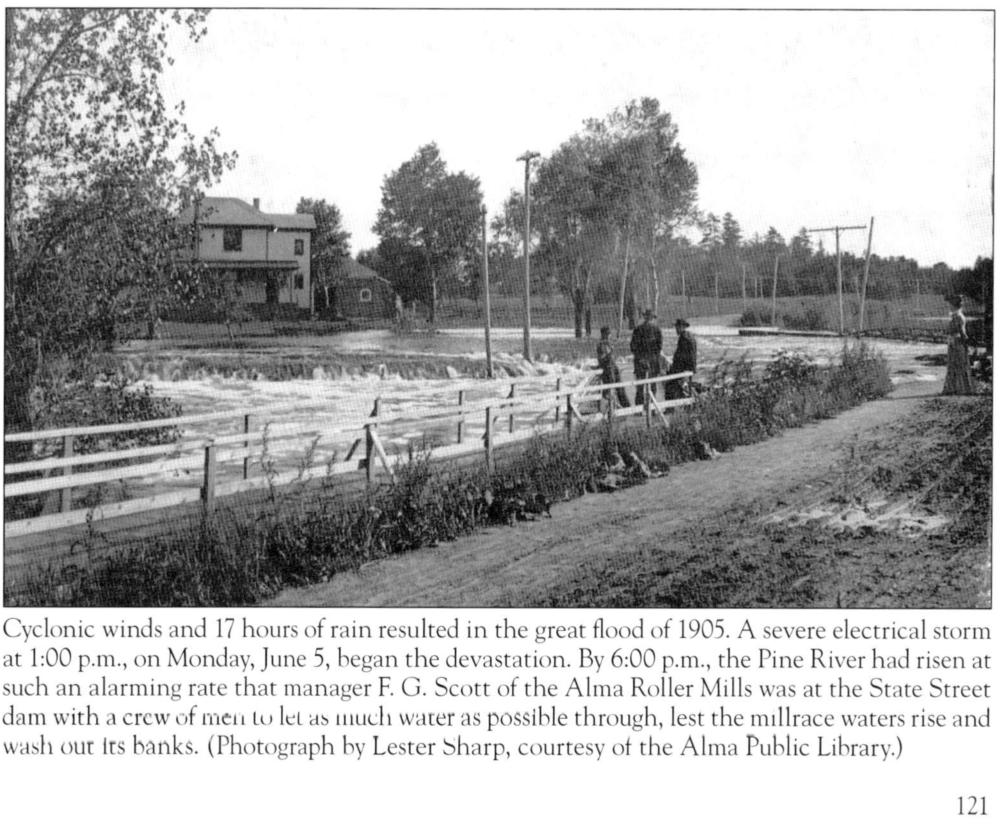

Cyclonic winds and 17 hours of rain resulted in the great flood of 1905. A severe electrical storm at 1:00 p.m., on Monday, June 5, began the devastation. By 6:00 p.m., the Pine River had risen at such an alarming rate that manager F. G. Scott of the Alma Roller Mills was at the State Street dam with a crew of men to let as much water as possible through, lest the millrace waters rise and wash out its banks. (Photograph by Lester Sharp, courtesy of the Alma Public Library.)

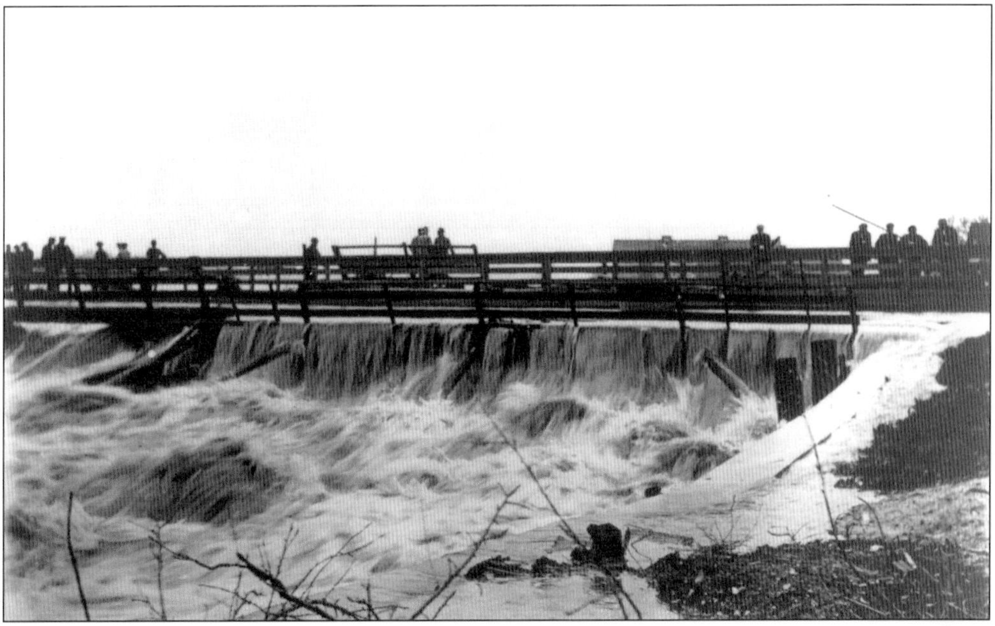

With floodgates open, the dam releases an immense flow of water. Still, the Pine River flows around the end of the dam, and city officials must keep track of the overflow. This picture was taken on Thursday, the fourth day of flooding in 1905. (Courtesy of Lucille Behler.)

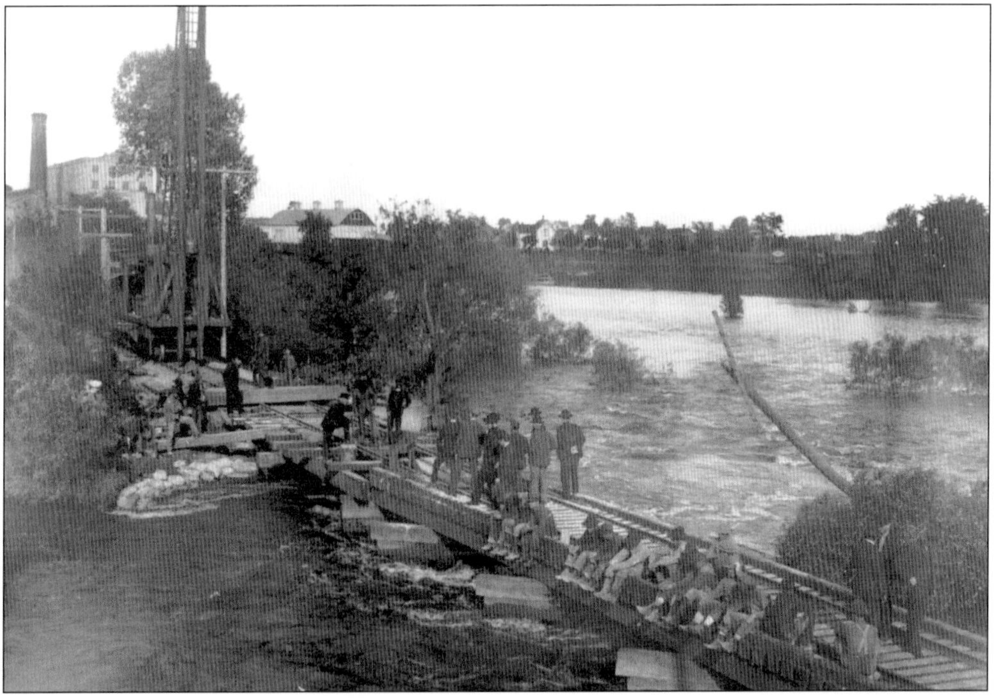

Water from the flooded millrace washed out the east end of the Pere Marquette Railway bridge and carried away 20 feet of grade and the railroad's electric signal target. The wrecking train with its pile driver arrived on Wednesday, and repairs allowed the first passenger trains into Alma in three days. (Courtesy of Lucille Behler.)

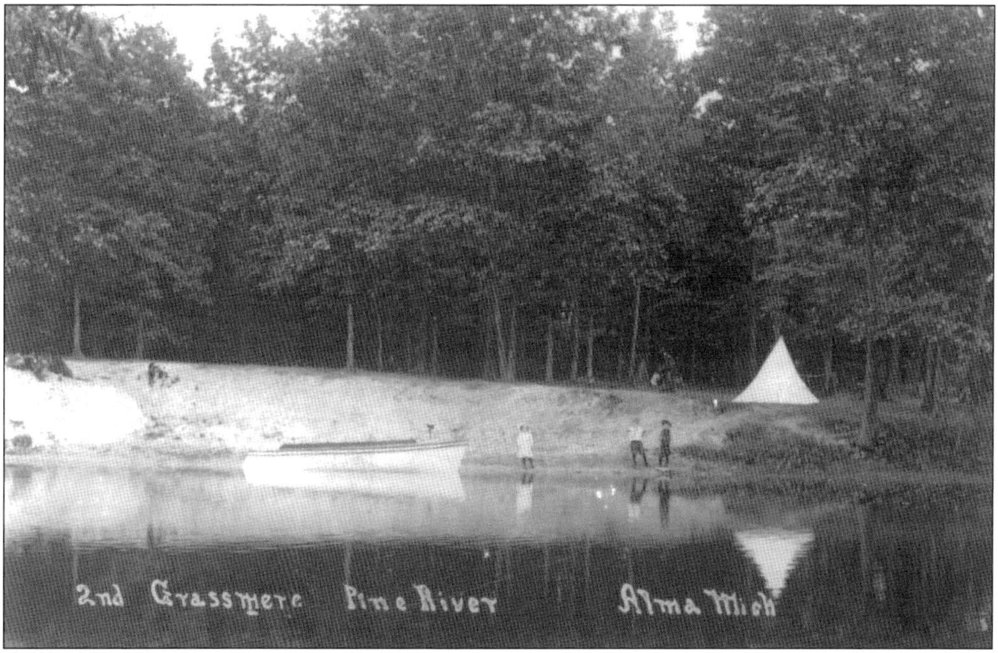


Several lovely locations along the upper reaches of the river not far from Alma were labeled grassmeres. Millionaire businessman and farmer Ammi W. Wright named one of his larger farms, bisected by the river, Grassmere Farm. Here a gentleman has pitched a tent, perhaps for the day, and his children are exploring along the riverbank. (Courtesy of Colleen Boyer.)

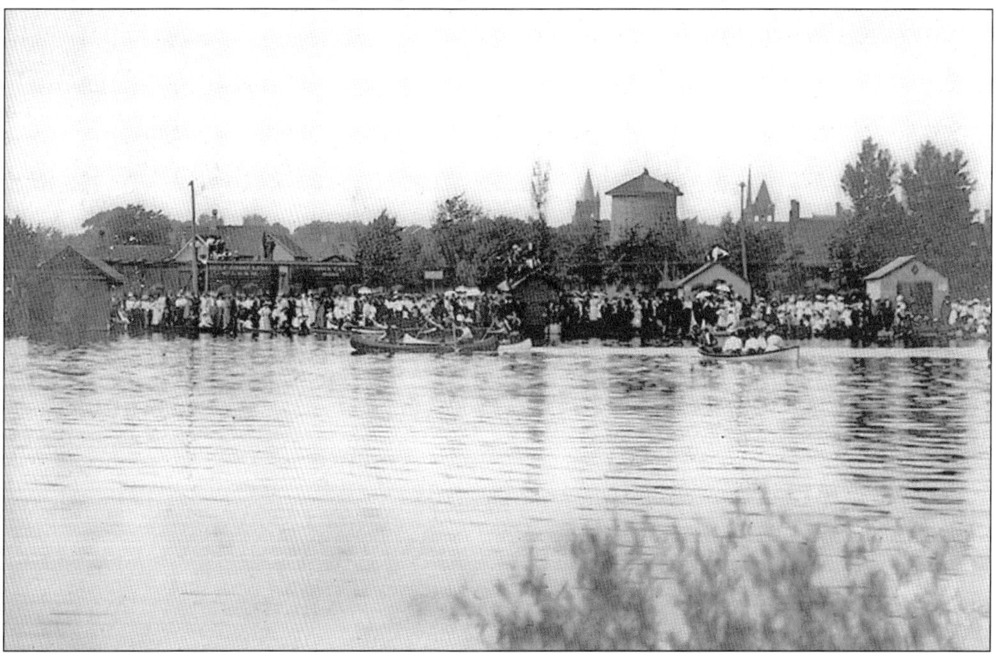

A crowd of 10,000 people crowded into Alma for the Fourth of July celebration in 1907. As activities began down at the river above the dam, 5,000 people gathered on the riverbank, even perching on the roofs of boat houses to view the activities. Here canoeists prepare to race. A small launch holds ladies dressed in their best. (Courtesy of the Alma Public Library.)

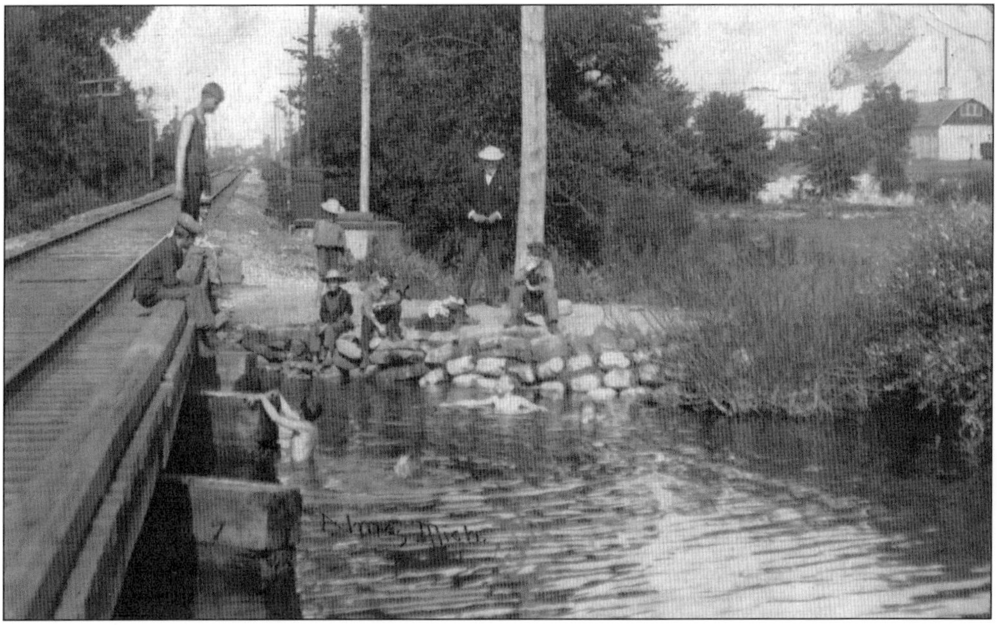

Four boys have abandoned their clothes to skinny-dip in the millrace at the railroad bridge. Several locations along the millrace, including a swimming hole near the roller mill and creamery, were popular with youngsters looking for a cooling dip. (Courtesy of Jan Caputo.)

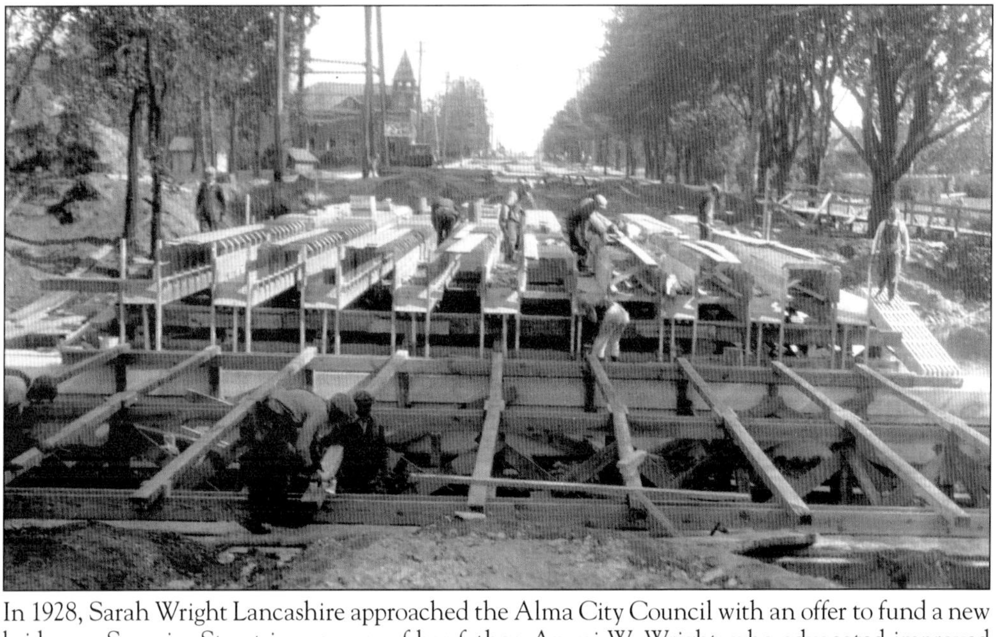

In 1928, Sarah Wright Lancashire approached the Alma City Council with an offer to fund a new bridge on Superior Street in memory of her father, Ammi W. Wright, who advocated improved roads. At the time, the city was widening Superior Street from Euclid Street to Pine Avenue. The unused millrace was filled, and the weakened millrace bridge on Superior Street was torn out, thus providing a wide approach to the new bridge. (Courtesy of the Alma Public Library.)

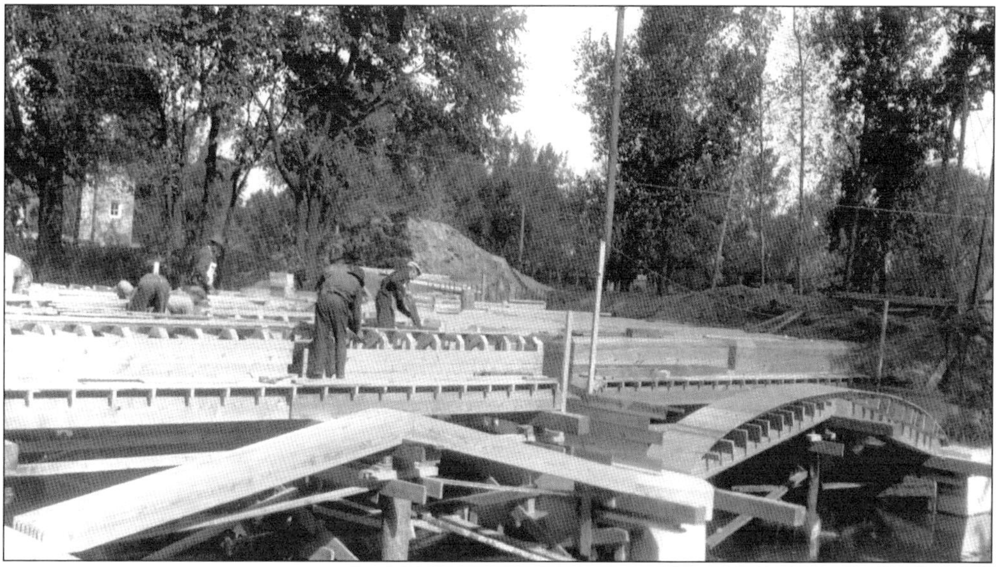

The total cost of the bridge was about $35,000, a considerable sum at the time. Lancashire covered the entire amount. Here workmen are building the forms for reinforced concrete beams. The forms, including the bridge's attractive arches, were intricately built. Concrete was poured over the forms, creating a strong, unified structure. (Courtesy of the Alma Public Library.)

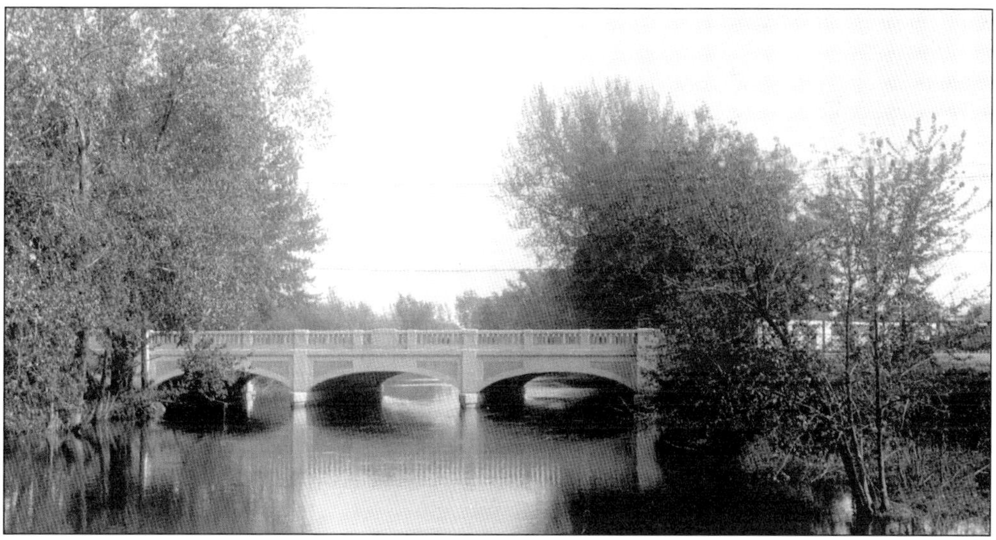

The finished Lancashire bridge was a model of beauty in a cast-concrete bridge. Its graceful arches and massive railings blended into an eye-pleasing unit. Lancashire came for the dedication of the bridge and reminded the crowd of her father's desire for better rural roads and his efforts to improve them. (Courtesy of the Alma Public Library.)

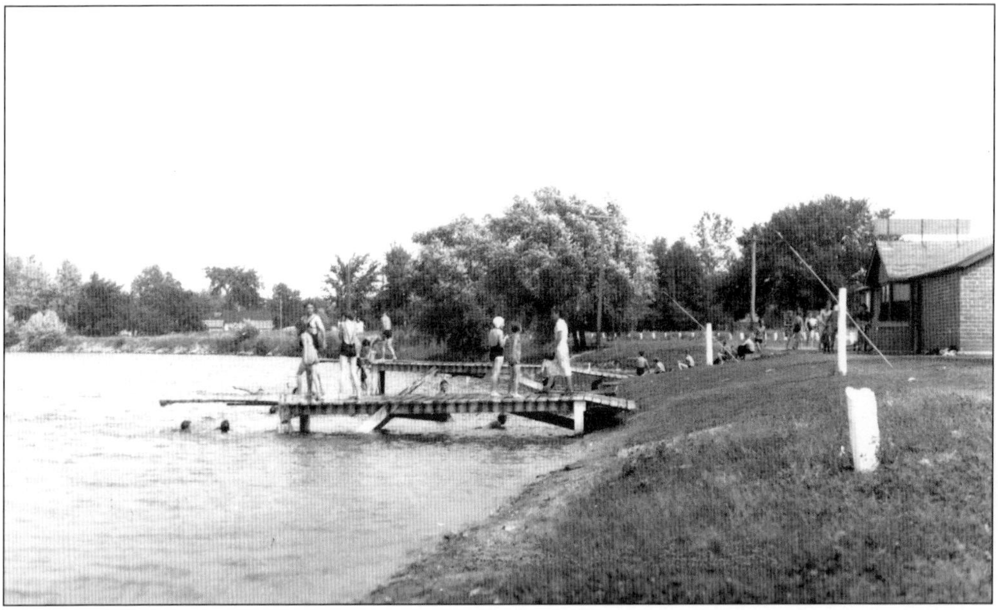

Around the bend from the State Street dam lay Turck's woods, later to be known as Conservation Park. This parcel was given to the city by businessman William S. Turck. Not far from Riverside Drive, a concession and bathhouse was built in the 1930s. The river was clean enough for swimming, and it became a popular summer spot for Alma youngsters. A water carnival was held here in the 1940s. (Courtesy of Richard Tesman.)

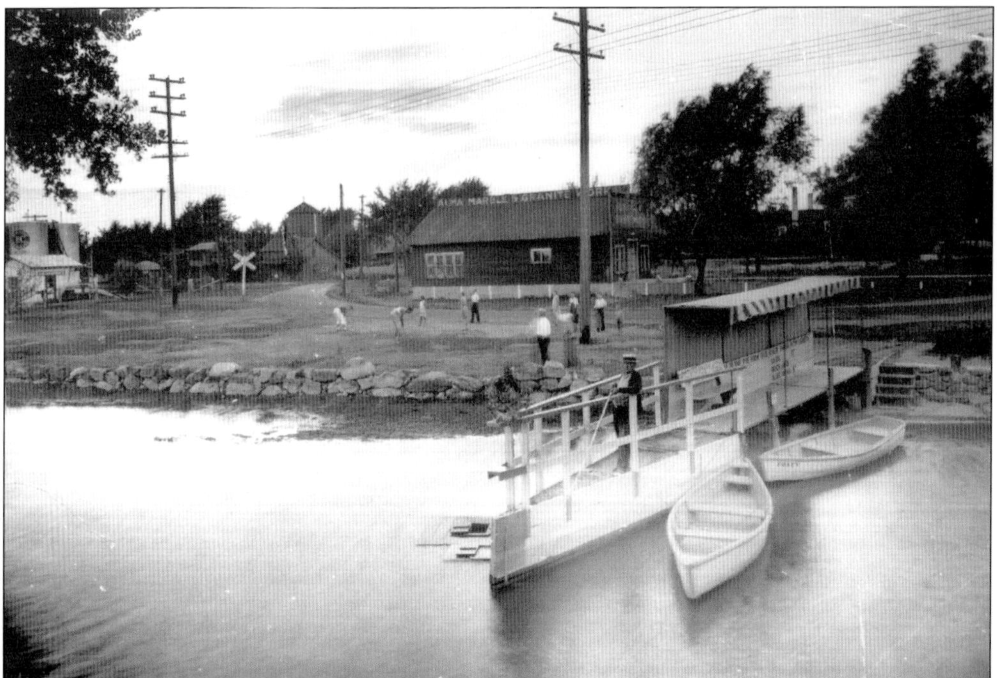

The north side of the millpond just above the dam was the scene of several large icehouses in the early days. Later boathouses occupied the banks of the river. Here a boat rental has been established. Youngsters play croquet in the background. (Courtesy of Lucille Behler.)

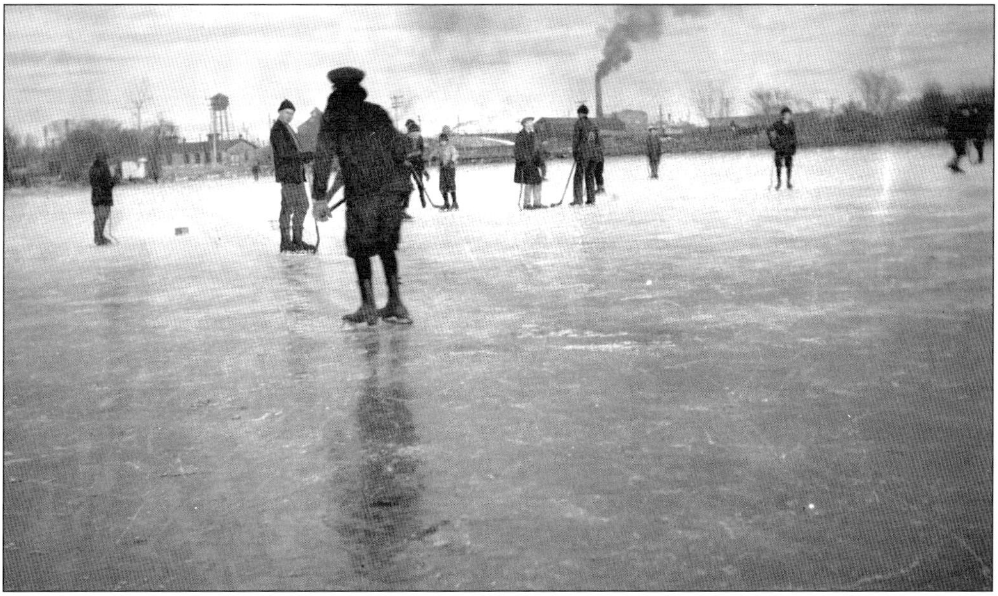

A smoothly frozen millpond was an invitation for ice-skating parties. Here the ice has drawn a number of boys for a game of hockey. Smoke rises from the Alma Sugar Company on this winter day. (Photograph by Hubert Elias, courtesy of Dale Kemler.)

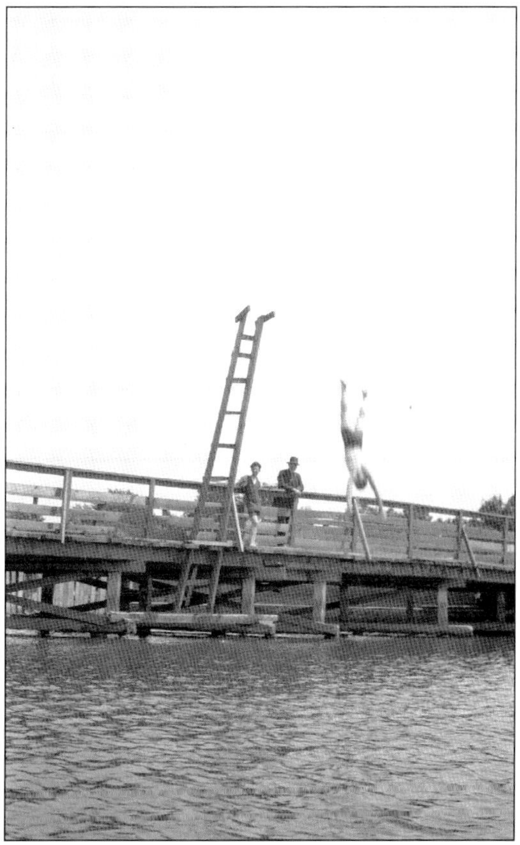

During the July 4, 1907, celebration, one of the attractions was a ladder attached to the State Street bridge and dam. In an age before diving boards, the ladder allowed youngsters to climb to the top, balance on extensions for their feet, and then catapult themselves into the deep waters of the millpond. (Courtesy of Dale Kemler.)

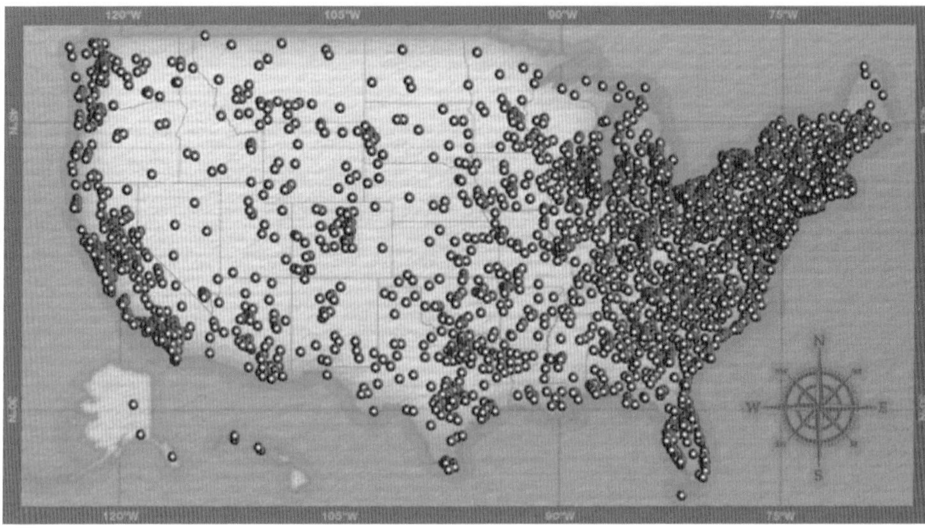